Mis/takes

Mis/takes departs from the bulk of screen discourse by applying Jungian and post-Jungian ideas on unconscious processes to popular film and television. This perspective offers a rich insight into the way that various myths infiltrate popular culture.

By examining the function of psychological motifs and symbols in cinema and television, Terrie Waddell opens up another way of thinking about how identity can be constructed and disrupted. *Mulholland Drive*, *Memento*, *The Others*, *The X-Files*, *Twin Peaks*, *The Sopranos*, *Spider*, *Intimacy* and *Absolutely Fabulous* all lend themselves to this approach. The close analysis of these films/programs are guided by a number of core archetypes from trickster and Self to incest and the grotesque. The book's four parts reflect these dominant patterns:

- Jung, trickster and the screen
- Mistaken identities, self-deception and the undead
- Redeemers, bad dads and matricide
- Excesses of the sad and the sassy

Mis/takes gives readers a chance to engage with screen material in an original and subversive way. This study will be of great interest to Jungian analysts and students of film, cultural studies, media, gender studies and analytical psychology.

Terrie Waddell is a Lecturer in Media Studies and Convenor of Gender, Sexuality and Diversity Studies at La Trobe University, Australia.

Mis/takes

Archetype, myth and identity in screen fiction

Terrie Waddell

This publication has been supported by La Trobe University
Internet: http://www.latrobe.edu.au

LA TROBE UNIVERSITY

Routledge
Taylor & Francis Group
LONDON AND NEW YORK

First published 2006 by Routledge
27 Church Road, Hove, East Sussex BN3 2FA

Simultaneously published in the USA and Canada
by Routledge
270 Madison Ave, New York, NY 10016

Routledge is an imprint of the Taylor & Francis Group, an informa business

Typeset in Times by
RefineCatch Limited, Bungay, Suffolk
Printed and bound in Great Britain by
TJ International Ltd, Padstow, Cornwall
Paperback cover design by Anú Design

This publication has been produced with paper manufactured to strict environmental standards and with pulp derived from sustainable forests.

British Library Cataloguing in Publication Data
A catalogue record for this book is available from the British Library

Library of Congress Cataloging-in-Publication Data
Waddell Terrie.
Mis/takes : archetype, myth and identity in screen fiction / Terrie Waddell.
p. cm.
Includes bibliographical references and index.
ISBN13: 978–1–58391–720–6
ISBN10: 1–58391–720–9
ISBN13: 978–1–58391–721–3 (pbk.)
ISBN10: 1–58391–721–7 (pbk.)
1. Motion pictures—Psychological aspects. 2. Television—Psychological aspects. 3. Identity (Psychology) in motion pictures. —4. Identity (Psychology) on television.—5. Archetype (Psychology) in motion pictures. 6. Archetype (Psychology) on television. 7. Myth in motion pictures. 8. Myth on television. 9. Jung, C. G. (Carl Gustav), 1875–1961. I. Title.
PN1995.W27 2006
791.43′6353—dc22 2006012516

ISBN13: 978–1–58391–720–9 (hbk)
ISBN13: 978–1–58391–721–7 (pbk)

ISBN10: 1–58391–720–9 (hbk)
ISBN10: 1–58391–721–7 (pbk)

For Peter Schmidt and Barb Fyffe

Contents

Acknowledgements

There's a long list of people to thank for contributing to *Mis/takes*. I am especially grateful to Peter Hughes, Head of Media Studies at La Trobe University, for enthusiastically helping to facilitate this project from beginning to end. Thanks to Jane Longmore, Head of the School of Humanities at the University of Greenwich, for supporting my 2005 Honorary Research Fellowship in the UK. It was at Greenwich that I was lucky enough to share my work with Susan Rowland. Susan generously read the manuscript and guided me through each chapter.

I appreciate the thoughtfulness of a number of friends and colleagues who read through various sections of *Mis/takes* and offered their much valued suggestions: Andrew Samuels, Mark Nicholls, Sue Turnbull, Bernie Neville, Hester Joyce, Lisa French, Mary Debrett, Bridget Magner, Chris Lloyd, Neil Baird, Peter Hughes, Dean Triplett, Anna Taifer, Rachael Kacan and Joanne Madden. A special thanks to David Tacey for his guidance, insight and gentle pushes.

My publisher Kate Hawes has been extremely encouraging and always supportive. The assistance of Claire Lipscomb and Helen Pritt at Routledge has also been very much appreciated. I am indebted to Caroline Haywood of The Picture Desk Ltd (The Kobal Collection) for her patience over the duration of this project, and to Francesco de Asmundis' translating precision.

Mis/takes was presented in various stages of development at a number of international conferences. Thanks to Rob Fisher of the Wickedness.net project, responsible for the organization of the following conferences in Budapest: the Second Global Conference on *Monsters and the Monstrous: Myths and Metaphors of Enduring Evil* (convened by Stephen Morris, 2004) and the First Global Conference on *The Erotic* (convened by Jones Irwin, 2004). Thanks also to the committee of the Second International Academic Conference of Analytical Psychology and Jungian Studies, *Current Connections: Creative Dialogues* (2005), and the Media, Communication and Sociology staff of Queen Margaret University College, Edinburgh.

Without the support of my colleagues at La Trobe University, I wouldn't have been able to present at the above conferences: Matt Ford, Darren Chau,

Frank Ryder, Chris Freeman, Alec Hyslop, Ian Armet, Marilyn Quinn, Kylie Gunn and Margaret Taylor. I would also like to acknowledge the financial assistance of La Trobe's publications committee and thank the School of Communication, Arts and Critical Enquiry along with the Faculty of Humanities for granting me a six month Outside Study Program so that I could concentrate on research and writing in London. I must add my 'Media and the Spectacular' and 'Women in Media' students to this list – your ideas and contributions have *always* been much appreciated.

Love and thanks to Melissa Agnew, Rosie John, Cathy Weate and Maya Waddell.

I gratefully acknowledge image permissions from The Kobal Collection, ABC Television Publicity (Kristine Way) and BBC Research Central. Preliminary versions of sections from Chapter 11 appeared in my 1996 article 'The Female Grotesque, Dionysos, Trickster and the Patsy/Edina Dyad: Archetypal Fusion and *Absolutely Fabulous*', *Practice*, 1: 22–32. Citations from the following volumes of *The Collected Works of C. G. Jung* are reprinted by permission of Princeton University Press:

Jung, C. G. (1970) *Psychiatric Studies*, Collected Works Volume 1, edited and translated by G. Adler and R. F. C. Hull, Princeton, NJ: Princeton University Press.

Jung, C. G. (1956/1977) *Symbols of Transformation: An Analysis of the Prelude to a Case of Schizophrenia*, Collected Works Volume 5, edited and translated by G. Adler and R. F. C. Hull, 2nd edn, Princeton, NJ: Princeton University Press.

Jung, C. G. (1966) *Two Essays on Analytical Psychology*, Collected Works Volume 7, 2nd edn, edited and translated by G. Adler and R. F. C. Hull, Princeton, NJ: Princeton University Press.

Jung, C. G. (1956/1970) *The Structure and Dynamics of the Psyche*, Collected Works Volume 8, edited and translated by G. Adler and R. F. C. Hull, Princeton, NJ: Princeton University Press.

Jung, C. G. (1969/1981) *The Archetypes and the Collective Unconscious*, Collected Works Volume 9i, 2nd edn, edited and translated by G. Adler and R. F. C. Hull, Princeton, NJ: Princeton University Press.

Jung, C. G. (1969/1979) *Aion, Researches into the Phenomenology of the Self*, Collected Works Volume 9ii, 2nd edn, edited and translated by G. Adler and R. F. C. Hull, Princeton, NJ: Princeton University Press.

Jung, C. G. (1956/1964) *Civilization in Transition*, Collected Works Volume 10, edited and translated by G. Adler and R. F. C. Hull, Princeton, NJ: Princeton University Press.

Jung, C. G. (1970) *Psychology and Religion: West and East*, Collected Works Volume 11, 2nd edn, edited and translated by G. Adler and R. F. C. Hull, Princeton, NJ: Princeton University Press.

Jung, C. G. (1968/1980) *Psychology and Alchemy*, Collected Works Volume

12, edited and translated by G. Adler and R. F. C. Hull, Princeton, NJ: Princeton University Press.

Jung, C. G. (1977) *Mysterium Coniunctionis: An Inquiry into the Separation and Synthesis of Psychic Oppositions in Alchemy*, Collected Works Volume 14, 2nd edn, edited and translated by G. Adler and R. F. C. Hull, Princeton, NJ: Princeton University Press.

Jung, C. G. (1966) *The Spirit of Man in Art and Literature*, Collected Works Volume 15, edited and translated by G. Adler and R. F. C. Hull, Princeton, NJ: Princeton University Press.

Jung, C. G. (1966) *The Practice of Psychotherapy: Essays on the Psychology of the transference and other subjects*, Collected Works Volume 16, edited and translated by G. Adler and R. F. C. Hull, Princeton, NJ: Princeton University Press.

Jung, C. G. (1981) *The Development of Personality*, Collected Works Volume 17, edited and translated by G. Adler and R. F. C. Hull, Princeton, NJ: Princeton University Press.

Jung, C. G. (1977) *The Symbolic Life*, Collected Works Volume 18, edited and translated by G. Adler and R. F. C. Hull, Princeton, NJ: Princeton University Press.

Introduction

While the work of Freudian influenced theorists dominates psychological approaches to film analysis, few studies draw on the work of Freud's colleague and later rival Carl Gustav Jung (1875–1961). *Mis/takes* is an attempt to do something about this. It's a way of saying, let's put Freud and the post-Freudians to bed for a minute, and go to the other/another side – for some, the dark side. Using Jung's ideas on unconscious processes to examine the way that identity is disrupted and developed in contemporary film and television involves drawing on the core archetypal patterns central to his understanding of the psyche and mythology. As interconnecting energies that merge with and borrow from each other, archetypes rarely operate as pure or undiluted things-in-themselves. Each part of *Mis/takes* artificially disentangles these motifs, bringing one or more forward for scrutiny. But in trying to approach and grapple with the import of archetypes in this way, it's still impossible to avoid referring to a number of impacting auxiliary patterns, symbols and mythic themes.

The three major concepts integral to Jung's 'analytical psychology' provide an obvious framework for analyzing the visual media: first, images common in dreams, myths and creative art are often projections of unconscious archetypal patterns; second, there is a 'collective unconscious' where these patterns are constellated; and third, the gradual conscious unraveling of these structures promotes the development of a more aware sense of self. Film and television are particularly receptive to theories of the archetype, the objective psyche (collective unconscious), and the fraught path to emotional and intellectual maturity. The way that both media rely on imagery, and are able to cyclically reinterpret common mythic themes, invites a Jungian/post-Jungian approach. The bulk of Jung's thinking about art, religion and the unconscious has been sourced from his eighteen volumes of *Collected Works*. This material is used in conjunction with the ideas of post-Jungian writers and relevant cultural theorists.

While taking on board the *intent* of particular directors or creators of the works discussed throughout the book, I'm more concerned with the subjective interpretation of film and television material rather than resorting to authorial intent as *the* key into a text. Of course I'm not saying that the 'author is dead' (in postmodern speak). I'm arguing that s/he is just one element, not *the* element in unraveling the import of screen material. The discipline of Media Studies in particular champions audiences as active participants in meaning making. The notion of readers/spectators as passive, à la crude 'hypodermic needle' thinking, where information is imagined to be 'injected' into pliable and uncritical receivers, was largely dismissed in the 1970s with 'uses and gratifications' theories and later 'reception theories' of the 1980s and 1990s. Today there is no dominant interpretive voice. What we can be grateful for is a plurality of ideas and the freedom to think that we can contribute to that pool.

The disciplines of Cinema and Media Studies commonly include television as means of reflecting on social issues, theoretical positions and artistic innovations. With this in mind the psychological import of film *and* television should be equally weighted. Apart from the dominance of cinema in the hierarchical ranking of screen cultures, another bias against television is the way that its content is often understood to be homogenous and disposable. During the process of writing *Mis/takes*, I co-edited *Lounge Critic: The Couch Theorist's Companion* (2004), a collection of theoretical perspectives from academics, journalists and industry practitioners on their favourite television programs and genres. When the book was reviewed in the popular news press, some exception was taken to the discussion of one particular series because it was fourteen years old (despite its considerable cult fan base). I mention this example because it's indicative of a wider bias: a bias that rarely, if ever, enters into public criticism or discussion of film texts.

I have never heard anyone dismissing the analysis of certain films because they weren't being screened in the local cinema. And yet no matter who the creators, writers, directors or actors are, and no matter how reflective, artistic or creative a piece of television might be, the assumption that all television has a used by/saturation date is a common enough prejudice. And all this despite the accessible DVD packaging of many television series that would tend to reflect the medium's cultural viability. I've looked at both *Twin Peaks* and *The X-Files* in *Mis/takes* to counter this discrimination. Both texts are particularly relevant to the kind of analysis I'm concerned with. Although a great deal has already been written about each program, I certainly hope that they will continue to be discussed and reinterpreted from a number of new and challenging perspectives.

The screen material selected for *Mis/takes*, after a considerable period of adding and scratching other possibilities, best serves my purposes because of the way that each text engages with the archetypal. Rather than trying to unravel these energies via characterization alone, I've always found it ultimately more satisfying to explore the way they pulse through the complex production, imagery and thematic threads of a film or piece of television. So while central characters are usually the primary carriers of archetypal projections, they often only amplify what is already propelling and fusing the interlinking elements of the narrative.

The first part of *Mis/takes* 'Jung, Trickster and the Screen' establishes the overall framework. Chapter 1, 'Analytical Psychology and Myth: The Bigger Picture' examines the development and key features of Jungian and post-Jungian ideas: the collectivity of the psyche; the importance of images; the distinction between symbols and signs; the nature of archetypes; the individuation process; and the concept of the Self. The chapter finishes with a discussion of myth's relationship to analytical psychology and its integration in contemporary media. The following chapter 'Mutability, Identity and the Farce of Fixity: Trickster' follows on from the previous discussion of mythology, through a detailed analysis of the trickster motif and its association (and disassociation) with the persona, or what might be called the 'social mask'. Because trickster is the dominant archetypal force running through *Mis/takes*, it's important to fully explore what is known of this energy and how it's able to bring about a greater sense of awareness.

The core discussion of films and television programs begins in Part II, 'Mistaken Identities, Self-Deception and the Undead'. The three chapters in this part specifically deal with trickster energy. I've selected *Mulholland Drive* (2001), *Memento* (2000) and *The Others* (2001) because of their focus on unstable or floating personae, the ensuing anxieties that this displacement brings, and the attempts of trickster to agitate for a more authentic awareness of identity. Chapters 3, 'The Obscure by the More Obscure', and 4, 'Setting the Conditions for Forgetting', explore the way that trickster can confront and initiate psychological shifts by forcing an awareness of unconscious material. While *Mulholland Drive* revisits the surreal 'dual personality'/'parallel-universe' thinking of David Lynch's earlier work (particularly *Twin Peaks* discussed in Chapter 7), Christopher Nolan's *Memento* is a less mischievous take on the film-noir genre. In each text the central protagonists murder, then psychologically try to resurrect their lover from the dead. This Orphic play with grief and guilt serves only to further fragment the fragile identities of these characters. There are no happy endings. Instead we might talk of *the frustration of archetypal intent*, where surfacing unconscious material, via trickster, is unable to bring about the necessary transformation.

Chapter 5, 'The Undead, Psychopomps and Filicide', focuses on Alejandro Amenábar's *The Others*. In contrast to the last two films, *The Others* ends on a somewhat higher note. It provides us with the opportunity to look at the ferryman or psychopomp (guider of souls) aspect of trickster. In this homage to Henry James' *Turn of the Screw* (1898), trickster as arch manipulator of reality and fantasy allows us to understand the import of the ghostly 'others' as containers for intermingling archetypal matter. This reworking of literary and screen Gothic fictions also exposes the paradoxes inherent in trickster. For while it breaches boundaries, it also operates to reinstate order or bring about a sense of stability. In this case it ferries the central character 'Grace' to the underworld, by forcing her to acknowledge her undead state.

Part III, 'Redeemers, Bad Dads and Matricide', discusses the divine, shadow and life/death archetypes particularly in relation to the child. Chapter 6, 'Dana Immaculate and Divine Children', applies the mythological motifs of the divine child and Self (a state of fluid conscious/unconscious interplay) to the Fox Network's *The X-Files* (1993–2002). The series poignantly captured the nature and significance of these archetypes through its dual sci-fi and religious drives to understand 'the truth' that's supposedly 'out there'. Although children feature throughout its nine year history as motivating forces for the central characters, it was only during the last two years of *The X-Files* that 'the saviour' was most fully realized with the birth of the ultimate alien/human hybrid, 'William'. Son of Federal Bureau of Investigation (FBI) agents Dana Scully (who became more Madonna-ish with each season) and Fox Mulder (her unidentified flying object (UFO) obsessed partner), little William allows for a parodic return to our mythic and spiritual past. As yet another contemporary reworking of the Christ myth, the creator Chris Carter plays on the theme of redemption and future potential through the divine child: the must-have paradigm of more established Eastern and Western religious faiths.

The next three chapters, 'Libidinal Frenzy', 'Incest by Goomah/Daughter Proxy' and 'Motherly and Slatternly Creatures', explore one of analytical psychology's more controversial concepts – libidinal regression to the incest archetype. Jung's main argument with psychoanalysis was the way that the libido was theorized. He wanted to remove the sexual focus of what he called this 'life-force', by positing that sexuality was merely one aspect of libidinal energy. He argued that when this energy becomes blocked, it regresses in a number of ways, one of which is retreat to the maternal matrix. To Jung this idea, firmly embedded in cross-cultural mythology, signified a desire for transformation. Regression to the incest archetype (and I must be careful here because I'm not referring to literal incest) was indicative of a critical need for renewal.

Although intimated in *The X-Files*, this myth is more clearly woven through David Lynch and Mark Frost's *Twin Peaks* (1990–1991), David Chase's *The Sopranos* (1999–) and David Cronenberg's *Spider* (2002). While these texts, particularly *Spider*, might be talked about as reworkings of the Oedipal drama and consequent complex, it's worthwhile looking at each narrative from a less clichéd angle. Jung was hesitant not to labour the Oedipal theory because it largely excluded the developmental processes of women. He offhandedly quipped about an Electra complex, but rather than taking this idea seriously, he argued that regression to incest imagery (as a desire for revitalization) was a genderless means of shifting a stifled libido.

The fourth and last part, 'Excesses of the Sad and the Sassy', considers the idea of excess from two very distinct perspectives: one where abandon is a way of avoiding confrontation with underlying distress, and the other where it becomes a way of challenging disempowering cultural conventions and ideologies. In Chapter 10, 'The Fear of Exposure and Connection', we look at Patrice Chéreau's dark and claustrophobic *Intimacy* (2001). The film is so tightly shot that there's little relief from the intense relationship of the central characters 'Jay' and 'Claire'. This reading follows Jay's story, and although I could have easily concentrated on Claire's situation, Jay, as the film's main problem to be dealt with, is more clearly drawn as a seething knot of inner conflict.

Instead of anima representing the 'feminine' aspects of the psyche as Jung argued (an *extremely* problematic idea), I have understood the archetype as it appears in *Intimacy*, as a non-gendered 'gearing' mechanism for the eros (love/sex) paradigm. In this particular film, anima works as a way of compelling Jay to anchor his free-floating eros energy so that he can have more control over his fear of personal attachment. This is not of course to argue that anima is 'moral' or 'judgmental' in relation to commitment, but for Jay, who *desires* commitment, anima becomes the most relevant psychological function that kicks in to help him along.

In Chapter 11, 'Grotesques, Bakhtin and Rupture', I examine the archetypal nature of the grotesque through medieval/Renaissance carnival and the BBC sitcom *Absolutely Fabulous*. Since the 1990s the concept of the female grotesque or unruly woman has developed into a hot topic for film/television studies and media debates. This type of character, as imaged in myth, carnival, film and television, can be understood to symbolize the tricksterish and Dionysian desire to subvert, transgress and initiate transformation. Although a number of key theorists discuss the female grotesque from the perspective of art, theatre and carnival (Mikhail Bakhtin, Geoffrey Harpham, Wolfgang Kayser), or contemporary female transgression (Patricia Mellencamp, Mary Russo, Kathleen Rowe), the archetypal properties of this spectacle have not adequately been explored.

Because this analysis focuses on the comic aspects of the grotesque rather than its darker (or monstrous) side, it's necessary to look in some depth at the social and political machinations of carnival as a cultural spectacle driven by laughter and the ubiquitous presence of the unruly (grotesque) woman. The archetypal motifs of trickster and Dionysos (the desire for ecstatic release), with their inherent drives to stretch emotional, physical and social limits, directly relate to the grotesque and are integral to understanding the nature of the pattern. Although the work of seminal theorists of grotesquery will be analyzed, the chapter concentrates more specifically on Bakhtin's *Rabelais and his World* (1965), a theoretical study of medieval and Renaissance carnival based on François Rabelais' satires *Gargantua* (1532) and *Pantagruel* (1534). The social and political impact of both writers will be discussed before looking at how their work informs *Absolutely Fabulous*.

Despite the relevance and popularity of Jung's work for contemporary readers or audiences, there's always some awkwardness in using specific disciplines of psychology to analyze visual texts. This kind of application must be understood as a means of grappling with the mythic nature of cinema and television as well as the 'bigger' cultural/emotional questions that these media offer up. Reading a text through the framework of one primary theorist helps us to more clearly understand the ideas that they are putting forward, and, if appropriate, revise them. With this methodology in mind, analyzing cultural material through psychological approaches is far from analogous to analyzing actual case studies. The body of work left by Jung, or Freud, or Bakhtin might better be understood as a 'tool' that we can use to help us wrestle with meaning. In the academic world the ideas of theorists are rarely taken to be absolutes. They fluctuate in status from fashionable to unfashionable. It is unfortunate that Jung has never registered very high in the theory fashion stakes. But maybe a change is in the air.

Part I

Jung, trickster and the screen

Chapter 1

Analytical psychology and myth

The bigger picture

> I don't know where ideas come from, but I think there's a big ocean of ideas and once in a while those ideas pop into our conscious mind and we, you know, go from there.
>
> David Lynch, *David Lynch Interview* (2001)

It has to be said that depth psychologies are a leap of faith. If the unconscious is 'all that *I am* that I don't know *I am*', we can really only make informed guesses about its content and function no matter how 'scientific' its pioneers and contemporary theorists claim/ed to be. Jung's analytical psychology, popularly distinguished from Freudian psychoanalysis by its theorization of the *archetype* and the *collective unconscious* (or *objective psyche*), has often been targeted, by academia in particular, as one of the greatest leaps. Although Jung repeatedly refers to himself as 'an empiricist' and 'a scientist' throughout the eighteen volumes of his *Collected Works*, I would argue that the creative and spiritual insight of the ideas he left us has more punch than their science. Analytical psychology's concentration on the cross-cultural and timeless language of images, filtered through art, myth, religion, dreams, and unconscious projections, also lends itself to the analysis of cinema and television.

This chapter initially focuses on the contentious tenets of analytical psychology central to *Mis/takes*, while the later section looks at the relationship and import of myth to screen imagery. Despite some of his more awkward theoretical positions, particularly his essentialist views on gender and sexuality, Jung was one of the most progressive thinkers of his day, groomed to be Freud's heir, but sacrificing the mantle to develop his own insights into the spiritual dimensions of the psyche largely overlooked in psychoanalysis. As I'll argue throughout this book, the sacred, mythic and archetypal are inescapable givens of many contemporary and classic screen stories. Because of this it's difficult to understand why the application of analytical psychology to these 'texts', or what might just as easily be thought of as recycled myths, has been so overshadowed by the *logos* (rationality) of Freudian and post-Freudian (predominantly Lacanian) psychoanalysis. The films and television programs in *Mis/takes* have been carefully chosen to illuminate specific aspects of Jungian and post-Jungian thought, and because of this they inevitably illuminate our mythic past. Rather than seeing tired repetitions of traditional myth and clichéd projections of archetypal patterns, what we're able to extract from each visual text is the absolute relevance of the archetype as it reworks and morphs its way into contemporary imaginings.

Jung's model of the psyche

Carl Gustav Jung (1875–1961) specialized in psychiatry at the University of Basel. This led to his appointment as a training psychiatrist at the Burghölzli Mental Hospital in Zurich under Eugen Bleuler, where he focused on the treatment of dementia praecox (an early term for schizophrenia). Jung sent Freud (1856–1939) a copy of his *Diagnostic Association Studies* (*CW* 2) in 1906 after being inspired by *The Interpretation of Dreams* (1900), but their ensuing intellectual, professional and intensely emotional 'father–son' relationship ended bitterly in 1912, when all communication virtually stopped. It was then that Jung published his *Theory of Psychoanalysis* (*CW* 4), a repudiation of Freud's fundamental theories.

In 1913 their links were inextricably severed as Freud worked to remove Jung from his presidency of the International Psychoanalytic Association and oust him from editorial responsibilities (Gay 1995: xli). The intellectual rifts between them were complex, but principally centered around Jung's questioning of Freud's theorization of the unconscious and libido. For Freud, the unconscious was largely a depot for repressed, once conscious material unacceptable to the ego. He formulated the libido as purely sexual in nature rather than, as Jung thought, understanding sexuality to be one of many expressions of this 'psychic energy' (Freud 1914, 1920).

While initially fracturing the psyche into three distinct areas, *conscious, preconscious* and *unconscious*, Freud finally consolidated his now familiar *super-ego, ego* and *id* configuration with the publication of *The Ego and the Id* (1923). Here he argued that 'all that is repressed is *Ucs.* [unconscious], but not all that is *Ucs.* is repressed. A part of the ego, too . . . may be *Ucs*' (Freud 1923/1961: 18). The *id*, the unknowable, unconscious site of instincts and drives (or 'the passions' as he put it) partially merges with the *ego*, conscious perception and reason. He likened these states to a rider (ego) directing and restraining a powerful horse (id). The *super-ego* or *ego-ideal*, a 'supra-personal' plane of the ego that he saw functioning as a moral arbiter, completes this triadic structure. In 1912 though, Jung began to modify the basic principles of psychoanalysis by theorizing the ego as the center or archetypal heart of consciousness, the *personal unconscious* as the repository for suppressed, personal material, and the *objective psyche* (unconscious) as the transpersonal, culturally collective site from which consciousness emerged (*CW* 5).

The notion that there existed a distinctive area of the psyche innately interconnected with consciousness dates back to the ancient Egyptians. St Augustine's (AD 354–430) 'I cannot grasp all that I am' was merely an articulation of this idea (Stevens 1990: 11). The work of Gottfried von Leibniz (1646–1716); the philosophies of nineteenth-century German thinkers Friedrich Wilhelm Joseph von Schelling (1775–1854), Georg Wilhelm Friedrich Hegel (1770–1831), Arthur Schopenhauer (1788–1860), Friedrich Nietzsche (1844–1900); *The Philosophy of the Unconscious* (1868) by Eduard von Hartmann; the research of hypnotists Franz Anton Mesmer (1734–1815), Jean-Martin Charcot (1825–1893), Pierre Janet (1859–1947), Joseph Breuer (1842–1925); and psychologists Francis Galton (1822–1911) and Theodore Flournoy (1854–1920), cultivated notions of unconscious functioning that paved the way for Freudian psychoanalysis and Jungian analytical psychology (Stevens 1990: 12–16). From this classical and complex history of ideas, Jung defined his model in this way:

> I would like to emphasise that we must distinguish three psychic levels: (1) consciousness, (2) the personal unconscious, and (3) the collective unconscious. The personal unconscious consists firstly of all those contents that become unconscious either because they lost their intensity and were forgotten or because consciousness was withdrawn from them (repression), and secondly of contents, some of them sense-impressions, which never had sufficient intensity to reach consciousness but have somehow entered the psyche. The collective unconscious, however, as the ancestral heritage of possibilities of representation, is not individual but common to all men, and perhaps even to animals, and is the true basis of the individual psyche.
>
> (*CW* 8, para. 321)

Jung embraced both logos and *mythos* (imagination, intuition and story) to develop a rounded philosophical and psychological position that attempted to fuse the rational and scientific with the creative and spiritual functions of the psyche. As Laurence Coupe (1997) explains, while classical antiquity flourished through mythos, this didn't discount logos opposition to mythic thinking. It wasn't until the Enlightenment that reason was privileged. Coupe laments modernity's push to 'demythologize' taking comfort in the transgressions of artists who push the mythological envelope, particularly during postmodernity where he claims that, 'we have witnessed, not a retreat from myth, but a much more pervasive sense of myth' (Coupe 1997: 19).

When Jung presented his work to the medical and academic community during the rise of modernity (with all its Enlightenment-hangover), the frustration it caused his peers and contemporaries, who saw the spiritual slant on his theories as unscientific philosophies, is really not surprising. His desire for scientific authenticity continues to take a backseat to his acute (postmodern) recognition of the spiritual and mythic dimensions of psychological processes. It's a legacy that, as David Tacey (2001) writes, is unfortunately attractive to 'New Age' movements quick to abridge and appropriate Jung's complex (and sometimes inconsistent) theories for their own purposes. Those more critically, clinically and academically engaged in Jung's work, though, can be divided into overlapping streams. The three categories Andrew Samuels developed in 1985 are still the most relevant: the *Classical* school, largely uncritical of Jung's theories; the *Developmental* school, privileging personal development and links with psychoanalysis; and the *Archetypal* school, interested in the primary nature of the archetypal image (Samuels 1985: 15).

Archetypes, instincts and complexes

The concept of the *archetype* is central to Jung's version of the objective psyche. He wrote of visions arising from the unconscious via dreams and fantasies that constellated into patterns similar in content to the interconnecting strands of myth. In 1912 Jung called the phenomenon *primordial images* (and archetypes in 1919), interpreting them as patterns of thought and behaviour universally common and recurring rather than features of personal memory. Samuels extends this idea of universality and collectivity by adding 'depth and autonomy': 'The primordial images are like fountains, subsequent imagery is derived from them. And primordial images have a certain independence, can pop up in the mind without warning in dream, daydream, fantasy or artistic creation' (Samuels 1985: 24). This concept also applies to media and cinema, and of course we can relate it back to the introductory citation where David Lynch talks about an 'ocean of ideas' that can 'pop into our conscious mind' every now and then.

Jung's theory of collectively inherited psychological *motifs*, a term he often used to characterize archetypes (*CW* 9i, para. 309), was developed from his association with patients at the Burghölzli Hospital, extensive research into myth, and self-analysis that took a more acute turn after his traumatic split with Freud. The images present in dreams, art, literature and religion were, to Jung's thinking, primordial and shared. He began to articulate with more clarity his theory of 'a collective a priori beneath the personal psyche' (Jung 1963: 185) from a dream where he imaged himself descending various levels of a house, each recalling an earlier period of history than the last.

The notion of a priori images was posited long before Jung in the form of Plato's *original ideas*: 'in some cases the name of the idea is not confined to the idea; but anything else which, not being the idea, exists only in the form of the idea, may also lay claim to it' (Plato 1992: 102). Elizabeth Grosz's (1994: 5) claim that Plato 'sees matter itself as a denigrated and imperfect version of the Idea' suggests that these 'ideas' can be understood only in terms of the Cartesian mind/matter binary. In an archetypal reading, Plato's notion of the 'idea' is similar to Jung's archetype. The 'forms' or matter that Grosz believes is demeaned by Plato can be understood as that through which the idea is realized. In the context of Jung's thought, the 'idea' (archetypal content) takes precedence over the vehicle in which it is conveyed to us (matter, bodily images, symbols, characterization, behavioural patterns). In this type of reading, matter is not denigrated, but understood as an active means of expression (if a secondary one) through which psychological energies resonate. Grosz however, inadvertently puts forward a moot point for post-Jungians (taken up later in a discussion of James Hillman's position); that is, which takes precedence, the archetype or the archetypal image?

Allusion to archetypal structures can also be found in Immanuel Kant's (1724–1804) notion of an a priori perceptive form in which sensory information is categorized (Samuels 1985: 23). Kant's thinking, along with the writings of Spinoza, Plato and Schopenhauer, significantly contributed to the theory of archetypes (*CW* 8, para. 275–277). In 1946 Jung differentiated between the archetype and the image that housed it, arguing that the archetype is not the image but a nucleus from which subsequent images arise (Samuels 1985: 25). The 'image' is a projection of the archetype, an invisible, universal component of the collective unconscious, whereas its imaginal representation is determined by social and historical influences. Jung distinguished the terms this way: 'We must, however, constantly bear in mind that what we mean by "archetype" is in itself irrepresentable, but has effects which make visualizations of it possible, namely the archetypal images and ideas' (*CW* 8, para. 417).

With his theorization of predetermined patterns of thought tempered by social and environmental factors, he saw the mind as matter; a biological structure like the body, genetically determined and programmed, yet open to variation through cultural and environmental factors. Walter Shelburne (1988) draws attention to the difference between Platoic ideas and archetypes by arguing that the former are 'eternal and unchanging' whereas the latter are 'a natural part of the developing human organism' (Shelburne 1988: 67). While Jung claimed that archetypes constitute a 'psychological instance of the biological "pattern of behaviour" ' (*CW* 11, para. 222 ff. 2), Shelburne cautions against accepting the notion that *all* human experience is archetypally patterned. This kind of thinking, he argues, places the whole concept of the archetype in danger of 'being over generalized into triviality' (Shelburne 1988: 40). Samuels succinctly sums up what Jung meant by the archetype in the following three generalized categories:

> (a) archetypal structures and patterns are the crystallisation of experiences over time. (b) They constellate experience in accordance with innate schemata and act as an imprimatur of subsequent experience.

> (c) Images deriving from archetypal structures involve us in a search for correspondence in the environment.
>
> (Samuels 1985: 27)

This issue of the genetic and biological nature of collective behaviours brings up the question of how archetypes are differentiated from *instincts*. In its most superficial form, these structures can be understood as analogous energies. Archetypes have a psychological and biological root, and instincts might be seen to operate on a purely physiological level. The archetypes therefore regulate instincts by directing the expulsion of instinctual energy. For Shelburne (1988: 46), the development of human consciousness facilitated the separation of the instinct from the archetype, unlike animals where (to his way of thinking), archetypes and instincts remain interwoven.

In his interpretation of Jung's instinct/archetype distinction, Shelburne emphasizes that the 'tension' between unconscious psychological drives and the way that these drives are channeled, realized and modified through archetypal processes, need not necessarily be a source of conflict. Jung's desire for the psyche to work toward a sense of integration, harmony and balance suggests that base instinct, and the transformation of the instinct, be understood as 'forces of tension' that function to balance and develop the human personality (Shelburne 1988: 48): 'The archetype, as a glance at the history of religious phenomena will show, has a characteristically numinous effect, so that the subject is gripped by it as though by an instinct' (Jung *CW* 5, para. 225).

Paradoxically, Jung repeatedly emphasized the unknowable nature of archetypes: accessible only through metaphor (*CW* 9i, para. 271). He imagined them as intertwining with each other and rising to consciousness when activated by personal or collective experiences. Casting the archetype externally (*projecting*) onto people, characters, races, subcultures and objects (although the central means of realizing these patterns) should not, according to Jung, be thought of as a way to disown archetypal material (*CW* 9i, para. 160). By this, he was talking about the unproductive and regressive act of expelling, via projection, these internal motifs instead of trying to work through their implications. When archetypes present themselves in a personal (non-collective) context, Jung referred to them as *complexes*, and rather than writing of them as communicated through the 'image', in 1911–1912 he began to use the Latin term *imago* (*CW* 9i, para. 89).

Jung's concept of the complex (the mother-complex for example, discussed in Chapters 8 and 9) refers to: 'a collection of images and ideas, clustered round a core derived from one or more archetypes, and characterized by a common emotional tone' (Samuels et al. 1986: 34). The mother-complex then is woven around the way that the mother archetype is fused with personal experience, one's own mother, experiences of mothering, fantasies of mother/ing, and possibly a number of other archetypal motifs. According to Christopher Hauke and Ian Alister:

> Jung opposed 'monolithic' ideas of personality, proposing that we have many selves or sub-personalities and that it is the complexes which constitute these minor personalities within us and which may, under certain circumstances, behave like independent beings.
>
> (Hauke and Alister 2001: 244)

Throughout his discussion of the way complexes manifest, Jung argued that they always operate as autonomous structures, often occurring spontaneously and gripping us with their *feeling-tone* or *affect*.

Image as archetype

Hillman developed his own interpretation of Jung's work and in 1970 named his movement *Archetypal Psychology*. He understood the archetype differently from Jung, insisting that the psyche functions to create images that are fundamental realities unto themselves and irreducible to any structure beyond this awareness:

> If archetypal images are the fundamentals of fantasy, they are the means by which the world is imagined, and therefore they are the modes by which all knowledge, all experiences whatsoever become possible. 'Every psychic process is an image and an "imagining", otherwise no consciousness could exist . . .' (CW 11: 889). An archetypal image operates like the original meaning of idea (from Greek eidos and eidolon): not only 'that which' one sees but also that 'by means of which' one sees.
>
> (Hillman 1983: 12)

For Hillman images are a source of interaction rather than interpretation. They are to be experienced and encountered much like we engage with artworks.

Hillman's view of the image as the prime reality led him away from the notion that archetypal patterns are grounded in the biochemical, socio-historical and behavioural to the *mytho poetic*. This area of oral, artistic and literary tradition was rich ground for understanding the significance of the archetypal experience; a view that contradicts Jung's aim for spiritual and scientific balance: 'For Hillman has taken up the cause of mythos and attempted to understand all experience in terms of it. Rather than aiming for a logos of the mythos as Jung did, Hillman wants to articulate a mythos of the logos' (Shelburne 1988: 8).

Jung believed that the images of myth were personifications of underlying archetypal content, whereas Hillman presumed that the pantheon of the gods, particularly in Greek mythology, were themselves archetypes not merely symbolic representations of primordial phenomena. He argued that because we're unable to distinguish between mythical characters and archetypes (which by their nature are unknowable), 'our descriptions of the archetypes and the classical descriptions of the Gods, heroes, and daemons have to be analogous' (Hillman 1976: 36). Jung saw the personification of archetypal material as a positive way to examine the unconscious as distinct and separate from consciousness, but not with the same 'analogous' sensibility as Hillman. In 1916 Jung called dialogue between the *patient* and the *images* s/he projects in fantasies and dreams, *active imagination*, and sought to develop a relationship between the two, whereby the patient would begin to understand the meaning of the image and eventually the dynamic of the archetypal pattern underlying it.

Audience interactions with film and television via fan clubs, websites, fan fiction, or joint interactive viewing operate in a similar way. The archetypal images surfacing in the framework of particular screen fictions become intrinsic to the shared dialogue of viewers as they collectively unravel the import of their favourite plots and characters. As Rowland (2005: 11) argues: 'art is a means by which the collective unconscious informs collective society'. This is indeed how Jung saw the functioning of cultural texts. For him they were symbolic of a culture's development or individuation process in the way that they educated, 'the spirit of the age, conjuring up the forms in which the age is most lacking' (*CW* 15, para. 130).

Individuation

Analytical psychology is based on the idea that only by becoming aware of unconscious material are we able to work toward a sense of unity, or what might be thought of as a utopian state of mind where once conflicting psychological energies no longer function as opposing disturbances, but operate as components of a unifying 'give and take' dynamic. A conversation, perhaps, that *appreciates* rather than *struggles* with difference. This might be visualized through the Möbius strip, a geometric shape named after scientist/mathematician August Möbius (1790–1868), formed by twisting a length of material 180 degrees and joining the ends together. The effect is a continuous surface rather than two distinct back and front sides. This twisted model of inner and outer exchange, as well as being a metaphor for the merging of conscious and unconscious contents, can also, according to Grosz, be used to debunk the Cartesian mind/matter duality, by 'showing that there can be a relation between two "things" – mind and body – which presumes neither their identity nor their radical disjunction' (1994: 209–210).

Throughout the *Collected Works*, and as we saw in the previous discussion of the way Jung linked archetypes to biological process, it becomes clear that rather than arguing for ongoing binary conflict, he was advocating the kind of mind/matter twist and exchange that Groz talks about. While he believed that the tension of opposites was necessary for psychological development, he theorized that the ultimate aim of this struggle was balance. The path to this goal was called *individuation*.

In 'Jung and Politics' (1997), Lawrence Alschuler sees individuation as a three-step process. The first stage involves the emergence of ego consciousness in early childhood; in the second the ego, *persona* (the social mask) and *shadow* (suppressed material unacceptable to the ego) are shaped, tested and sometimes pitted against each other via complexes and projections in a struggle for identity that often climaxes in mid-life; and the third stage is about integrating the ego with the 'greater' matter of the psyche, or in other words, dissolving projections by becoming to more familiar with, and accepting, the workings of one's unconscious (Alschuler 1997: 285–287). Because this conscious/unconscious melding appears to be more of an 'ideal' than a practically lived psychological process, Samuels holds reservations about the concept:

> A holistic vision perceives the world as inextricably united. Though I *do* doubt that such a phenomenon exists to the extent wished for, personal experiences of oneness mean that I partly share the holistic ideal. But holistic thinking tends to be utopian-what Jung referred to as 'preaching' about unity and wholeness.
>
> (Samuels 1990: 298)

Tacey (2001) understands the merging of unconscious processes with consciousness in the individuation process not as a fusion or blending, but a meaningful interaction between these contrary energies: 'The whole point is not to get the opposites to coalesce and subside into a undifferentiated soup, but to allow them to work toward a state of complementarity and interplay' (Tacey 2001: 67). For this to occur, Samuels (1989: 224) argues that binary tensions must be withdrawn and replaced by an appreciation of a more free flowing plurality without the presumption of 'unity' as its aim.

Again it's helpful to image the Möbius strip. Each side of the strip maintains its autonomy and yet, in Tacey's (2001) terms, works as a 'state of complementarity and interplay'. It's possible to run a finger over one side of the geometric configuration and watch it magically find its way to the other side without lifting the skin. While the navigation of individuation requires rigorous conscious effort, Jung saw this energy as an unconscious motif, so that according to Tacey it's 'not just Jung's "theory", but a psychobiological process to be reckoned with . . . The individuation process indeed appears to be archetypal, and if we do not co-operate with it, it runs its course without our assistance' (2001: 127).

Psychology and Alchemy (*CW* 12) and *Mysterium Coniunctionis* (*CW* 14) deal specifically with Jung's interest in medieval alchemy. On the surface this was a covert form of chemistry developed with the specific intention of turning base metals into gold, but to Jung, it was a practice and philosophy rich in the symbolism of individuation (*CW* 12, para. 40). He saw this tradition steeped in a mix of empirical science and mysticism where chemical transformation was analogous to psychological transformation (*CW* 12, para. 332–333). Much of his research was drawn from the *Rosarium Philosophorum* (1550), an alchemical text where he claimed: 'The anonymous author was very definitely a "philosopher" and was apparently aware that alchemy was not concerned with ordinary gold making but with a philosophical secret' (*CW* 12, para. 99). The various procedures and images that alchemists detailed to describe the process of 'change' (much of it 'coded' to avoid the looming threat of religious heresy), was nevertheless overtly pious in its overarching allusion to Christ/God as the ultimate marker of the individuated state.

Jung reads the turning of base metals into gold as an analogy for the perforation of unconscious contents to consciousness that effect psychological development as they transform from one state to another (*CW* 12, para. 564). The alchemists illustrated this merging of opposites through the notion of *coniunctio* (divine marriage), a concept developed further in Chapter 3's discussion of *Mulholland Drive* (2001). This union, often illustrated through the hermaphrodite or an often incestuous heterosexual coupling (Sol/sun/masculine and Luna/moon/feminine), pre-empted the rise of the individuated state. The product of this symbolic coitus adopted a number of forms including gold, the divine child, the figure of Mercurius, the lapis philosophorum (philosopher's stone), and Christ (*CW* 9ii, para. 73).

Like the metaphors the alchemists set up to explain the process of individuation, the films and television programs in *Mis/takes* also contain images that suggest a reworking of the same desire for integration, utopian 'wholeness', or genial inner dialogue. Each of the central characters strives to come to terms with uneasy 'truths' about their lives and in the process begin to either realize (or fail to realize) that only by recognizing and accepting these unnerving aspects of themselves, are they are able to discover an identity beyond misplaced/mistaken façades. The individuated state that either eludes or illuminates, often takes the form of what Jung saw as spontaneous symbols arising from the unconscious. These dream, religious and artistic images that he believed primarily took the form of *mandalas* (Sanskrit for circle) and *quaternities* (because of their four-pronged and whole-number structure) symbolized the ambiguous and abstract notion of the *Self*: 'I have called this wholeness that transcends consciousness the "self". The goal of the individuation process is the synthesis of the self' (*CW* 9i, para. 278).

Big 'Self', small 'self' and the bigger picture

In classical Jungian terms, the Self is often concretely defined as the unifying principle of the psyche (the 'wholeness' archetype) *and*, like all archetypes, a principle beyond comprehension. The concept is further confused in the *Collected Works* because Jung doesn't consistently distinguish the 'self' by capitalization, parenthesis or italics, from the notion of individual character. As the following quote shows, the difficulty implicit in this slippery use of language seems to escape him:

> I have defined the self as the totality of the conscious and the unconscious psyche, and the ego as the central reference-point of consciousness. It is an essential part of the self, and can be used *pars pro toto* when the significance of consciousness is borne in mind. But when we want to lay emphasis on the psychic totality it is better to use the term 'self.' There is no question of a contradictory definition, but merely of a difference of standpoint.
>
> (*CW* 14, para. 133)

To clarify this problematic syntax, some post-Jungians began to discriminate between the two terms by capitalizing the 'Self' when discussing this utopian state of psychological wholeness/dialogue, and leaving the 'self' in lower case when referring to personal identity. *Mis/takes* follows this precedent for clarity, only sliding into non-differentiation in citations.

In juxtaposing Jung's views of the Self with Freud's hostile ego–id relationship, Hauke (2000: 56) writes that: 'Jung called the whole of the conscious-unconscious psyche the *self*, of which the ego was but a small part that the psyche as a whole uses to consciously relate to itself and the outer world'. In Alschuler's (1997: 285) view, the Self can be read as both the drive toward psychic integration as well as the image of integration. As mentioned earlier, this imagery takes on a variety of forms, cross-culturally similar in configuration: to the mandalas and quaternities we can also add the figure of the divine child (discussed in Chapter 6).

Throughout his writings, Jung saw the Self as a numinous concept fundamental to both organized religion and nonsectarian spiritual practices. He argued that although an archetypal motif remains a latent possibility in all of us, it's only fully realized (if ever) through exhaustive self-analysis and synthesis of unconscious/conscious material (*CW* 9ii, para. 297). When he quotes Clement of Alexandria (*c.*150–*c.*215) as saying, 'it is the greatest of all disciplines to know oneself; for when man knows himself, he knows God' (*CW* 9ii, para. 347), he suggests that the concept of God, rather than being an external impacting force, can be seen as a symbol of ultimate psychological maturity or evolution. And yet in his characteristic slip sliding of positions, he argued that the Self extends beyond the individual so that the concept of 'I' is overshadowed by an experience of a larger, more unified sense of existence; 'the bigger picture', commonly presented to us through, but of course not limited to, religious doctrine (*CW* 9ii, para. 57).

Rather than reading the Self as an attainable embrace of consciousness and the unconscious, the goal of the individuation process, or a plausible state of psychological regulation and balance, it might also be thought of as an impossible otherness. To talk about the Self as a *desire* for synthesis and a *desire* for ultimate potential, makes more sense in the light of the way that the concept is embedded in the screen texts under discussion. When Jung equates the Self with the numinous qualities of the god-image, the concept becomes intangible and abstract, collective and personal. It's more easily read as a *want* rather than a *promise for the individuated.* Throughout *Mis/takes*, the symbolism of Self is seen as both symptomatic of a yearning for cohesion, and a signifier for an illusive state of unification – another of Jung's leaps of faith.

Chapters 3 and 6 in particular look at the Self through symbolic and recurring imagery in the film *Mulholland Drive* and the Fox Network's *The X-Files* (1993–2002). There's a jarring edge, though, in reading very conspicuous images of 'wholeness', an ostensibly modernist concept, into these overtly postmodern texts. Both embrace the postmodern aesthetic by eroding high/low cultural distinctions, interlacing parody and pastiche, diffusing the metanarrative, and drawing on what Fredric Jameson calls the 'schizophrenic experience' of 'isolated, disconnected, discontinuous material signifiers which fail to link up into a coherent sequence' (Jameson 1985: 119). So although I am fashioning *a* meaning or *a* narrative from these texts, I acknowledge that there is no decisive reading, interpretation, or narrative strand. In a way this follows Jung's line of reading art, which as Rowland (2005) argues, he never makes explicit enough, but still clearly legitimizes as a way of interpreting creative material.

If modernity is ultimately a gateway to a unifying experience, a concept that Jean-François Lyotard (1979) in his critique of Jürgen Habermas dismisses as a pacifying illusion, then how do we position the Self and the texts that allude to it, if not in a modernist frame? Jung's characteristic ambiguity, his insistence on plurality and duality, and his refusal to nail down the unconscious and the archetype to a definitive meaning, carries the seeds of postmodern thinking. We can see this in his understanding of the Self as: 'a term on the one hand definite enough to convey the essence of human wholeness and on the other hand indefinite enough to express the indescribable and indeterminable nature of this wholeness' (*CW* 12, para. 20).

Like the disparate intertextual fusions of contemporary cinema and television, where genres and disciplines of our cross-cultural past and present synthesize to form both narrative and non-narrative structures contained within the concept of 'the text', so the Self has 'a paradoxical, antinomial character' that forms a 'complexico oppistorum' (*CW* 9ii, para. 355). If the Self is the product of the balance of unknowable psychological material that endlessly reveals itself in diverse symbolic imagery, it must also be unknowable, multilayered and postmodern. It must be a fusion of multiple influences *and* their impossible containment. More postmodern than the products of the postmodern era, it can never be the sum of its parts, only an enigmatic sense of possibility without beginning or end.

Yet the *desire* for oneness fixed in the notion of the Self, the same desire that drives the characters under discussion throughout this book, takes us back to that which Lyotard dismisses as pacifying. It has more in common with the notion of modernity as an unfinished project of Enlightenment, that is, the ongoing search for unity. In the films and programs I've selected, this concept of modernity within postmodern texts can be seen as playful appropriation or an ambiguous and canny plurality. So for instance while *Mulholland Drive* can be talked of as being influenced by dada and surrealism (modernist movements) as well as embracing the push for a sense of 'wholeness', David Lynch, like all postmodernist scavengers, can be understood to merely borrow and pluck, rather than claim a position.

Sign and symbol

Jung clearly makes the distinction between *signs* and *symbols*, by claiming that signs represent the known, and symbols the unknown and ultimately unknowable. In his terminology, symbols describe the wide variety of references to the Self. These spontaneously occurring and autonomous images are understood to be as cross-cultural and atemporal, and although changing and shifting in appearance depending on the context in which they present themselves, they often retain the integrity of the basic circular or four pronged template that suggests a sense of harmonious coexistence.

Because symbols refer to the Self, other archetypal motifs, and complexes (all ultimately unknowable energies), they should never be thought of as representing something tangible and recognizable as in the classic semiotic schema established by early structuralists, Ferdinand de Saussure (1857–1913) and Charles Sanders Peirce (1839–1914). Peirce's structure for instance divides the sign-image into three central categories predicated on already learned and shifting cultural understandings: *iconic* where we see a direct resemblance to the signified (the image of a horse represents the animal we call 'horse' in English), *indexical* where the signified is shown through an associated image (the Sydney Opera House indicates Australia) and *symbolic* where the signifier does not resemble the signified but alludes to it through cultural convention (the dove as a symbol of peace).

In analytical psychology, a mandala image for example, is seen as a *symbol* of the Self, because the concept of the Self is beyond definition. As Don Fredericksen (2001: 37) in 'Jung/sign/symbol/film' argues in relation to Jung's terminology: 'one comes to realize that while symbols come from us individually, they escape our attempts to enclose them within the wholly or essentially personal, and irrevocably link us to the transpersonal'. While for structuralists, signs and their various sub-categories (including symbols) are fixed within a system of established meaning and representation, for post-structuralists like Michel Foucault, Jacques Derrida and Lyotard, there is no single fixed meaning, all signs are fluid and negotiated within a social context. Even though

Jung can easily be regarded as a structuralist primarily because of his archetypal schema, he slips into post-structuralist and postmodernist territory by distinguishing between the sign and the symbol:

> A symbol is an indefinite expression with many meanings, pointing to something not easily defined and therefore not fully known. But the sign always has a fixed meaning, because it is a conventional abbreviation for, or a commonly accepted indication of, something known.
>
> (*CW* 5, para. 180)

Mis/takes follows Jung's reasoning to make clearer the way in which sign, symbols and the symbolic can be applied to screen texts as a way of extending the discourse beyond conventional denotative and style discourses in cinema analysis. Sympathetic to Jung's development of the sign/symbol relation, Fredericksen puts his position as a film theorist in this way:

> I want to counter the thesis that every time one entity 'stands for' another, we have an instance of one known thing 'standing for' another known thing. This inflation of the narrower notion of sign to encompass all semiosis leaves no room for the symbol as Jung defined it and denies legitimacy to his symbolic attitude . . . The primary aim is to argue for the meaning in, and the meaningfulness of, film situations in which a known entity 'stands for' a relatively unknown one.
>
> (Fredericksen 2001: 21)

While symbols must necessarily be read to provide a textual analysis, I'm not presuming any conclusive/absolute definition of these images, and in keeping with the classical and post-Jungian schools of analytical psychology, maintain the ambiguity of the symbol as it appears in relation to both the characterization and thematic trajectory of screen texts. As mentioned earlier, Chapters 3 and 6 take exactly this position in the way that the symbol of the Self within the text, is never a closed and defined concept for the characters or the spectator. The hermetically sealed cubes in *Mulholland Drive*, I've read as quaternity images, defy definition but serve to point toward the central character Diane's desire for a sense of unity. Similarly the mandala imagery of UFOs in *The X-Files* can never be explained or concretely nailed down to a rational absolute. The closest one can get to the meaning of these often spontaneously appearing images in the series, is the way that they reflect a search for 'the truth' and 'God' for each of the main characters. Both concepts are ultimately unknowable and yet able to encompass a sense of ultimate potential, for as Jung argued: 'symbols act as *transformers*, their function being to convert libido [his term for psychic energy] from a "lower" into a "higher" form' (*CW* 5, para. 344, original emphasis).

Had these texts been looked at through a Freudian perspective, the cubes and UFO images, might have signified something of an altogether personal nature – repressed desires seeking acknowledgement. The marked difference in the Jungian and Freudian approaches hinges on the transpersonal and transforming nature of the symbol in the former discipline, and the personal, once 'known' nature of the symbol in the later (Fredericksen 2001: 37). We shouldn't be surprised when UFO obsessed Fox Mulder lets us know that he is *not* a Freudian ('Clyde Bruckman's Final Repose' 3×4).

Myth in film and television

Throughout Jung's writing, myth is prioritized as a potent psychological given and the best representation and shaper of the psyche. In 'Jung and Derrida: the Numinous, Deconstruction, and Myth', Rowland (2006) elaborates on our ability to create stories by arguing that, 'the myth-making quality of the psyche is a weaving together of body, consciousness and unconscious.' To her way of thinking mythology 'makes elements of the textuality of the psyche into the equivalent of sublime works of art: pregnant with meaning that can never be wholly absorbed into logocentric rational knowledge, yet neither wholly dissipated in the dissemination of psychic signifiers.' Myth is an inescapable given in analytical psychology that is under constant review, and as Rowland writes, beyond any sense of the absolute. Jung argued that the conflicting and intertwining images of mythology emanate from the structure of the objective psyche, so that rather than audiences *having* these myths, the myths *have* them (*CW* 9i, para. 314, original emphases). Myth is then, in essence, symbolic. It's because of this unknowability that I want to argue for the 'open' nature of contemporary mythic fictions (that is, texts beyond fixed definition), where symbols flourish. I'm being almost classically Jungian here, because this is Jung at his most postmodern. As Rowland writes of his take on symbolic art, it is 'autonomous of the author because it is rooted in the *collective* unconscious, not reliant upon the author's *personal* life, but rather his impersonal one. For symbolic art, the author is not a guide to the work' (Rowland 2005: 8, original emphases).

As well as producing material riddled (both intentionally and unconsciously) with allusions to myth and archetypal patterning, television creators and filmmakers, like Chris Carter (*The X-Files*) and Quentin Tarantino (*Kill Bill* Vols. 1 and 2, 2003, 2004), talk enthusiastically in their DVD featurettes, of the self-styled 'mythology' embedded in their various epics. Even though these contrived and conscious appropriations of mythic patterns follow the tradition of Joseph Campbell influenced work like George Lucas's six *Star Wars* epics (1977, 1980, 1983, 1999, 2002, 2005) or George Miller's *Mad Max* trilogy (1979, 1981, 1985), they have evolved in the way that both play with (and on) the use of myth in their highly postmodern compositions, to create intricately textured events resonant with archetypal tension; in particular allusions to the concept of the Self ('the Bride's' child in *Kill Bill* for instance, or UFOs and the divine children in *The X-Files*). Despite this self-conscious playing around with the symbolic, *Mis/takes* maintains that audiences are the ultimate authors, the ultimate readers, of any screen text.

The similarity between the psychic processes and structural elements of ancient myths and fantasies/dreams is linked to the way that the content of each is forced from the unconscious in the form of archetypal patterning (*CW* 9i, para. 259). This view is counter to Roland Barthes (1972) reading of myth as part semiology, part ideology, and closer to anthropologist Claude Lévi-Strauss' idea of myth as a series of units or *mythemes*, similar to the concept of archetypes which have no original authors and move in a circular discourse of repetition where content and meaning can be varied (Paz 1970). *Twin Peaks* (1990–1991, discussed in Chapter 7) and *The X-Files* are examples of this kind of activity. They blatantly enfold the fictions of literature, television and film in an intertextual borrowing intrinsic to the mythic tradition itself, so that in line with Lévi-Strauss: 'Each myth reveals its meaning in another one, which, in its turn, refers to another, and so on in succession to the point where all these allusions and meanings weave a text: a group or family of myths' (Paz 1970: 38).

The interlocking of Greek tragedies are clear examples of what Lévi-Strauss is talking about. But in terms of popular culture, we can also see blatant parody/pastiche fusions of interlocking Greek myth in the soap opera, or within the daytime soap cannon itself, when a character from, for example, *The Bold and the Beautiful* (1987–) also appears in *The Young and the Restless* (1973–) and continues their storyline across the two programs. A similar interweaving also informs the current 2005 prime-time *Crime Scene Investigation* and *Law and Order* spin-offs. Although from the structuralist school, Lévi-Strauss, like Jung, slips into postmodern terrain when trying to articulate the overarching dynamic of the multifarious cross-references and split-off threads within mythology:

> There is no end to mythological analysis, no hidden unity to be grasped once the breaking-down process has been completed. Themes can be split up ad infinitum. Just when you think that you have disentangled and separated them, you realize that they are knitting together again in response to the operation of unexpected affinities.
>
> (Lévi-Strauss 1970: 5)

Lévi-Strauss also likened myth to music, seeing both as languages that rise above the strictures of speech and have the power to suspend a sense time, 'so that when we listen to it we accede to a sort of immortality' (Paz 1970: 61). It's telling in relation to the mythic allusions in *Twin Peaks* to hear composer Angelo Badliamenti, in the short documentary *For One Week Only: David Lynch* (1990), talk about the way Lynch described the five segment structure of the theme he imagined for the series:

> I'm looking for a multi theme that can work throughout the pilot as well as some of the episodes . . . I think you've got to start with something very dark and very slow and almost scary, and then it's got to build into some switch from minor to major, and start this most beautiful single note climb . . . let it build and reach a climax that should tear the hearts out of people . . . stay on that climax a bit and then come down in a falling gentle way, and then make it segue back into that first minor dark thing.

The mythic strands in *Twin Peaks* are looked at later in the book, but at this point it's worth noting the way in which this signature theme, like Lévi-Strauss' music–myth relationship, is clearly trying to access a sense of the atemporal and transcendent, so that the shifting moods conveyed in the score, reflect the poignant mythic trajectory of the central narrative. These five segments also echo the major archetypal twists that help shape the character and story arc of the tragic 'Laura Palmer' as well as the secondary characters who mirror her inner multiplicity. Without knowing what the series is about, Lynch and Badliamenti's composition helps us to tap into the mythic/musical language of the unconscious in order to prepare for further narrative explication – or some might say, onslaught. It's easy to sense the influence (conscious or unconscious) of Lévi-Strauss' thinking:

> Music and mythology bring man face to face with potential objects of which only shadows are actualised, with conscious approximations (a musical score and a myth cannot be more) of inevitably unconscious truths, which follow from them. In the case of myth we can guess the reason for this paradoxical situation: it is a consequence of the irrational relation between the collective and the particular manner in which it is experienced by the individual.
>
> (Lévi-Strauss 1970: 18)

Mythology as an expression of unconscious patterning has always influenced screen fiction. As far back as the 1970s, before the splurge of digitally hyped mythic epics or the Joseph Campbell/Jung influenced rash of screenwriting guides (Seger 1987; Vogler 1992; Bonnet 1999), Fiske and Hartley (1978: 85) went some way toward acknowledging the function of television as a conduit for the mythic constellations of the collective unconscious, by claiming that the medium, 'functions as a social ritual, overriding individual distinctions, in which our culture engages in order to communicate with its collective self'. They appear sympathetic to the mythic dimensions of the psyche when they claim that projecting 'abstract ideas into material form is evident in such social activities as religious ritual. But the television medium also performs a similar function' (Fiske and Hartley 1978: 90). While the technologies of information transmission continue to develop, allowing audiences to experience the media in a variety of forms, the essence of these messages can be traced to our earliest systems of communication, largely religious and artistic expressions.

As mentioned earlier in relation to Hillman, Jung understood the characters of myth (gods, demi-gods and mortals) to personify specific archetypal patterns of experiencing the world: the Self in the form of the divine child – Christ, Buddha or the alchemists 'Mercurius'; *anima/animus* syzergy as Sol and Luna; trickster as Hermes or Wakdjunkaga; intoxication and ecstasy as Dionysos; shadow as Mephistopheles, Satan, Mara; Great Earth Mother as Gaia or Chomolungma (Mount Everest). If archetypal images are culturally modified, it's not surprising that these and related figures of ancient mythology are periodically reimagined on the screen, for as Jung argued: 'The most we can do is *dream the myth onwards* and give it a modern dress. And whatever explanation or interpretation does to it, we do to our own souls as well, with corresponding results for our well being' (*CW* 9i, para. 271, original emphasis).

Although an archetype can be interpreted as 'an unobservable, hypothetical construct' (Shelburne 1988: 57) that adopts form and definition only through projection, it has to be implicitly understood that these projections are never uniform, but subjectively coloured. The impact of the visual media (film, television, video, photography, DVD, CD-Rom) has revealed how diverse the representations of archetypal content can be, and how the core/fundamental figures of mythology still prevail. This modification can also be seen in the way archetypal content is projected in images of both genders.

Established by strongly male-dominated cultures to preserve their ideology, the politics that shapes and reshapes mythology is problematic. The ancient female deities of Western culture (generally speaking) are divided into images of fertility, virginity, seduction, war, horror and the maternal. Expressions of laughter, autonomy, transgression and spectacle without violence or monstrosity are not as prolific. However, if archetypes spring from the *collective* unconscious then no matter how they have been culturally imagined, they must, in their essence, be genderless. The pattern of trickster for instance, predominantly imagined as a male figure of laughter, mischief, power, redemption, play and transformation, *is*, for contemporary audiences, just as easily realized through female projections (Chapters 2 and 11). Superman shares his childhood divinity with Buffy (*Buffy the Vampire Slayer*, 1997–2003); boxer Maggie Fitzgerald in *Million Dollar Baby* (2004) embodies the heroic paradigm or the archetype of ego-consciousness in the mythic tradition of more macho male protagonists; the nurturing and protective mother archetype governs lawyer Atticus Finch (*To Kill a Mockingbird*, 1962) and child psychologist Malcolm Crowe (*The Sixth Sense*, 1999); and not only are the *drag* spectacles of *Little Britain*'s (2003–) Matt Lucas/David Williams and Australian export Dame Edna Everage grotesque, but so are Patsy and Edina from the series *Absolutely Fabulous* (1992–).

Jung was conspicuously unreflective about the way he assigned gender to archetypal images: anima (feminine) and animus (masculine) energies the most obvious examples. But as Hillman argues in *Anima: Anatomy of a Personified Notion* (1985), the archetype is at its core, gender neutral. Although archetypal patterns are often projected into characters and their various story arcs, this narrow 'spot the archetype' concentration is problematic when applying analytical psychology to screen texts. An archetypal dominant, more often than not entwined with a number of motifs, is infused throughout the structure of a film or television series. For example, while we can read the character of 'Leonard' in Christopher Nolan's *Memento* (2000) as a trickster figure, we can only really do this through the way this archetypal theme is amplified throughout the fabric of the film, via characterization, dialogue, open-ended narratives, bodily markings, set design, and various psychological approaches to Leonard's 'condition' of memory loss. These signifiers, in conjunction with what we know of the archetype through mythic representation, contributes to the textual analysis and also helps broaden our understanding of how archetypes can be understood through the complex intertwining of oral and visual cues in cinema.

It's then obvious to ask just how much, if at all, the archetypal and mythic threads of screen texts are consciously integrated by the filmmaker/s or television series creators. *Mis/takes* adopts a 'reader response' or 'audience reception' approach to screen analysis. It might be considered a limited position to cinephiles, but in this particular study, I'm not interested in the author's intention as much as responding to the text with all the subsequent *making of meaning* that this involves. David Lynch in his various interviews and press conferences, for instance, hesitates entirely from exposing his 'game-plan'. It's a shrewd position that suggests respect for whatever reading/s the audience takes from his material, rather than burdening the spectator with an overarching meaning that they need to 'get' before the work can be 'suitably' appreciated.

A number of the directors/creators that *Mis/takes* draws on, knowingly embrace the mythic (Chris Carter's *The X-Files* for example), but my analysis isn't built on his assumption. For if myth is a psychic phenomenon, not a conscious construction, then despite intentionality, the mythic can pervade art at an unconscious level as invasively as it does dreams and fantasies. Consequently the various myths and archetypal structures that can be read into, or perhaps 'felt through' screen fiction, says something of the spectator's personal and collective relationship to the imagery before them.

Film and television seduce us into a world of illusion, excess and permeable boundaries, where we, as interactive spectators, are invited to juggle mixed ethical, moral, philosophical and political messages. Keeping all these balls in the air, while being pleasured, allows us to come to our own conclusions about the viability of the positions we are watching and how they might apply to our lives beyond the screen. Thinking through the framework of analytical psychology, it's possible to argue that this intricate activity is presided over by the energy of *trickster*. The archetype can be read as governing the form and function of cinema and television, and to varying degrees, each of the screen texts in *Mis/takes*. I haven't included any discussion of the motif here because it deserves more than a cursory paragraph or two. This is why the next chapter is dedicated to analyzing the complexity of the trickster paradigm in past and present popular culture. So, having set down the prime concepts that I'll be drawing on throughout the book, it's time to indulge in something a little more profane, marginal and unruly.

Chapter 2

Mutability, identities and the farce of fixity

Trickster

> There is an idea of a Patrick Bateman, some kind of abstraction, but there is no real me only an entity, something illusory, and though I can hide my cold gaze and you can shake my hand and feel flesh gripping you and maybe you can even sense our lifestyles are probably comparable, I simply am not there.
>
> Mary Harron, *American Psycho* (2000)

Mary Harron's film version of Bret Easton Ellis' (1991) scathing allegory of America in the 1980s is a prime example of the chaotic, fluid and elusive nature of trickster. In all its mythically imaged forms this archetypal energy remains a constructive *and* destructive catalyst for psychological movement on a range of interlocking emotional and intellectual levels. Although trickster has been personified as shape-shifting shamans, clowns/fools and primitive animal–human hybrids able to play in the sacred and profane, the motif is far more complex than its cultural projections. The memories and projections of others that help shape our sense of self can all be manipulated by this function. In this way the archetype forces us to acknowledge the mutability of identity. By turning the signifiers of who we are topsy-turvy, it allows a respite from, and a more knowing re-evaluation of, the self as distinct from an outward show presented to the world as a defense against either real or imagined threats. The ability to 'trip up' the psyche through wily behaviours, unconscious slips, lapses, moral ambiguity, or foolery enables trickster to alter perceptions and consequently initiate personal and collective change.

The key protagonists in each of the film and television series under discussion in *Mis/takes* can develop a more realistic understanding of their motives and inadequacies only by playing out, meeting, or embodying trickster. Before working through these texts, it's important to understand the nature of the archetype and its ability to stimulate awareness of veiled and/or stuck psychological material. This chapter concentrates exclusively on the multidimensionality of the trickster paradigm by interspersing anthropological studies and the way that the motif has been theoretically 'decoded', with a broad sweep of its manifestations in popular culture, its (often) antagonistic relationship to the persona (social mask), and its role as redeemer.

Anthropological readings of trickster

The American mythic tradition of trickster was popularized through Paul Radin's (1956) study of the trickster in Siouan-speaking Winnebago Indian culture (Eastern Nebraska and Wisconsin). The Winnebago imaged the motif as a mediating figure able to traverse and straddle a number of complex and contradictory positions. Radin's work is divided into two cycles, the Winnebago Trickster and the Winnebago Hare, with supplementary summaries of the Assiniboine and Tlingit trickster myths. Sam Blowsnake, the primary source for the first cycle, translated the stories in 1912 from Winnebago syllabary, a rare nineteenth-century script (Radin 1956/1972: 111). Radin considered his accounts to be versions of more ancient trickster myths exclusive to the Winnebago, prompting Jung to describe the motif as 'an archetypal psychic structure of extreme antiquity' or psychologem (*CW* 9i, para. 465).

Radin found not only that the primary trickster figure Wakdjunkaga, meaning 'trickster' or 'cunning one' (1972: 174), dominated Winnebago mythology, but also that varying forms of the mythologem also pervaded global cultural traditions. This research, published with chapters by Karl Kerényi, 'The Trickster in Relation to Greek Mythology', and Jung, 'On the Psychology of the Trickster Figure' (in *CW* 9i), is often cited as one of the principal sources that most acutely reflects the trickster's impact on the psyche (Campbell 1959; Spinks 1991; Hyde 1998).

Jung concentrated on the Winnebago tradition to support his thesis that trickster represented a movement from a base, 'rudimentary stage of consciousness' to one more developed and discriminatory (*CW* 9i, para. 467). Within the evolutionary schema symbolized by trickster, the motif in its present more mature form, has the capacity to effect change and progression of the individual and the collective by transforming the seemingly 'meaningless into the meaningful' (*CW* 9i, para. 458). It does this by generating and shattering illusions. But as Robert Pelton (1980: 228) comments in his study on West African tricksters, Jung's focus on Wakdjunkaga as a 'normative' example of the archaic trickster's 'movement from an undifferentiated psychic state to an adult capacity for differentiation' is questionable. While Pelton stresses the importance of looking beyond Jungian appropriations of the figure as an archetypal projection to anthropological structuralist and neo-Durkheimian readings, this chapter concentrates, for the most part, on how cultural projections of trickster can be read through the framework of analytical psychology.

The most common feature of the mythic trickster is its unruly desire to transgress and manipulate societal laws, ethics and morality as a means of shifting awareness from the imposed to the 'authentic'. This longing to disrupt convention and so 'see beyond' the confinement of cultural constructs, is integral to personal and collective psychological development. In reference to Wakdjunkaga, Samuels acknowledges trickster's flexible, amoral and 'omnipotent infant' aspect, but goes way beyond these signifiers of mischief and noncompliance when he argues that, 'to my mind he represents the psyche itself' (Samuels 1985: 270). The unknowable nature of trickster, its ambiguity, its penchant for loitering at crossroads, thresholds and boundaries, its drive to make the meaningless meaningful through chaos, sensuality and the mediation of dualities, and the way it oscillates between the conscious and unconscious, can be understood as analogous to the cryptic nature of the psyche, that while appearing to work against us, ultimately, according to Jung, works for us.

Kerényi is not as enthusiastic in his summation of trickster as Samuels; nevertheless he endows the archetype with considerable power. In the following description, though, it's still worth keeping in mind the trickster/'psyche itself' relation:

> nothing demonstrates the meaning of the all-controlling social order more impressively than the religious recognition of that which evades this order, in a figure who is the exponent and personification of the life of the body: never wholly subdued, ruled by lust and hunger, for ever running into pain and injury, cunning and stupid in action. Disorder belongs to the totality of life, and the spirit of this disorder is the trickster. His function in an archaic society, or rather the function of his mythology, of the tales told about him, is to add disorder to order and so make a whole, to render possible, within the fixed bounds of what is permitted, an experience of what is not permitted.
>
> (Kerényi 1972: 185)

Traversing boundaries

While embodying, juggling and rousing right/wrong or moral/amoral polarities, trickster makes no judgment as to which is a more politically or socially correct means of guiding its subject/s toward inner and outer action. This function pervades the many cultural representations of the fickle and insatiable trickster. Don Giovanni from Mozart and Da Ponte's opera (1787) was one of the most notorious seducers, a reinvention of Molière's *Dom Juan* (1665) and Don Juan of Tirso da Molina's play *El Burlador de Sevilla* (1630):

> A Burlador is a trickster and hence the original play draws attention to the characteristic that was to become fully incorporated in the popular version of the Don Juan story. Don Juan is not simply a desperate sinner, he is also a trickster.
>
> (Mitchell 2000: 255)

The aversion to choosing between culturally loaded notions of appropriate and inappropriate behaviour, embodied in Don Juan's sexual play, elevates trickster above and beneath the web of completing moral ideologies.

Like his fellow more ancient mythic tricksters, Hermes/Mercury in particular, Don Juan is constantly in flight, detached, climaxing and running to the next romp. As Julia Kristeva (1987) writes in relation to Don Juan's cyclic conquests and his refusal to be confined either physically, emotionally or morally: 'he makes of it the principle of an abstract quest, a nonrepresentable ideal, an esthetic or an erotics for which visible objects, although not devalorized, are only ephemeral stops on the way to an impossible absolute' (Kristeva 1987: 195). It may appear that trickster achieves nothing and that its perpetual desire for the unattainable renders it empty of value, but I would argue that in its refusal to take a moral stand, a position, or ownership of any thing or anyone, trickster enables those it plays upon to formulate and constantly renegotiate their own sense of morality. This becomes obvious throughout the screen texts in *Mis/takes*.

Trickster's more general traversing from the known to the unknowable is expressed in the Western myths of Hermes/Mercury, messenger of the immortals, demi-god of commerce, thief, and bearer of souls to the underworld:

> Hermes, too, operates outside the fixed bounds of custom and law. I have described his field of operations as a 'no man's land, a sealed off, Hermetic region between the fixed bounds of property, where finding and thieving are still possible'.
>
> (Kerényi 1972: 185)

As with other trickster manifestations, he symbolizes mediation between immortal/mortal, life/death, honesty/dishonesty, reality/fantasy. In his study of the semiotics of trickster, C. W. Spinks (1991: 178) connects the motif with all marginal signs and argues that it is 'at the margins of self, symbol and culture' that trickster operates, ready to question the authority of the demarcator and the meaning of the demarcated.

As a figure that personifies the unfixed and fabricated nature of cultural margins, trickster calls into question the ideological 'spin' surrounding us by drawing attention to the tenuous nature of official 'truth'. Yet it is a figure of contradictions. Although bent on destabilizing the establishment, in whatever form, it also needs to operate within convention to best undermine, and ironically, strengthen, established norms. For as we'll see in Chapter 5's analysis of Alejandro Amenábar's *The Others* (2001), trickster inevitably effects a stronger sense of stability while subverting order through what might appear to be anarchy. According to Radin, this is a common disposition of the archetype: 'He possesses no values, moral or social is at the mercy of his passions and appetites, yet through his actions all values come into being'

(Radin 1972: xxiii). The paradox here demonstrates that while the motif is ultimately beyond fixity and above culturally fluctuating mores, it operates to reconfigure or, if appropriate, reconfirm boundaries.

Rowland (2005) acknowledges Jung's view of trickster as a means of cornering and incorporating the shadow (the container of material unacceptable to the ego): 'Without the self-consciousness only possible through individuation with the inner "other", the outer "other" may be subjected to devastating "mindless" violence. Jung evokes the modern soldier who does not know how to subject his orders to ethical scrutiny' (Rowland 2005: 186). Without inner/outer conflict facilitated by trickster, one merely 'follows' rather than makes a moral choice whether to, or not to follow. As the paradigm that spurs on collective and moral development, Jung warns, as Rowland reminds us, that by, 'forgetting trickster, the modern European pays no attention to the shadow. What is only perceptible to him in "fate playing tricks" is completely unintelligible to him as personal ethical responsibility' (Rowland 2005: 189). While amoral, trickster is therefore the prime agitator of moral and ethical accountability.

Cultural trickster figures

Trickster infiltrates the popular imagination in innumerable guises, some more convoluted than others. While popularly mythologized as a personal and collective shadow element able to manifest in both positive and negative forms, it nevertheless remains a catalyst for psychological movement throughout its various incarnations. It's easy to see this ability to drive narrative action through subtle and gross forms of disruption in, for example, the farces of Shakespearian fools who emerge as the most enlightened philosophers of the text; commedia dell'arte; late medieval/early Renaissance Farce, Sottie and Moralité comedies; television sketch comedies and sitcoms like *The Simpsons* (1989–), *Absolutely Fabulous*, *Just Shoot Me* (1997–2003), *The Games* (1998–2000), *The Office* (2001–2003) or *Kath and Kim* (2002–), well as the more sinister figures of film like *American Psycho*'s Patrick Bateman, or prime-time television's Bob (*Twin Peaks*), Cancer Man (*The X-Files*) or Livia and Uncle Junior (*The Sopranos* 1999–).

Vicky Pollard, the sometime teen mum from the sketch comedy *Little Britain*, is a striking example of trickster made flesh. Implicit in her pink track-suited excess and the seeming meaninglessness of her chaotic syntax is the need to fix her as chav princess-cum-subcultral stereotype-cum-parody of class-bound British culture. She's elusive, irresponsible and avoids any moral position. As her audience, moral positions are our job. From her convoluted dialogue and multiple pregnancies, to the male–female transmutation of alter ego actor Matt Lucas, Vicky embodies the trickster energy of past and contemporary comedy. While it's impossible to chart the exhaustive projections of trickster through myth, literature, performance and the electronic media, the representative examples throughout this chapter will help clarify the archetypal current that shapes and propels what can be known of this highly unpredictable aspect of the psyche.

In *CW* 12, Jung draws on eleventh-century alchemical imagery of the Italian Mercury or Greek Hermes, often depicted as a dragon bird/snake hybrid or the uroboros, a circular snake-like creature ingesting its tail to symbolize unity/Self. Through these configurations trickster is elevated to, 'the god of revelation, and in unofficial nature philosophy of the early Middle Ages he is nothing less than the world-creating Nous itself' (Jung *CW* 9i, para. 193). In his spiritual reading of the art of medieval alchemy, Jung sees this ability of trickster to contain and fuse the contradictions of the material world and the psychological states of the unconscious and consciousness manifest in Mercurius, as a significant component of the psyche:

> Mercurius is the divine winged Hermes manifest in matter, the god of revelation, lord of thought and sovereign psychopomp . . . When the alchemist speaks of Mercurius, on the face of it he means quicksilver, but inwardly he means the world-creating spirit concealed or imprisoned in matter.
>
> (*CW* 12, para. 404)

The substance Mercury was of prime significance to ancient alchemists. As a liquid forming metal able to solidify, it clearly reflects the shape-shifting and conflicting nature of trickster.

Mercury (Hg in the periodic table, from the Latin *hydrargyrum*) is also known as liquid silver, a substance found in Cinnabar and Calomel ores that doesn't steep into surfaces, but remains in spherical 'blobs'. It does, however, alloy with metals like silver, tin and particularly gold (the alchemical symbol of perfection) that it 'wets' or absorbs to form an amalgam. In keeping with the trickster imagery it was named after, Mercury doesn't stick to anything other than the above metals. It passes from one material to another without committing itself along the way. This unattached and fleeting contact corresponds to the mythic representations of Mercury as the 'fleet footed' courier god of commerce and communication who merely passes information and money without owning either. In a similar homage, the planet Mercury, discovered around the third millennium BC, was also named after the Italian god because of the relatively breakneck 88 days it takes to revolve around the sun compared to Earth's 365 day orbit. Mercury as trickster is not only slippery, but also first to arrive at and leave the scene.

The action in *The Homeric Hymns*' ode 'To Hermes' is set within the first day of Hermes' birth. Son of the nymph Maia (meaning old mother) and Zeus, he treks mischievously from womb, to cradle, to the outer world. He first makes a lyre from a tortoise shell after brutally killing the tortoise, fashions sandals to cover his tracks when rustling his brother Apollo's cattle, and seduces Apollo, Zeus and Maia into forgiving him after he is caught. As a consequence of this obsequious toadying, he finds himself appointed lord of 'all herds' of animals and 'sole messenger to Hades' (Homer 1976: 47). Although Hermes is often exposed in his various acts of double-dealing, creating, destroying, charming, stealing, passing sleekly from one ruse to another, lying and profiting from the misfortunes of others, true to his mercurial 'teflon' nature, he manages to avoid retribution.

According to Bernie Neville's (2003) analysis of Hermes as an archetypal paradigm of contemporary culture, a shift has taken place from previous hero stories. He argues that Western/masculine thinking begun in the second millennium BC and driven by the Promethean myth of emancipation and technological advancement has been outmoded by a way of experiencing the world more profoundly influenced by the anti-hero Hermes. Neville (2003) locates the archetypal pattern in the slippery deregulation of money markets; the lack of community and familial relations; the collapse of 'grand narratives'; the fast paced exchange of information technology where volume and image are valued over content; the reliance on consumerism as a way to better ourselves; and the restructuring of the education system where 'Debates about what is worth teaching have been replaced by debates about what will sell' (Neville 2003).

Yet despite this seeming dissipation of structure, Neville credits 'Hermes' consciousness' with subverting the stifling nature of Apollonian rigidity. This move from a dependence on 'ordained' order to a confidence in our own ability to navigate the complex/multiple networks of the emotional and material world, have allowed for the development of, 'imagination, flexibility, intuition, the sense of the sacred, playfulness, irony, delight in paradox, grace, magic, heterogeneity, complexity, multiplicity, luck, healing and connection with the feminine' (Neville 2003).

Mercury/Hermes is among the most cited trickster figures in analytical psychology, but this is not to diminish other mythic projections, like the Bamapana of Australian Murnging mythology; the Chinese Sun Wukong/Monkey King; the Raven in North American and Eskimo mythology; Merlin of the Celts; Loki the more nefarious Norse trickster; and Loki's sister tricksters, the Valkyries, powerful female death angels (psychopomps) able to transform into birds or horses. In Pelton's (1980) comprehensive study – the spider trickster Ananse of the Ashanti (West African Ghana), Legba of the Fon (West African Togo and Benin), Eshu of the Yoruba (West African Nigeria) and Ogo-Yurugu of the Dogon (West African Mali) – the archetype is not so much seen as a psychologically redemptive figure able to unite by creating 'order from disorder', but as an anthropomorphic or personified mirror of the complexity, irony and multifaceted dimensions of reality. He argues that exposure to the chaotic quality of existence, via trickster, enables us to deal with, rather than become overwhelmed by, the nature and consequences of this internal/external havoc (Pelton 1980: 45).

Lawrence Goldman understands the trickster Iba Tiri (Iba-water, Tiri-fool) as an 'imaginary comforter-companion' (Goldman 1998: 91) for children of the Papua New Guinean Highlands. Iba Tiri shares the typical trickster traits of previous studies, but its particular association with water as the source of life adds to its marginal and cosmological importance as a pervading force of nature and human physiology that segregates land and bodily spaces. For the Highland population, water/waterways are productive and destructive forces of nature that as Goldman (1998) argues, divide, unite and preserve the physical and cultural boundaries of the many New Guinean peoples. Iba Tiri's relationship to water also links it with the psychopomp/ferryman aspect of the Hermes trickster where water symbolizes the regenerative flow between life/death and the unconscious/conscious aspects of the psyche.

Shape-shifting

The ability to shape-shift is a given of all trickster figures whether represented in character or symbolic form as in the liquid/solid transmutation of mercury. This can be seen literally in the morphing from animal to human and male to female in oral/written mythology, Western animation/Japanese anime, and the digitally manipulated special effects of fantasy/adventure/sci-fi films like *Dracula* (1992) and *The Mask* (1994), or the trilogies of *The Terminator* (1984, 1991, 2003), *Species* (1995, 1998, 2004), *The Matrix* (1999, 2003, 2003), *Lord of the Rings* (2001, 2002, 2003), *Harry Potter* (2001, 2002, 2004, 2005) and *Spider-Man* (2002, 2003, 2007). A striking play on the female shape-shifter is incorporated into Chris Cunningham's video clip, *Frozen* (1998), where a Goth/Celt ornamented Madonna morphs into a large black dog and a flock of ravens, well documented trickster birds central to the North and North-West coast of America (Lévi-Strauss 1963: 224; Radin 1972: 156).

Although images of trickster move from human to animal they're more frequently presented as anthropomorphic or theriomorphic figures (human/animal hybrids specific to myth). Radin argued that the primacy of Wakdjunkaga's laughter and language in the Winnebago mythic canon, demonstrated the intrinsically human quality of trickster, for although animal in appearance, its speech and humour was clearly aligned with human consciousness (Radin 1972: 125). He also claimed that trickster originated in the form of an old man driven by sexuality, hunger and wanderlust. Generally though, among the indigenous peoples of western North America, the motif was identified as an anthropomorphized shape-shifting animal (Radin 1972: 165).

The elasticity of trickster to modify itself into any form that serves its purpose corresponds to the proficiency with which the psyche can forget and camouflage uncomfortable memories or experiences to avoid psychological conflict. This slippery morphing ironically works to 'reveal', for as mentioned earlier in relation to Hermes, trickster myths incorporate exposure. He/she/it rarely 'gets away with it' undetected, yet the literal or figurative justice that seems inevitable upon discovery, is continually thwarted by trickster's lack of remorse and refusal to moderate its behaviour. When caught, trickster merely turns the other cheek and continues to play with disguises.

This slick transition from exposure to 'smoothing over' (and sometimes even exoneration) is clear in Apollo's discovery and ultimate forgiveness of Hermes' cattle rustling, Wakdjunkaga and Hare's endless getaways and slick back-peddling from one swindle to another, and even the ongoing yet thwarted attempts to 'unmask' performer Michael Jackson as a paedophile (sparked by Martin Bashir's British documentary exposé *Living with Michael Jackson*, 2003). With his modified facial features and skin colour, musical style, *puer aternis* (eternal boy) persona, ambiguous sexuality, and mercurial celebrity façade, Jackson, like his mythic predecessors, is a consummate self-reinventor who patently personifies aspects of trickster.

Although often depicted as an adolescent or infantile figure, closely aligned with Jung's delineation of the archetypal patterns puer and *puella* (eternal girl), trickster is nevertheless nearly always endowed with an intense sexual insatiability (à la Don Juan). This kind of intoxication though, doesn't preclude rationality, for although never afraid of sensual pleasures, trickster is not subject to the laws of either Apollonian rationalism or Dionysian ecstasy. It mediates both psychic fields. In maintaining that trickster can be epitomized by the phallus, Kerényi claims that the exaggerated penis is so aligned with trickster that it alone can epitomize the archetype, particularly in the form of Hermes, who is 'represented either by the phallus alone, set up as a "Kellenic image", or by the ithyphallic herm, the erect phallus and pillar bearing the god's head' (Kerényi 1972: 182). As Neville (2003) claims, this demi-god presides over 'getting lucky' and the 'one night stand'.

Like Hermes, Iba Tiri's generous genital endowment is compared to 'the probing incisors of ogres' (Goldman 1998: 109). Eshu's giant penis shaped hairdo similarly signifies fertility along with his pipes and whistles that are indicative of 'insatiable orality' (Pelton 1980: 129). Similarly in the film *Sex and Zen* (1992), trickster Mei Yeung-Sheng, a scholar of sexual enlightenment, has a horse-sized penis surgically sutured to his body. The penis is so exaggerated that it's often strapped to the back, or in the case of the Wakdjunkaga, detached and carried around in a container or box, as though, writes Radin (1972: 183), 'he were carrying his own essential core about in it'.

Despite these overt allusions to male potency, Kerényi (1972) points out that sexuality is used metaphorically to further emphasize trickster's transgressive edge. Even though the motif is associated with the phallus, its shape-shifting function allows for multiple gender readings: 'Even his sex is optional despite its phallic qualities: he can turn himself into a woman and bear children' (Jung *CW* 9i, para. 472). The inclusion of the 'box' accessory is interesting in terms of trickster's ability to switch from male to female. The word box is also a Western euphemism for cunt/vagina, so it's not a stretch to read a penis curled or squashed into the interior of a 'box' as an act of intercourse or male/female synthesis; mythically personified as the Hermaphrodite, child of Hermes and Aphrodite:

> He [Hermes] is the hermaphrodite that was in the beginning, that splits into the classical brother-sister duality and is reunited in the *coniunctio*, to appear once again at the end in the radiant form of the *lumen novum*, the stone. He is metallic yet liquid, matter yet spirit, cold yet fiery, poison and yet healing draught – a symbol uniting all opposites.
>
> (Jung *CW* 12, para. 404)

In Jung's writings on alchemy, coniunctio (as we saw in Chapter 1), is a term used for a merging or dialogue of opposites in the process of individuation. It's usually imaged as an incestuous heterosexual coupling, but also takes the form of a same sex fusion. Trickster can thus be rendered god-like it its ability to draw together the more disparate and/or conflicting elements of the psyche (*CW* 9i, para. 295).

Male/female transmutations

The literal gender morphing inherent in trickster denotes an ability to move beyond the culturally defined and precarious margins of the physiological body. Despite no direct references to the male/female metamorphosis in New Guinean culture, the very masculine Iba Tiri is understood by Highlanders to embody hermaphroditic qualities (Goldman 1998: 103). The primary gender of trickster projections has traditionally been male (not surprising in male-dominated cultures), but if the unconscious knows no gender boundaries, trickster, as with all archetypal structures, can be interpreted as a fluid, non-fixed image; intrinsically neither male or female. Pelton (1980: 52) writes of Ananse's 'monthly period'; Wakdjunkaga transforms himself into a woman by shaping a vulva from an elk's liver and breasts from its kidneys (Radin 1972: 22–23); and the Asiniboine trickster cycle details the shifting genders of tricksters Sitconski and particularly Inktumni who gives birth to a litter of rabbits after mating with Rabbit (Radin 1972: 101–103). Garth expresses a similar sexual preference to Inktumni in *Wayne's World* (1992) when he asks Wayne if he ever found 'Bugs Bunny attractive when he put on a dress and played a girl bunny?'

Although the grotesques of carnival (discussed in Chapter 11) are more strongly identified with female physiology (childbirth and its associations with bodily excretion), the male body can take on grotesque proportions when it adopts female characteristics. This notion of the body metaphorically adopting 'femaleness' (penetrability, seepage, boundlessness, merging inner with outer etc.) is grotesquely illustrated in Monty Python's film *The Meaning of Life* (1983) where the character 'Mr. Creosote' enters a restaurant, consumes vast amounts of food and then explodes, projectile vomiting and gushing bodily fluids onto neighbouring diners.

While penetrability doesn't necessarily involve a mimesis of the female body, the adoption of a sex other than that to which one is born, is yet another way of understanding the trickster pattern manifest in grotesque imagery. In the case of transsexual procedures this type of imitation can surgically involve the body exceeding its own limitations and abjectly spilling and seeping. The phenomenon/practice of couvade (male nemesis of pregnancy) in myth, literature, theatre, film and television (particularly comedy) also contributes significantly to our understanding of the way in which the shape-shifting trickster filters through popular culture by playing with, and challenging, conventional ideas of sexuality, the sexed body and gender ascription.

The French couvade (to brood or hatch), introduced into anthropological studies by Sir Edward Taylor, was used as a term for birthing rites (Hall and Dawson 1989: 49). These customs were developed by a number of indigenous tribes and involved men adopting the preparation rituals and sometimes the trauma of childbirth as an act of reverence for the birth process. Hall and Dawson (1989: 40) argue that what was once considered a ritual act appears to have taken on larger psychological dimensions which allowed for a way of 'entering and dwelling in the domain of the other', an act akin to the coniunctio process. This points to a strong link between 'couvade consciousness' and trickster's desire to access a greater range of physical and psychological experiences by dissolving conventional sex/gender categories.

Transvestite and transsexual practices have the potential to operate on a similar psychological level as couvade. One gender can to some degree merge with the other, whether in terms of emotional empathy and/or physical mimesis. This type of comparison suggests itself in the following Aboriginal ritual where according to Hall and Dawson, an 'initiated Aboriginal man made womanly by sub-incision can imitate the womb's ability to open' (1989: 16). This is achieved by cutting the penis in such a way that it takes on the form of a bleeding (menstrual) vulva. Hall and Dawson (1989: 26) also note that Count Ludwig von Zinzendorf applied this practice of becoming womanly or wombly, to the wound made in Christ's side at the crucifixion.

When considering that the purpose of rites of passage customs was/is to transform the initiate from one state of reality to another, it's plausible that the wounds of Aboriginal men could symbolize 'new life', regeneration, and fertility. This kind of thinking is reinforced by another Aboriginal initiation ritual where male children are placed into sunken caves and then removed by 'male mothers (men with vaginal engraving)' (Hall and Dawson 1989: 39). Both the celebration of the birth/death cycle and the severing of flesh joining the inner body to the outer world imply that couvade was a powerful ritual that involved the fusion of the archetypal mother and trickster with all their associated abjection, femaleness and reproductive qualities.

The complex narratives of ancient mythologies also included episodes of male pregnancy. Zeus, the most powerful deity in the Greek pantheon not only experienced the pangs of childbirth, but also gestated and delivered the gods Athena and Dionysos. After burning his mortal and pregnant lover Semele by exposing himself in his god-like form, Zeus stitched the unborn fetus from her ashes into his thigh. Dionysos was born from the wound after a three month gestation period. When Zeus swallowed the pregnant Titan Metis, the fetus of Athena worked its way to his head, leading to pressure on the brain. He called on Hephaistos to cleave an axe through the painful area and Athena sprang fully grown and armed from the wound.

It's interesting that Zeus presents an image of physical penetrability yet remains a dominant patriarchal figure. In his mother/father/hermaphroditic mode, he doesn't appear to be a closed and classic male image, which according to Mikhail Bakhtin (1984: 25) is usually 'cleansed, as it were of all the scoriae of birth and development'. In a tricksterish parody of the supernatural male births of Hellenistic mythology, satirist François Rabelais details how his character Gargantua was born from his mother Gargamelle's ear. Chapter 6 of *Gargantua* (1532), entitled 'How Gargantua Was Born in an Extremely Odd Way', details the mythical material Rabelais exploited:

> Wasn't Bacchus spawned by Jupiter's thigh?
> And the giant Rocquetaillade, wasn't he born from his mother's heel?
> And Croquemouche, wasn't he born out of his nurse's slippers?
> And what about Minerva: wasn't she born out of Jupiter's head – and through his ear?
> And Adonis, didn't he appear through the bark of a myrrh tree?
> And Castor and Pollux, out from the shell of an egg laid and then hatched by Leda?
>
> (Rabelais 1532/1990: 22)

Bakhtin (1984) finds evidence of male pregnancy readily available in Rabelais' work and also cites a number of other examples of the pregnant man in carnival comedies, including the seventeenth-century character Gros Guillaume (Fat William) whose rotund body adopted the shape of a wine barrel (Bakhtin 1984: 292); the obese and glutinous monks in twelfth- and thirteenth-century Latin literature (1984: 294); and more specifically the medieval figure of the king of Torelore (Torelore being a topsy-turvy realm) who 'bears children while the queen fights a war' (1984: 297). The illustrations of figures in commedia dell'arte also display noticeable protrusions that suggest symbolic pregnancy. 'Brighella' the lazy servant is a good example of this, but 'Pulcinella' or 'Polichinelle' (popular in Punch and Judy puppet shows) is more visibly extreme with his noticeable paunch, large nose, and hunchback that became more exaggerated over time (Speaight 1970: 67).

Bakhtin draws attention to Punch specifically to emphasize the reproductive nature of carnival play: 'For all these images', he says of carnival participants, 'have a dual body; everywhere the genital element is emphasised: pregnancy, giving birth, the procreative force (Pulcinella's double hump, the protruding belly)' (Bakhtin 1984: 256). George Speaight tells us that Pulcinella was not a recent Renaissance invention, which suggests that since ancient times couvade has been a significant aspect of carnival roguery and grotesque play. Another form of male pregnancy noted by Bakhtin centers on the physical exertion of a stuttering character in a commedia dell'arte sketch. In this farce, the prime trickster of the ensemble, Harlequin, encourages the stutterer to articulate what he is saying. Bakhtin takes this as an act analogous to giving birth (delivering the word); a gesture of fertility and abundance fundamental to trickster mythology (Bakhtin 1984: 308).

As a tricksterish ploy to provoke an awareness of gender stereotypes, couvade remains a component of contemporary commedia dell'arte, sitcom, and stand up theatre comedy. In the mid 1980s Australian comedian Sue Ingleton performed 'Bill Rawlings, the pregnant man' on the Melbourne cabaret circuit. Ingleton developed the concept while seven months pregnant, a single mother and vocal feminist. She previewed 'Bill' in *From Here to Maternity* at Melbourne's Comedy Cafe and followed it with the sequel *Mother's Courage*. In a parody of lactation, Ingleton had Bill wearing a bra of two rubber dish-washing gloves, one filled with Milo (chocolate milk) and the other with vegemite flavoured milk, 'so that the baby would have a choice' (Harris 1994: 69). As mimetic behaviour or actual male pregnancy in the fictions of theatre, television, literary texts or myth, couvade has the potential to agitate prevailing notions of maleness or femaleness by introducing the possibility of merging sex and gender.

Couvade and the related practices of drag and transvestitism, in a tricksterish fusion of male/female synergy, highlight the possibility that sex-roles are socially imposed. However, in keeping with trickster's ambiguity, male pregnancy can also be used as a ploy to reaffirm sex-role conventions. In the contemporary television sitcom, male pregnancy subplots are not always gender subversive. In *The Young Ones* (1982–1984) episode 'Crash' (2×2), Vyvyan, the token punk of a surreal 1980s shared house, bloats into what the other characters imagine is a state of advanced pregnancy. Similarly, in a 'homage' to this classic UK cult show, the more recent Australian *Kath and Kim* episode 'Another Announcement' (2×2) has Kim's husband and father-to-be, Brett, develop a phantom pregnancy in sympathy with Kim's condition.

Vyvyan and Brett's improbable story arcs are resolved when both characters give birth to an enormous fart. This not only reminds us of the absurdity of male pregnancy and the male body exceeding its 'clean and proper boundaries', but also revalidates appropriate gender behaviours. In these programs, particularly *Kath and Kim*, it seems as if the humour is not as much generated by the fact that the men think they are pregnant, but by the nurturing/fragile/helpless qualities they adopt in their delusion. If laughter can be generated through a switching of socially 'legitimate' gender roles, over and above the switching of physiologically sexed bodies, then the comedic farce even more potently operates as a means of maintaining the status quo. On the other hand, perhaps this is yet another tricksterish method of allowing us to make up our own minds about the slippery nature of essentialism/anti-essentialism.

Transvestism

While role reversal in the topsy-turvy world of carnival and ritual functioned to reinforce the existing organization of society, it also disrupted these structures. Social conventions of the seventeenth century were somewhat tested by the transvestism of commedia dell'arte's clowns and fools. Natalie Zemon Davis (1975: 132) cites black-faced Harlequins who dressed in frills and bows, masquerading as the goddess Diana: 'The result is so absurd that not only are the boundaries between high and low effaced . . . reality itself seems to dissolve'. Related to this dissolving of boundaries is the possibility of 'spill over', where behaviour allowed in carnival could be carried beyond its boundaries and in so doing provoke reflection on the nature of subordination (Davis 1975: 143).

The Wiltshire riot of 1641 was an example of non-carnival disruption. During this upheaval a male mob was spurred on by men in drag who referred to themselves as 'Lady Skimmington', a popular figure of fifteenth- to eighteenth-century carnival inspired by 'Skimmington ladles' used to beat misbehaving husbands (Russo 1994: 58–59). While Mary Russo argues that caricatures of brutal women in this type of comedic play can allude to a form of transgression and transformation, she also recognizes that the image of Lady Skimmington could well have served to mock strident women (Russo 1994: 59). It's a tricksterish double-edged sword, whereby the interpretation of the violation is up to the reader. Trickster doesn't take sides but merely presents 'spill over' options that can either reinforce or challenge the rule.

Outside carnival play, private/public, group/individual cross-dressing practices are threatening and entertaining. Transvestites appearing as guests on the talk-show circuit generate a mix of audience tolerance and intolerance, and while championing transvestism as a lifestyle choice, they are nevertheless coded as popular and marketable spectacles. Not only do these guests challenge the conventions of appropriate sex-role behaviour, but also they can, by their very 'otherness', reinforce established sex-role boundaries. This suggests that gender-appropriate behaviours are still firmly entrenched in the fabric of popular culture.

Epstein and Straub (1991) believe that public displays of cross-dressing and sexuality serve only (much like the talk-show phenomenon) to maintain gender systems: 'Festivals – Halloween or Mardi Gras; lesbian music weekends or drag shows – still do the work of defusing gender ambiguity by incorporating it into institutionally available and culturally demarcated spaces' (Epstein and Straub 1991: 21). Their point is valid if a little narrow. Davis' (1975) concept of the 'spill over' effect of carnival ideology and politics implies that activities taking place in these demarcated venues can be influential within these spaces and beyond them. If cultural projections of trickster indicates a need for collective/personal introspection, it's unhelpful to think in terms of marked and demarcated spaces able to specify the beginning and end of the archetype's influence, especially in a Jungian reading where trickster is unconfined by time and space – flourishing in 'appropriate' venues, but never restricted to them.

Women adopting 'maleness' dates back to ancient mythology. Aristophanes' comedy, *The Ecclesiazusae* or *The Congresswomen* (*c*.392 BC), a political satire about Athenian women who rose to dominate government by disguising themselves as men, is an early example of gender topsy-turviness. While the play celebrates a world upside down, the women maintain their heterosexuality and impose laws to ensure that the older, rather than younger, women of the city have first choice of all potential sex partners. In the manner of carnival revelry, *The Ecclesiazusae* concludes with feasting, dancing and lustful bravado. Aristophanes' comedy *Lysistrata* (411 BC) also uses the device of role reversal. Women gather at the Acropolis to plot a method of ending the war between Sparta and Athens. Led by Lysistrata, they refuse to have sex with men on both sides of the conflict and as a consequence the war ends. Although not focused on female transvestism, the play concerns itself with the adoption of (what was considered) maleness by women, evident in their ability to initiate and secure political stability. In a similar fashion to *The Ecclesiazusae*, unruliness and gender bending is a necessary aspect of the women's governmental coup d'etat.

The medieval legend of Pope Joan a.k.a. Johanna VIII (ninth century), initially chronicled by Boccaccio (1473), is either a morality myth or a suppressed Vatican embarrassment. Either way her accession to the papacy through a cross-dressing ruse is yet another example of trickster in its shape-shifting aspect. In a mockery of religion, politics and gender conventions, Joan gives birth during a papal procession. This leads to her unmasking and eventual death through childbirth, torture or repentant old age (depending which version you read) (Van der Helder 1988). Caryl Churchill's play *Top Girls* (1984) includes the transvestite spectacle of Pope Joan among her collection of historical figures gathered together for dinner at a contemporary restaurant. Churchill evokes the archetypal trickster in its female grotesque mode through a monologue in which Joan details her labour during the papal parade:

> We were in a little street that goes between St. Clement's and the Colosseum, and I just had to get off the horse and sit down for a minute. Great waves of pressure were going through my body, I heard sounds like a cow lowing, they came out of my mouth. Far away I heard people screaming, 'The Pope is ill, the Pope is dying.' And the baby just slid out onto the road . . . One of the cardinals said 'The Antichrist!' and fell over in a faint.
>
> (Churchill 1984: 17)

Davis' (1975) hesitancy in claiming Pope Joan as an example of social transgression is based on Joan's heterosexuality and supposed female insatiability for power. Marjorie Garber (1992: 215), who outlines Joan's fall as the result of a tragic love affair with a Benedictine monk, is similarly unconvinced that Joan poses a threat to hierarchical standards. Not surprisingly many examples of unruly female gender-bending in the medieval, classical and Romantic periods were undermined by idealizing the female (drag) protagonist as a romantic or ultimately divine heroine. This plot device maintained, rather than disrupted, traditional gender roles. Nevertheless in turning religious, sexual and power relations topsy-turvy, the spectacle of Joan as trickster can also provoke reflection on supposed assumptions about the inadequacy of women to assume dominant religious positions. After all, it was only on the discovery of Joan's sex that her wisdom and authority were discredited. Had she remained an undiscovered cross-dresser, her papacy may not have been unquestioned.

Shakespearian plays also dabbled in female–male transvestism: in *The Merchant of Venice*, Portia disguises herself as a doctor of civil law and her maid Nerissa as a lawyer's clerk; in *As You Like It*, Rosalind becomes Ganymede; and in *Twelfth Night*, Viola passes herself off as the young Cesario. The mythical figure of Ireland's Macha was the inspiration, along with the goddesses Badb and Ana, for one of the three witches in *Macbeth* (Kennedy 1994: 67). The elements of laughter and gender ambiguity apparent in Shakespeare's 'three weird sisters' (as in the Irish myth) suggest the presence of trickster. Banquo's speech on encountering the trio lets us know the transgressive nature of their physical (male) appearance and behaviour: 'you should be women, and yet your beards forbid me to interpret that you are so' (Shakespeare 1980: 862). The threat that the witches pose lies in the absence of overt heterosexuality and female passivity, a state which the other three characters in the comedies mentioned earlier, return to upon revealing their original identity. The witches control the affairs of state through their power over Macbeth. It's their presumed 'maleness' in this function that contributes to the fear they incite.

Although the witch is a clear version of trickster in female form, her power in myth and folklore is less balanced than most male projections because it is often tipped in favour of the motif's destructive aspect (Morgan Le Fay,

Medusa, Circe, the Sirens). Even the ever-so-affable characters of the 'magi-sitcom' Samantha Stevens, *Bewitched* (1964–1972) (inspired by the 1943 film *I Married a Witch*) and Jeannie, *I Dream of Jeannie* (1965–1970) are diminished through their eagerness to operate under the law of their husbands/masters. Samantha's mother Endora however, as a 1960s version of trickster who balked at any form of submission, can be read as a clear forerunner to contemporary incarnations in *The Witches of Eastwick* (1987), *Buffy the Vampire Slayer* and *Charmed* (1998–). The three witches under the rule of Hecate in Macbeth, though, remain among the most potent female versions of trickster in popular culture. They wield magic not to excite evil, but to engender reflection on the nature of evil and power. Their dark duplicity, transgressive nature, moral ambiguity and brazen laughter parallel that of their traditional male counterparts.

Laughter for the witch, as for less maligned trickster figures, is not only a subversive and aggressive form of defiance, but also a signifier of unconscious tricksterish eruptions surfacing to challenge the illusion of seriousness, rationality and control. In her first autobiography, *My Life as a Woman* (1989), 1980s–1990s comedian Roseanne Barr had something to say about this in a poem she wrote for her Jewish grandmother's funeral. She called on her female ancestors to 'Come! With your seared flesh and toothless mouths, with torn bowels and uteruses stuffed with fetishes' so that they could 'dance upon the earth, smelling fetid and of olives' (Barr 1989: 18). She closes with a tribute to the Old Testament's 90-year-old Sarah, who, in the ultimate act of defiance when learning of her pregnancy, laughed at god (Genesis 18).

Trickster's uneasy relationship with the persona

Jung first introduced the concept of the persona in his 1917 essay 'The Relation between the Ego and the Unconscious' (*CW* 7), arguing that it was an 'arbitrary and fortuitous segment of the collective psyche': in other words, 'a mask that feigns individuality, making others and oneself believe that one is individual, whereas one is simply acting a role through which the collective psyche speaks' (*CW* 7, para. 245). To identify too closely with the persona, is to risk ego-inflation, while a floating or unhinged persona signifies a lack of ego development. In order to understand the persona for what it is, a fairly stable sense of self must exist beneath it. That is, a coherent understanding of what the persona is protecting, facilitating or filtering has to be in place in order to psychologically fashion the most serviceable 'outer mask'.

Jung argued that for the persona to function appropriately it must be acknowledged as merely one among many interconnecting components of the objective psyche that helps shape the personality, not as is often thought, a prime signifier of the self. Understanding this more or less perfunctory role of the persona is a significant part of the individuation process. When the trickster function kicks in to address the unstable, erroneous and splintered identities of the chief protagonists of the films and television programs in the following chapters, the brittle nature of the persona, 'semblance', or 'two-dimensional reality', as Jung called it, is made patently clear (*CW* 7, para. 246).

If trickster demonstrates the elastic mutability of gender through male/female shape-shifting behaviour, then it can be assumed, in line with the anti-essentialist idea, that sex-roles can be discarded or switched at will. It also implies that these roles are imposed 'guises' not necessarily innate or essential dispositions. The persona can take the form of a personality with which one identifies, but far from being fixed, it fluctuates. A facilitator of social interaction, the persona as psychological complex, determines which roles are played and for whom, including sex-roles. It also functions as a protective psychological device: 'a complicated system of relations between the individual consciousness and society, fittingly enough a kind of mask, designed on one hand to make a definite impression upon others, and, on the other, to conceal the true nature of the individual' (Jung *CW* 7, para. 305). Discovering a deeper level of identity involves penetrating the persona and consequently coming to terms with the shifting nature of social conditioning, often entrenched in the personal unconscious via relentlessly reinforced ideologies.

An example that Jung cites in relation to this notion of persona versus self is the hypothetical situation of a man, who while putting on a highly masculinized, rigid and controlled personality, is liable to regress to an infantile emotional state when away from the public gaze (*CW* 7, para. 307). It's an extreme and stereotypical scenario, but one familiar enough to understand what he's getting at when he talks about the futility of identifying with social expectations, over deeper and more personal emotional needs and desires. If trickster operates to expose the veneer of conventional structures and behaviours, gender pigeonholing for example, then it's also able to bring awareness to the function and mutability of the persona. Through this ruthless agitation, the struggle with, and for, a more authentic sense of self-awareness begins. Radin (1972: 169) writes that even in Wakdjunkaga's apparent destructiveness, there was a positive reflection of the complex reality of the world. Like all tricksters he perched on precarious margins to expose the multiple layers of life around him. Pelton (1980: 45) writes of Anase in a similar way: 'He may disclose that what helps also hurts and that what hurts also helps, but in every instance he is an agent of the many-sidedness of what is'.

Out of the seemingly incoherent, trickster restores a sense of order, even if this comes in the form of simply understanding that nothing is fixed, or that trying to strike a balance between warring energies is the optimum outcome. This sense of liberation through an acceptance of diversity and constant change can also be applied to the way that we relate to the persona. Trickster keeps shifting the margins of identity by challenging what appears to be a stable self-image. It's through this constant questioning of how we fashion our personae that we're able to come to grips with its ephemeral and shape-shifting nature. For to acknowledge that the psyche is in constant movement, and that the personality can reflect these inner shifts, is to understand that maintaining an inflexible persona is nothing more than a futile attempt to control a force beyond containment.

Saviour, creator, destroyer

In triggering a re-evaluation of how we operate and react to external and internal situations, and how we relate to the various persona we adopt, trickster becomes an agent of both life and death. Re-evaluation often leads to change. Change/rebirth in turn is often the result of death. The sexual hunger and concentration on phallic power/energy, pregnancy and birth (literal or metaphoric) inherent in trickster mythology, once again reinforces this life/death nexus that is the very core of sexual abandon central to Bakhtin's (1965) carnival and even George Bataille's (1956) philosophical porn fictions. In the 'giving over' of the body and ego to 'the little death' of orgasm, sex and death become synonymous. Out of this dying new beginnings arise. The procreative nature of the sex/death theme is central to the perpetual cycles of regeneration within trickster mythologems.

As is so common in the Winnebago sequences, trickster, fresh from copulating with anything that has a pulse, cheating, birthing and being caught out, moves without pause to yet another rotation of adventures. Its creative energy is renewed with each conquest and swindle. Without attachment to the past or fear of the future, trickster cyclically reshapes itself in fresh skin. It's fair to argue that this is the component of ourselves that never gives up: the part of our psyche that 'fucks us up' to give us another chance at getting it 'closer' to right.

In this light, it's easy to identify the saviour elements of the archetype. Hermes' snake entwined staff, the Caduceus, is used as a medical sign, and the prolific use of Mercury during the height of alchemical practices around the seventh century where the substance was thought to be instrumental in the production of gold (perfection/individuation), signifies the archetype's healing properties. Jung sees trickster as analogous to God, particularly in his alchemical writings of Hermes/Mercury (*CW* 12, para. 404). He talks of it as a duality of the 'bestial' and 'divine' that in accord with his utopian notion of psychological individuation, ultimately functions to create a Möbius strip-like harmony (*CW* 9i, para. 458).

Trickster though is not so much a figure of supreme healing powers or an energy that we should endow with religious awe, but rather a transformative aspect of the psyche that 'continually provokes intercourse between what is outside man and what is inside him' (Pelton 1980: 234). In this light, trickster figures are no more or less than projected images of our ability to heal and unite disparate psychological material. Goldman (1998) sums this up in his analysis of the Iba Tiri trickster in Papua New Guinean children's folklore: 'Children are "kings" of the universe because, like tricksters, they control transformations between reality and make-believe' (Goldman 1998: 114). As the child-like part of us able to play with, and pierce through, illusion, trickster takes us back, as Goldman writes, to a place of extreme power. It's here where the potential to dislodge manicured social façades and sift the authentic from the illusory bubbles away.

As this chapter demonstrates, while the trickster myth permeates popular culture in a directly 'classical' form, it more often than not operates through a fusion of mythic ideas and positions. The following chapters aren't as detailed in their discussion of trickster; they assume an understanding (gleaned here) of the way that the motif has been mythically and psychologically realized on a personal and collective level. Lynch's *Mulholland Drive* is a good place to start putting theory into practice (or some might say, theory into theory). We don't just experience trickster as a projected archetypal pattern, but also as a 'texture' embedded in the structural layers of screen texts.

From each production element to the characters themselves, Lynch, as an exceptional illusionist, produces work that is heavily inscribed with trickster energy. His cinema is a rich minefield of possible readings, so what we're going to experience in Chapter 3 is only one version of *Mulholland Drive* . . . but I would argue, whichever interpretation you choose, it is, in the end, a trick crafted by a trickster to emotionally agitate and disrupt black and white moral thinking. Rowland reiterates Jung's position on this kind of archetypal resurfacing when she argues that the continual 'retelling of the myth must have therapeutic properties for it would not occur if it did not tap into living imaginative energy' (Rowland 2005: 188).

Part II

Mistaken identities, self-deception and the undead

Chapter 3

The obscure by the more obscure

Mulholland Drive

> Love, they say, enslaves and passion is a demon and many have been lost for love.
>
> Jeanette Winterson, *The Passion* (1987: 154)

David Lynch's *Mulholland Drive* (2001) is an elaborately drawn story of desire, but even more than this, I'm going to argue that it's the story of a fragile anti-hero in thrall to her merciless trickster. Lynch's starlet wannabe 'Diane' (Naomi Watts), who kills her lover and is killed, epitomizes the plastic nature of reality and the need to find the still point that lies beneath it. My approach focuses on the idea that the film's surrealist structure and imagery work to accentuate both the tenuous margin between dream/waking states and the struggle for psychological liberation. This is achieved through potent symbols, configurations, and locations where inner dialogue and movement take place. We might call these sites expressions of the Self, Jung's concept of psychological unity now more popularly thought of as an ideal fantasy of unconscious/conscious conversation.

The trickster energies that work through Diane's story arc, while struggling to redirect her troubled conscience, climax in unbearable confrontation, annihilation and post-suicide 'baptism'; an extreme realization of the death/rebirth paradigm. I'm going to suggest that what we're left with up to the point of her death is an unambiguous *frustration of archetypal intent*, where despite all the self-preserving qualities of the unconscious, Diane is unable to save herself. Here is a classic myth retold; another Orphic trip to the underworld where lovers are reunited. This more byzantine version, though, has a disturbing undercurrent where, to haul out Nietzsche's (1974: 85) old maxim, 'that which is done out of love always takes place beyond good and evil'.

Mulholland Drive centers on Diane Selwyn's yearning for, and vengeance toward, her unfaithful girlfriend Camilla (Laura Harring). Diane's splintered self-awareness is played out and caught in an intricate web of fantasy/reality binaries as her dream persona 'Betty' gradually unravels and merges into the nightmare of her waking life. The more secondary characters, although crucial to the unfolding story, function as subordinate archetypal motifs to the overarching imagery of the Self (discussed in Chapter 1). The film's dream sequence, marking the first two-thirds of the text, is played out as a collection of reinventions, memory grabs and compensations from a fateful dinner party where Diane decides to have Camilla murdered. From the scripting and highly stylized imagery to its complex shape-shifting, the film is able to highlight the psyche's capacity to unmask through projection, the forbidden, vulnerable and thwarted nature of desire. Diane can never return Camilla's gaze. She can only gaze at herself and what she has done, through a labyrinth of underworld images.

Although this analysis doesn't presuppose any theoretical game-plan on Lynch's part, his previous work suggests a taste for psychological distress and conflicting realities. *Eraserhead* (1977), *Blue Velvet* (1986), *Twin Peaks, Wild at Heart* (1990), *Twin Peaks: Fire Walk with Me* (1992) and *Lost Highway* (1997) to a greater degree than his other work, draw on clear trickster imagery, usually in its shadow aspect. He consistently creates personalities who struggle (often ineffectively) with internal duality, and then projects this tension of opposites onto secondary characters, dialogue, music, set design and intertextual allusions. More arthouse-cum-mainstream than avant-grade, *Mulholland Drive* is a complex play on time/space dimensions and mis-takes. The alchemists' self-referential catchphrase *obscurum per obscurius* (the obscure by the more obscure, *CW* 12, para. 41) is an apt description of the film and the psyche of its central characters. In the process of finding gold, Jung argues that the alchemists and the chemistry they practiced dealt 'with the same, or very similar, processes as those involved in active imagination and in dreams, i.e., ultimately with the process of individuation' (*CW* 12, para. 448). In illustrating and unveiling the illusions that retard Diane, Lynch engages in a similarly obscure form of gold spinning.

Watching a hundred minutes of sleep

The screen initially fills with overlapping combinations of dancers jitterbugging to Badalamenti's swing score. A ghost-like, overexposed image of 'Diane Selwyn' eclipses the action with a synthetic 'ingénue-in-Hollywood' giddiness. Lynch idiosyncratically shifts mood, sucking the lightness of these images with a hollow industrial hum overlaid with heaving breathing. In blurred close-up the camera pans across an unmade bed from the visual perspective of a disembodied character before homing in on a pillow as if the unknown subject, whose point of view we have, is pressing their face into the fabric. The feel is narcotic and suffocating, suggesting a drug induced state or sleep. In a tricksterish three-way contract binding for the next 100 minutes, the camera and audience are positioned as Diane, falling into the pillow, the dream, the unconscious.

From this allusion to an altered state of mind, the imagery switches to a night shot of 'Rita's' limousine cruising up Mulholland Drive, the infamous and exclusive Santa Monica mountain stretch that divides the San Fernando valley from Hollywood. Lit only by the car's headlights and the neon glow of the city below, the winding climb inducts us/Diane into another partially visible reality. This commonly used Lynchian technique of paralleling dark isolated roads with passageways to other times and spaces (*Twin Peaks, Lost Highway*) signifies what is likely to be a highly image based and psychologically dense text. The trajectory into the unconscious is complete with a close-up of the female passenger's face. The film now seems to settle into the polymorphous dream narrative where Diane will reinvent herself as 'Betty Elms' and refigure her lover Camilla Rhodes as the enigmatic 'Rita'. In this imaginary hermetically sealed 'space', Camilla/Rita, the limousine's passenger, is a luminous presence on screen. She is the camera's focus – the heart of Diane's dream. As is made explicit throughout the film, 'this is the girl'.

Mulholland Drive continues in the dream for most of the film before easing its way into Diane's waking life for the last half hour. Although the placement of each sharply divided scenario has a chronological rationale, the dream is illegible until Diane's circumstances in the waking sequence are explained in present time (after the dream) and flashback (before the dream). The twinning throughout the dream, where characters in the waking scenes are reinvented and embellished with trickster and shadow material, alludes to the intricate way that the psyche is able to deal with the chaotic and unacceptable extremes of conscious life. Jung argued that projected archetypal constellations often take on separate identities and should be treated as 'autonomous factors' rather than 'fugitive images' (*CW* 9ii, para. 41). This insistence on the independence of personified material and symbols is woven into Lynch's construction of the characters/projections within the dream. Each has a life and function of their own within the container of Diane's agitated imagination. The pivotal waking events that help us make sense of this very specific unconscious material take place at a pool-side dinner party and 'Winkie's' diner.

Although Camilla has ended their sexual relationship, she invites Diane to director Adam Kesher's (Justin Theroux) dinner gathering. Diane is chauffeured by limousine to the party at 6980 Mulholland Drive and is greeted seductively by Camilla, who leads her through a secret garden entrance to the patio. When they reach Adam's house, Lynch establishes brief snapshots of characters connected to Camilla and highlights anonymous guests who have played key roles throughout the previous dream sequence. During the night Diane grieves the loss of her relationship while Camilla sadistically revels in her celebrity, sexuality, and as is announced during the dinner, impending marriage to Adam. In the following scene Diane meets a hit man in 'Winkie's' and, pointing to an agent's portrait photograph of Camilla, tells him, '*This* is the girl'. After she hands over a wad of cash, he passes her a blue key and cryptically lets her know that 'when it's finished you'll find this where I told you'. The blue key and the phrase 'this is the girl', both signifiers of the 'contract', feature ominously in the seemingly incongruent twists of Diane's fantasy.

There is of course no definitive interpretation of the dream sequence, but Jung's insistence on the potency of collective mythological patterns and images in dreams, along with his claim that dream figures represent 'personified features of the dreamer's own personality' (*CW* 8, para. 509), are valuable approaches to Lynch's ambiguous metaphors. Jung understood unconscious images to be intricate autonomous fusions of archetypal energies that may or may not be based around sexuality or frustrated wants depending on the subject and their circumstances. He argued that because dreams often transcend the personal, they're capable of embracing a complex and irrational fusion of not only the subject's individual memories, but collective physiological and psychological memories as well (*CW* 8, para. 527).

Jung maintained that dreams generally compensate for conscious material and divided this premise into three aspects: *prospective*, where there's an anticipation of what is likely to occur upon waking and provides clues to problematic situations; *reductive*, where emotionally loaded aspects of the dreamer's personal life are repressed and the unconscious, in regurgitating this material, confronts and attacks the dreamer; and *compensatory* (similar to reductive, but with more directed 'one-step-further' intent), where by bringing up content that has been held at the threshold of consciousness, the unconscious balances out a problematic conscious situation.

While these classifications are central to his reading of dreams, Jung cautioned against treating them as conclusive interpretive methods (*CW* 8, para. 499). In the next chapter we'll look at current reservations about the validity of repression, nevertheless all three of Jung's approaches are clearly woven into *Mulholland Drive* in an attempt to bridge conscious and unconscious states. We are after all talking about a piece of art and not an actual case study. In the following sections I'll argue that the dream sequence provides a form of compensation for the malleable and fluctuating state of Diane's fragile ego by dramatically advancing the illusive concept of conscious/unconscious dialogue through various permutations of the archetypal Self: 'If I were succinctly to state what Jung considers the primary function of dreams,' says Michael Vannoy Adams (2004: 21), 'I would say that it is compensation in the service of individuation'.

Persona, trickster and twinning

Diane's dream is more than a girl's-own-adventure fantasy intensified by idyllic love and jarring allusions to a loss of oneself in another. It is a tricksterish interplay of independent images that sporadically erupt to pierce her romantic misreadings of Camilla's motives, confront her with the impending murder she has arranged, and introduce the possibility of her own death. The dream can also be seen as a confusion and synthesis of identities that represent aspects of Diane's psyche. As this ambiguous sequence of unconscious material develops, the bleeding of love-object Camilla/Rita into Diane/Betty becomes more extreme. The merging of personae is easily read as a topsy-turvy play to create a fusion of opposites necessary to the individuation process.

Although the unconscious has no rational agenda, the complex network of symbols and signs within the dream suggests the search for that which might bring together and help regulate her splintered energies. Despite their seeming incongruity, when taken as an overarching pattern, the various permutations of persona twinning point directly to a sense of coniunctio, the psychological coitus or merging of opposites that takes place during the process of individuation and the emergence of the Self (*CW* 12, para. 44). This concept will be discussed in more detail later, but for the moment it's important to briefly identify the shape-shifting aspects of the various coupling combinations within the Rita/Betty/Diane/Camilla dynamic.

A number of short and ostensibly unrelated episodes weave in and out of the central Betty/Rita scenario as if Diane is framing her dream-scenes from confused movie plots. When the overlapping surreal sensuality of the fantasy, typical of Lynch, is viewed as a complete composition, it becomes clear that these initially disjointed vignettes have a direct relationship to the waking sequence. Lynch embellishes the central dream plot of a blond innocent unwittingly caught in the romance and intrigue of a murder-mystery, with a 1950s Hitchcock-like sensibility. Diane's make-over as Betty (still played by Watts), a naive-young-actress-in-Hollywood cliché, is an obvious compensatory fantasy for her more abysmal waking life as an unsuccessful bit-player trapped in the tawdry underbelly of Hollywood, a version of Hades personified by the cold-blooded Camilla.

In comparison, Laura Harring's Camilla is revamped as a bewildered, helpless and seductive object of the more proactive Betty's curiosity. The sexual and professional power tensions between Diane and Camilla are replaced by a compassionate partnership devoid of destructive ambition or jealousy, although it has to be said that Diane has an air of 'head prefect' officiousness about her, à la 'Tracy Flick' (*Election*, 1999). While the growing fusion of Rita and Betty dominates the dream sequence, Lynch also sets up obvious dualities: Betty/Diane's slim blonde form contrasts with Rita/Camilla's more voluptuous body and dark hair; Betty and Rita's wardrobe is often contrasting in style and colour; and Betty plays the 'active', successful and motivated partner while Rita is more passive and displaced. While these contrasts complement the partnership, Diane and Camilla's duality is far more brutal.

The dream's character fusing begins with initial close-up shots of Rita in the limousine. 'What are you doing? We don't stop here', she says to the driver as he pulls the car over to the side of the road (a line Diane will repeat in the waking sequence to her limousine driver when he stops at Camilla's garden rendezvous prior to the pool-side party). In film-noir mode, Rita's driver orders her out of the car with a gun, echoing Diane's 'contract', but the hit is foiled when drag racers crash into the limousine.

Rita, the only one to survive, wanders dazed around neighbouring streets until she finds refuge in an apartment on Sunset Boulevard. Fresh off the plane from Deep River Ontario and eager to make-it-in-the-movies, Betty arrives at her aunt's vacated apartment and discovers a bruised and concussed Rita in the shower. The failed assassination not only sets up an intriguing femme fatale mystery that guides the central storyline and offers a returning focus for the arcane vignettes, but also highlights the *reductive* and *compensatory* aspects of the dream. Diane is not just willing Camilla's resurrection, but compensating for the trauma of her murder by nullifying the act and consequently the *affect*.

The tricksterish twists of identity fusion and persona swapping continue when Rita, with no memory of who she is or what has happened to her, spots a mounted poster of Charles Vidor's *Gilda* (1946) reflected in one of the twin bathroom mirrors. Rita Hayworth, popularly dubbed the 'love-goddess' of her day, poses seductively under the eye-catching caption 'There NEVER was a woman like Gilda.' The reference to Hayworth and Camilla as successful exotic actors parallels the relationship of the character Gilda and Camilla, both femme fatales who revel in creating episodes designed to rouse the jealousy of their ex-lovers. It's no wonder that Diane dreams Rita into adopting this name. Although Gilda/Camilla/Rita/Hayworth are endowed with the same qualities of beauty and sexual charisma, the manipulative nature of Camilla and Gilda is erased from Diane's Rita. Diane not only reinvents Camilla and the dynamics of their relationship, but also, as the now more dominant, active partner, she reaps the acting acclaim that had eluded her. In this repositioning of interpersonal dynamics and the usurping of her lover's professional success, Diane *is* a combination of Rita, Betty and Camilla, all figures who personify at this rudimentary level both her ideal self and her shattered illusions.

Under Betty's guidance Rita finds a wad of money and a triangular shaped blue key in her handbag, both signifiers of Diane's 'contract killing'. As they sit in Winkie's diner, where Diane's hit on Camilla was arranged, they try to piece together the mystery surrounding the accident, but all Rita remembers is the name 'Diane Selwyn'. Having no context to frame it and thinking it might be her real name, she and Betty set out to track down 'Diane' in the phone book – 'strange to be calling yourself', Betty whispers conspiratorially to Rita. The twinning intensifies with the introduction of the dreamer's name, a twist that lends itself to the *prospective* aspect of Jung's dream theorem. When the couple break into 'Diane's' neglected bungalow apartment, they discover her decomposing body on the bed, the face contorted and stuffing from the pillow scattered over the sheets as if a bullet had pierced both the body and the linen.

Although the long stringy blonde hair of the corpse tells us that this is clearly not Watts a.k.a. Betty/Diane, the use of Diane's full name for this woman is enough to indicate that she is yet another aspect of the dreamer. In retrospect, this scene in *prospective* and *compensatory* readings takes on imagery that personifies Diane's emotional turmoil. It pre-empts a planned suicide in *prospective* mode, and in an act of compensation (via doubling), allows her once again to trade places with the, by now (in waking time), decaying Camilla. We might read this trading of places, as a relief of guilt, and/or as the fulfillment of Diane's desire to 'dwell in the other'; to make herself into Camilla. The corpse is useful in propelling the narrative of the murder-mystery fantasy of the dream space, by setting up the suggestion that the same person who killed 'Diane Selwyn' might be after or connected to Rita, an intriguing spin on the proposition that Diane's mind may be playing on the anxiety that the same person who killed Camilla, might be after her (which is of course herself). In other words Diane may be anticipating her own suicide. In the most blatant act of fusion, Betty disguises Rita in a blonde wig. The effect is a synthetic reproduction of Betty and Bettiness. It's an act of intimacy that triggers an escalation in their relationship from friends to lovers.

This more literal physical/emotional mimesis, a pointed allusion to Hitchcock's 'Madeleine/Judy' twinning in *Vertigo* (1958), functions as a passport to another dimension and sets in motion a chain of events that lead to the dissolution of both characters. As if led by a higher calling, Rita insists that she and Betty hop a cab to a small theatre, Club Silencio, tucked at the back of a deserted inner city lane. Like the half lit Mulholland Drive limousine episode, the alleyway to the club suggests a channel from one psychological space to another.

Firmly positioned inside the hermetically sealed theatre, Betty and the artificially blonde Rita watch as an MC trickster figure introduces performers miming to prerecorded music. In reference to these acts, while also a glaring allusion to the dream itself, he announces that, 'it's all a tape. It is an illusion'. The final act, Rebekah Del Rio's Spanish version of Roy Orbison's *Crying*, taps into the emotional trauma of Diane's unrequited love and its disturbing consequences. Clasping each other and reacting in unison to the energy of the performance space, Rita and Betty's caricatured personae surrender to a more unified embodiment of Diane's emotional agitation and from this synchronized state of distress Betty pulls a square blue cube from her handbag. The introduction of the cube, its puzzle-like quality, and its obvious colour connection to the blue key provide a surreal closure to the dream sequence.

Back in their apartment bedroom, Betty mysteriously disappears. Rita takes the blue key from her handbag filled with cash and turns it in the small triangular opening of the cube. The camera moves in as though Rita, whose point of view the spectator now has, is being sucked into the void of the puzzle box. The screen blackens, the cube falls to the floor, and the bedroom warps into Diane's flat. A 1950s Cowboy figure, seen in an earlier dream vignette and fleetingly as a guest at Adam's pool-side party, stands at Diane's bedroom doorway, a replica of the bedroom where we earlier saw the dead decomposing 'Diane'. The body of the dream 'Diane' and Diane, who lies in the same position on the bed, merge as the Cowboy/psychopomp (conductor of souls) leads her from the unconscious dream space with the phrase, 'Hey pretty girl time to wake up'.

Coniunctio/divine marriage

The Rita/Betty narrative and the many other surrogate dream characters, like the Cowboy and those mentioned later in the chapter, are easily read as archetypal elements of Diane herself. The amoral trickster pervades the dream sequence in the form of individual personifications, a melding of these 'characters', and the principal framework governing the trajectory of the dream. All work to confront Diane with her multiple selves. Not only does the twinning momentum of the Betty/Rita attachment and duality allow for a more complete understanding of Diane's interior selves, but also it reveals the desire for an illusive state of unity, merging of opposites, or alchemical coniunctio that would enable Diane to rise above her chaos and save her from the deaths (Camilla's and her own) signified in the dream. This drive to bring conflict to a meeting place, via the contrasts, doubling and sexual/emotional union of Betty/Rita, is plausible if looked at through Jung's understanding of the Self, for as he argues: 'The self, however, is absolutely paradoxical in that it represents in every respect thesis and antithesis, and at the same time synthesis' (*CW* 12, para. 22).

In *Mysterium Coniunctionis* (*CW* 14) Jung argues that the archetype of the coniunctio is not merely the union of opposites, but also the 'divine' product of that union. This process can be represented in a number of ways, but in alchemy it's usually symbolized through concepts and images like the divine marriage of mother–son/brother–sister (Sol–Luna) or the turning of base metals into gold via the amalgamating agent of mercury (a trickster allusion). Edward Edinger (1994: 18) goes so far as to regard the process and product of the coniunctio as 'the creation of consciousness, which is an enduring psychic substance created by the union of opposites'. In this sense, the bridging of unconscious and conscious material to swell awareness can be seen as a coniunctio of sorts that might ideally lead to a state of individuation.

In a more philosophical and psychological reading of the alchemical stages of transformation, union precedes death, the soul reunites with body, and from this process a resurrection takes place that creates a more complete state of being, or realization of ultimate potential. Diane's dream points to this process through its attempts to compensate for her brittle psychological state bordering on self-annihilation. Although this Orphic-like crossing, where Diane descends to the underworld, seems to be about reviving Camilla, I would argue it's more of a last-ditch effort for Diane to raise herself from Hades.

From the beginning of Christianity the fourfold phases of alchemical transformation were denoted by the colours black, white, yellow and red, aligning with the quaternity of the seasons, elements and humours, but after the fifteenth-century yellow was discarded. The first stage of the process, the union of coniunctio (coitus) and the resultant death (*mortificatio*) was marked by the colour black (*nigredo*); the baptism, rebirthing or reuniting of the soul with the body that arose from this mortificatio, was represented by white (*albedo*); and the ultimate fire-like intensity of this transformation was signified by red (*rubedo*) (*CW* 12, paras. 333–334). Both Camilla and Rita are seen only in these three colours. As the pivot on which the action of *Mulholland Drive* turns, she 'is the girl' who needs to be integrated by Diane for the Self to surface.

The initial overexposed and dazzling white, image of a Diane in the opening sequence, is repeated again at the end of the film, but this time with the blonde-wigged Rita by her side. Both images are telling in relation to the alchemists' colour chart. The first suggests Diane's baptism into the world of Hollywood, a trip she won through a jitterbug competition; the second though is more directly related to the coniunctio process of death and rebirth. Betty and Rita disappear at the end of the dream sequence, as if sucked into the same fate. This surreal episode mirrors the final waking scene where Diane shoots herself, and in the canon of classical romantic tragedy, is united in death with Camilla. The over-exposed image of Betty and Rita (Diane in her twin aspects), when read through the coniunctio paradigm, represents the ablution or baptism after union and death that allows for the reuniting of body and soul.

Further hints that Diane is attempting to access the Self erupt throughout the various stories in the dream, that although appearing to diverge from the central Betty/Rita coupling, actually work to support the process of divine union. Just as the film plays with the tensions of this alchemical merger, and the 'afterglow' of whitened images intimates a uniting of the two lovers, the dream sequence also suggests an unconscious desire on Diane's part, to stave off suicide. In other words she is trying to both confront and bring together the disparate parts of herself and so rise above her chaos. As Jung argues:

> The analysis of his [the patient's] situation will therefore lead sooner or later to a clarification of his general spiritual background going beyond his personal determinants . . . This phase of the [psychoanalytic] process is marked by the production of symbols of unity, the so-called mandalas, which occur either in dreams or in the form of concrete visual impressions,

> often as the most obvious compensation of the contradictions and conflicts of the conscious situation.
>
> (*CW* 12, para. 32)

Mandalas or quaternity symbols that signify the Self archetype, appear in three significant modes throughout *Mulholland Drive*: Mr. Roque's room, the blue cube and Club Silencio.

Hermetically sealed squares

In one of the divergent dream scenarios, Camilla's fiancé Adam, as the director of a new film project, is intimidated into casting the female lead according to the wishes of Mafiaesque men who answer to a sinister tricksterish superior called Mr. Roque (Michael J. Anderson). Roque inhabits a sparsely furnished airtight room where he views the action around him via cameras, giving orders and receiving information through speakerphones. The line 'this is the girl' filters through Adam's story arc via Roque and his cronies' insistence on casting actress 'Camilla Rhodes'. The Mafiosi stipulate that the phrase 'this is the girl' is to be said by Adam after 'Camilla Rhodes' (in the form of actor Melissa George) has auditioned for him. The casting deal is then secured in a mirroring of Diane's line to her hit man that seals the actual Camilla's fate.

The blue cube is initially presented as a three-dimensional shape within the autonomous dream dimension of Club Silencio, which in turn, like an unfolding of Russian Babushka dolls, is situated within Diane's dream, the film itself and the cinema (other more or less closed-off spaces). It is as if Rita and Betty, as aspects of Diane, are moving through multiple layers of the psyche, suggested by the hermetically sealed autonomous spaces connected to Diane's emotions. The only other aspect of the dream sequence to have any similarity to the cube and Club Silencio, is Mr. Roque's room.

It is significant that these spaces presided over by trickster projections (even the cube as will be discussed later) are intricately connected to one of the two main signifiers of Diane's contract killing, the blue key or the line 'this is the girl'. In a link to more traditional ways of imagining trickster, Radin (1972: 185) identifies Hermes as a structure that operates beyond social laws and rites as if it inhabited an enclosed 'hermetic' space pregnant with the opportunity to steal and discover. In a similar fashion to these hermetic zones, the three spaces mentioned above variously represent containers for acts of coercion, finding and ultimately taking. All echo Diane's 'contract' and consequent death.

Jung's notion of the quaternity, a four-fold archetypal mandala formation symbolizing the Self (*CW* 16, para. 405), is directly relevant to the box-like spaces of Club Silencio, Roque's room and the blue cube. While symbols of psychic antithesis and synthesis are usually represented in circular form (as mentioned in Chapter 1, mandala is Sanskrit for circle), Jung also directly talks about quaternities in the formation of squares (*CW* 10, para. 767). Each confronts Diane with her predicament, agitates awareness, and therefore has the potential to trigger a more advanced state of knowing. Drawing on the square-shaped Gnostic alchemical quaternity figuration, *the time-space quaternion*, which Jung regards as, 'the organizing schema par excellence among the psychic quaternities' (*CW* 9ii, para. 398), he reasoned that:

> If we look at this quaternion from the standpoint of the three-dimensionality of space, then time can be conceived as a fourth dimension. But if we look at it in terms of the three qualities of time – past, present, future – then static space, in which changes of state occur, must be added as a fourth term. In both cases, the fourth represents an incommensurable Other that is needed for their mutual determination.
>
> (*CW* 9ii, para. 397)

When understood in terms of these time qualities that Jung talks about, the cube, the club and the sealed-off room, suggest atemporal sites where 'past, present and future' meet and where 'changes of state' take place (this interplay of time and space is also a given of the cinema experience). Each of the three spaces has a shape-shifting function: 'Camilla Rhodes' is reimagined in Roque's room, a nerve center for the manipulation of her star-turn in Adam's film; Club Silencio is the magnetic performance space where Del Rio's *Crying* reflects Diane's malady and catapults Betty into a heightened state of agitation before offering her the cube; and the cube itself has the power to dissolve Betty and Rita, transporting Diane from an unconscious to a conscious state as if it were a gateway to another dimension.

All three spaces point directly to the trickster function; the other that forms the *fourth* mediating aspect of Jung's Gnostic quaternion that he directly associates with Mercurius (*CW* 9ii, para. 397). He also mentions the relationship of Hermes, often called 'quadrangular', to the notion of 'roundness' and 'squareness' (*CW* 12, para. 172), arguing that it's 'easy to see why such qualities made Mercurius an eminently suitable symbol for the mysterious transforming substance of alchemy; for this is round and square, i.e. a totality consisting of four parts (four elements)' (*CW* 12, para. 173). This puzzle of squared time-spaces that Lynch presents is analogous to archetypal symbols for the Self that hint at the need for dialogue between the unconscious and consciousness. In this case a dialogue initiated by the trickster paradigm, but frustrated by Diane's inability to cope with, or even recognize, these messages.

The frustration of archetypal intent

'I thought when I woke up. I thought sleep would do it', a concussed Rita tells Betty early in the dream. But although Diane is really telling herself this, and the unconscious is furiously working to pierce the membrane of consciousness (a concept Jung called the *transcendent function*), the waking reality of Diane's situation is too irreconcilable for such a subtle negotiation to take place. In one last telling image, an androgynous tramp figure, seen in an almost subliminal 'shock' shot accompanied by a loud jarring soundtrack at the beginning of the dream sequence, reappears in the closing scenes of the film.

Whether a symbol of death, the demonic, or the nefarious shadow, the trickster paradigm is a clear aspect of the tramp image, only ever seen at the back of 'Winkie's' diner where both Diane and Camilla's deaths are set in motion. In the final shots of the film, the tramp fingers the blue cube (the Self/mandala) as if s/he has been toying with it in some way, and then dismissively places it on the ground. This gesture of discarding 'the Self' foreshadows Diane's gunshot suicide. Knowing that there is a sense of complete loss of identity to that ungraspable, underworld other, a part of Diane casts aside any hope of resurrection within the illusion of coniunctio she has presided over, and the desired balance of opposites doesn't take place until the 'baptism' scene after her death.

The *archetypal intent* of the dream has been frustrated by the sheer fragility of an ego incapable of rising to the impossible challenge put before it. We might therefore see why the ego, the waking Diane, needs to die for there to be any sense of stasis as a trope of forward movement. Interpreted in this way *Mulholland Drive* is a dark and complex myth. If there's a happy ending to be extracted, it lies in the film's ability to show us how trickster might play with and perforate what in Hindu and Buddhist mythology is known as *maya* – the dream-like nature of the material world. Lynch's work is comforting and confronting because it illustrates the capacity to see through illusion and the fear of living without it.

In the next chapter we'll look at Christopher Nolan's *Memento*, a more film-noir stylized flirtation with trickster, maya and the lost other than *Mulholland Drive*. Through overlapping versions of reality via the blurring of time-space dimensions, Nolan's memory challenged 'Leonard Shelby', echoes Diane in his attempt to redress the murder of his wife by calling upon, and battling, the ruthless trickster. Like Diane, he revives his lover and recreates an illusory (better) history. But is this longing to resurrect, a poignant sign of love and grief, or is it more self-centered? Are both characters only compelled to wipe out the deaths of 'the beloved' as a way of escaping the brunt of their conscience?

If the kind of love that obliterates a sense of self (obsessive love perhaps), can be understood as a projection of one's essence/soul in another, then the killing of that other must surely lead to an attrition of one's core. Although prompted by trickster to confront their actions and integrate their romantic projections in order to access a sense of identity and becoming, Diane and Leonard are ultimately unable to function outside their symbiotic love relationships or peel back the maya of their downward spiraling worlds. As we'll see in the next chapter, *Memento*, like Lynch's work, while not as much of a hallucinogenic-dream trip, is still the stuff of classic mythology and alchemical ambiguity.

Chapter 4

Setting the conditions for forgetting

Memento

> Now, when thou wak'st, with thine own fool's eyes peep.
>
> Shakespeare's Puck, *A Midsummer Night's Dream* (1980: 208)

Christopher Nolan's earlier feature, the black and white film-noir thriller *Following* (1998), and the blockbuster *Batman Begins* (2005) demonstrate an ongoing interest in the anxieties attached to identity, anonymity and the way that time fragments in the process of recalling the past. Unlike *Mulholland Drive*'s conjuring of the unconscious through a juggling of time and space, Nolan's *Memento* (2000) attempts to capture the way that memories are distilled from the personal unconscious by retracing interlinked events through a more 'forward-reverse' linear framework. The film steers clear of saturating its flawed hero Leonard Shelby (Guy Pearce) in surreal unconscious imagery, but manages to probe the conscious/unconscious margins of his agitated existence through a shrewdly crafted play on the concepts of forgetting and disavowal. Nolan's backward sequencing of scenes shapes a puzzle decipherable only after reaching the beginning of the narrative rather than the end. This kind of regression, while cleverly evoking a sense of remembering, also reflects the internal trickster's capacity to simultaneously suck us back to the recesses of the psyche while pushing us toward conflict and understanding.

In a parallel approach to *Mulholland Drive*, the shift into psychological terrain is suggested early in the film through fairly obvious allusions to the unconscious; not a dark Lynchian stretch of road, but an isolated underground room in a deserted building. It's here that Leonard is first seen flapping a polaroid of the man he's just murdered. In rewind mode the photograph fades rather than sharpens with the developing image, an apt introduction to Leonard's 'condition' of anterograde amnesia or short-term memory loss. Footage of the murder is reversed until the victim, Teddy (Joe Pantoliano), is shown pleading for his life: 'Let's go down into the basement, let's go down you and me together', he says, hoping to trigger Leonard's memory, 'Then you'll know who you really are'. This practice of signifying the unconscious and notions of the underworld/hell through allusions to the subterranean, is a well-trod cinema cliché and a common Jungian metaphor.

Teddy's plea eerily echoes one of Jung's much quoted dreams where he imagined himself descending levels of his home, each dating to an earlier historical period than the last until eventually reaching the grotto-like floor of 'prehistory'. Jung's feeling that the dream was 'a summary of my life, more specifically of the development of my mind' (1964: 43) led him to more clearly understand the importance of interpreting dreams in direct relation to the dreamer's experience rather than through any preconceived theories on the analyst's part (ironic in light of his numerous dream interpretations scattered throughout the *Collected Works*). Although Jung understood his dream to be revealing a personal interest in history and human evolution, he is obviously referring to layers of the psyche when he talks about 'the development of my mind'.

If each level revealed a more primitive period of collective history, it must also have revealed differing stages of human psychological maturity. It's not too much of a stretch to read the lower prehistoric level he described as a cave, a tomb, 'still, dark, and obviously uninhabited' (Jung 1964: 43), as a metaphor for the 'unknowable' primordial collective unconscious. Nolan's audience is able to experience a sense of this space via Leonard's precarious oscillations to and from the known, half glimpsed and hidden corners of each reality he moves through. Despite his resistance to 'go down' to Teddy's basement/underworld, this plane is familiar territory. Ultimately we come to understand Leonard's pattern of cyclically passing through portholes to the unconscious while desperately attempting to negate the experience.

Through backward steps briefly intercut with jumps to and from the present, the film traces Leonard's search for his wife's imaginary murderer. His brain damage, the result of a brutal house robbery where he was severely beaten and his wife raped, inhibits the formation of new memories, but has no effect on his ability to recall memories encoded before the assault. The last thing Leonard remembers of this period is the image of his wife's body wrapped in a plastic shower curtain, a romantic fusion of beauty, serenity, and assumed death, reminiscent of Lynch's 'Laura Palmer' (*Twin Peaks*) and Hitchcock's 'Marion Crane' (*Psycho*, 1960). To cope with the condition he rigorously records each clue as it presents itself by trying to capture moments through instamatic polaroid images and tattooing accumulated 'facts' on his body. The action throughout the film is punctuated with claustrophobic interior scenes of Leonard trying to retrace the previous sequence of his movements while also working through his 'man-hunting' investigation. These enclosed spaces, mostly anonymous motel rooms, reflect the vacant, alienated entrapment of his present life.

Despite his efforts to identify a phantom murderer, the investigation climaxes in the discovery of his wife's survival, subsequent death and the role he played in her assisted suicide. Unwilling to relinquish the bogus 'killer' scenario that drives his need for purpose, nourishes the memory of his wife, and props up his ego-ideal, Leonard decides to ignore this version of reality, and so his search continues through deliberate forgetting. Nolan's play on the beautiful, perfect, dead beloved as hero's muse is a romantic device often used to soften the edges of cinema's more macho aggressors like *Gladiator*'s 'Maximus' (2000), *Braveheart*'s 'William Wallace' (1995) or *Sin City*'s 'Marv' (2005). This 'softening' has predominantly been theorized as a form of female subjugation (Dijkstra 1986) and 'death by proxy' (Bronfen 1992: x) where femininity and death are synonymously marked as a form of otherness.

Yet neither of these readings seems to motivate Leonard's fantasy. While he maintains faulty images of his wife's death, it's not the disavowal of death itself that sustains him (as Bronfen argues in relation to similar fictional idealizations of beautiful dead women) it's the need to substitute the assisted suicide memory with a romanticized murder scenario. Rather than resisting death by displacing it onto another, he is much more terrified of the meaningless/guilt ridden life that his wife's actual death signifies. *Memento* exposes the ambiguous and ambivalent psychological ruses of Leonard's primitive trickster-psychopomp aspect. This half-lit man, when he does surface from the underworld later in the film, deliberately reduces his brief flash of lucidity to numbing blankness. He ultimately has no vested interest in either tracking down a killer or 'finding out who he really is'. It's not surprising that Teddy's invitation to 'the basement' is resisted.

Sammy fusion

Throughout *Memento* Leonard compulsively repeats to others and himself the cautionary story of Sammy Jankis. Leonard's gradual disclosure of the incident, threaded throughout the backward sequenced action scenes, not only gives historical context to his handicap and the way he manages it, but also provides the psychological still/stuck point that propels his investigation. Prior to the burglary when he worked as an insurance investigator, Leonard dealt with a car accident compensation claim bought forward by Jankis' wife on Sammy's behalf. The crash left Sammy with a similar, but even more severe case of anterograde amnesia that prevented him from remembering anything longer than a few minutes.

Leonard decided the claim was untenable, arguing that Sammy's inability to remember was psychological rather than physical and consequently outside the terms and conditions of his insurance contract. Taking Leonard's assessment to heart, Sammy's diabetic wife began to test Sammy's memory. She became so distraught with her lack of success that she repeatedly asked him to give her insulin shots in the hope that the gravity of what he was doing would jog his mind. Genuinely unable to make new memories, he continued to administer each shot (forgetting the last) as requested, until she fell into a coma.

Ignoring or perhaps forgetting his 'never answer the phone' tattoo, Leonard tells this story in detail to an anonymous caller making it easy for us to see the dribble-down effect of his thoughts, to speech and then to the ambiguous 'Remember Sammy Jankis' tattoo on his left hand. 'Remember Sammy Jankis' is a frequently repeated sign of disability and decay; a brief punch of indelible words Leonard organizes to confirm his otherness to Jankis. From his thoughts, to his conversation, to the inscription, he confines the Jankis warning to a tight absolute certainty. 'I'm disciplined and organized. I use habit and routine to make my life possible', he says of his copious documentation of 'the facts', unlike Jankis who had no practical system to counterbalance his disability.

Leonard's sanity hinges on what appears to be a firm pre-accident memory of the Jankis case, but this series of recollections are proven flawed when Leonard learns that he exposed Sammy as a fraud and that he *himself* repeatedly injected his diabetic wife at her request. This displaced memory of the unwitting murder in its surreal distortion, is the one thing that appears to save Leonard from the abyss: 'I guess it [memory] can only make you remember the things you want to be true', Teddy tells him. Ironically Leonard defies his condition because the insulin incident, despite being distortedly encoded, occurred *after* the critical accident that impaired his short-term memory. It could be argued that ultimately Leonard's wife succeeded in shifting his awareness.

In *The Psychopathology of Everyday Life* (1901), Freud theorized the now popular concept that disagreeable memories could be repressed: 'It is probable that many instances of *disowning* which we encounter in our medical work are to be traced to *forgetting*' (Freud 1960: 144–145, original emphases). He also coined the term *paramnesia* for 'faulty recollection' of certain impressions and events (1960: 148), arguing that forgetting and paramnesis can, although not always, be motivated by repression. Jung's early word association experiments also supported this notion of forgetting as the result of repressing undesirable feelings/thoughts. The longer the patient took to respond to the stimulus-word given, the more likely it was, according to Jung, that the delayed recall could be related to complexes (autonomous structures of the personal unconscious in conflict with the ego) or their feeling-tone (affects) (*CW* 2, para. 650).

Leonard has repressed an act too traumatic for his ego to accept by disguising or reinventing his memory of the event. As well as assuaging his guilt, the persona swapping also enables him to allay his fears of invalidism. The black and white flashback shots of Jankis and his wife are heavily endowed with a claustrophobic sense of inaction, dependency and purposelessness that in hindsight suggests either the reality of Leonard and his wife's post-accident situation, or the fear of what their relationship might become.

Contrary to the early theories about repressed memory and the prolific incidence of 'recovered memories', particularly those of so-called forgotten childhood sexual abuse that swept across America in the 1980s and 1990s, contemporary research into the memory's relationship to trauma, reveals that survivors rarely repress distressing episodes, rather, they remember then all too vividly (McNally 2003). As a cinematic device, Freudian driven narratives and surreal imagery revolving around trauma, memory repression, displacement and recovery, make for suspenseful drama (Huston's *Freud*, 1962, or Hitchcock's *Spellbound*, 1945). Although *Memento* sits comfortably in this tradition where the credibility of Leonard's repression, when read literally, requires some suspension of disbelief, it is nevertheless a challenging commentary on the complex and subjective nature of memory.

The individual is the only reality

In writing about his multileveled dream house, Jung was adamant that the imagery should be treated as intrinsic to his experience of reality and was therefore averse to the possibility that it be read through any kind of rigid theory. He concluded, in relation to dream matter and projections of unconscious material, that 'the individual is the only reality' (Jung 1964: 45):

> The further we move away from the individual toward abstract ideas about Homo Sapiens the more likely we are to fall into error. In these times of social upheaval and rapid change, it is desirable to know much more than we do about the individual human being, for so much depends upon his mental and moral qualities. But if we are to see things in their right perspective, we need to understand the past of man as well as his present. That is why an understanding of myths and symbols is of essential importance.
>
> (Jung 1964: 45)

There seems to be a contradiction in this idea, for it is unclear whether Jung is talking about the individual as subject, or representative of a collective. The former response can be extended to read 'the individual's reality is the only reality', and therefore the only way an analyst can legitimately grapple with the authenticity of a patient's situation, while the later implies that the analyst can introduce, or read into the patient's experience (when interpreted at the archetypal level) symbolic/mythic images and meanings. *Memento* plays much more on the concept of reality as a subjective construction through the way in which Leonard both consciously and unconsciously modifies his memories and the meaning of the images he photographs to suit his situation. His version of reality is the only reality tolerable.

Teddy, Leonard's prime contact for information and eventually the one he kills for his wife's 'murder', tells him during the final scenes that they have already caught and shot the actual intruder (and fabricated murderer). Leonard is also told that he was responsible for blacking out words and passages from the copious police reports and investigation notes that he accrued in order to thwart his own investigation and prevent a rediscovery of the event. 'Can I just let myself forget what you've told me?' he says in voice-over before writing 'don't believe his lies' on the back of a polaroid of Teddy, knowing that the memory of Teddy's admission will be wiped blank.

Not only does Leonard choose not to note this confession down so he can use it as a referent to his troubled situation, but also he once again sets himself up to follow false clues that will propel a pointless investigation and, more menacingly, create an illusion of Teddy as a liar and future target despite the possible consequences of these actions. The intimation at the climax of Nolan's puzzle, is that Leonard has also been made aware of his wife's death before, and each time refused to record it, knowing that an unaccounted for incident would soon be forgotten and paramnesia would kick in as a protective shield against his conscience and the fear of meaninglessness.

Although Leonard creates his own reality by cleverly misinforming himself, he is merely a reflection of the way in which reality is continually shaped by the individual, for as Adams (2004: 8) writes: 'Reality is relative to fantasy, to how we imaginally construct it. This is what I might call the *theory of imaginal realativity*' (original emphasis). While Leonard tattoos 'memory is treachery' along his upper arm and caustically reminds himself (in voice-over) that 'memory can change the shape of a room, it can change the colour of a car, and memories can be distorted. They're just an interpretation, they're not a record', the way he distortedly remembers and forgets is his most reliable survival technique. In *Remembering Trauma* Richard McNally (2003: 35) argues that in recalling a past event, 'we reconstruct it from encoded elements distributed throughout the brain. There are very few instances in which remembering resembles reproducing'. As Leonard continually, compulsively, retells the story of Sammy Jankis to anyone who will listen, he is inscribing it in his imagination as an actual event, which of course it is and is not. This kind of repetition, according to McNally's research on the problematic nature of recovered memory therapy where a therapist may lead the patient into fabricating recollections of childhood abuse, is a powerful method of maintaining false memories:

> Thinking or talking about memories of both imagined and perceived events prevents their details from fading. The more someone thinks about an imaginary event, the more likely the person is to confuse it with an event that really happened. Individuals scoring high on measures of imaginary ability and disassociation are especially prone to confuse imagined with real events, and a focus on one's own emotional response fosters confusion among external sources of information.
>
> (McNally 2003: 43)

Leonard and trickster

The subjective nature of reconstructing past events can be understood as a tricksterish ploy to shield, develop or safeguard one's sense of self. In *Memento*'s extreme account of deceptively tripping consciousness and unconsciously displacing memories, the trickster archetype is clearly functioning, not only as a possible force for change, but also as a mechanism for self-preservation. In an interesting link, Spinks (1991: 185) notes that Jung associated the play of trickster to 'the articulation of the unrecognized, he is the embodiment of things to be remembered and things to be discovered'. The irony of Leonard's fear of purposelessness is that in his desperation to structure a meaningful existence, beyond mere subsistence, his search has to be pointless.

Like mythic tricksters Wakdjunkaga's or Anase's perpetual movement from one ruse to another (Chapter 2), there is no inherent substance or closure in each episode, rather, it is the ambiguity of trickster's cyclic play that can reflect, according to Pelton (1980: 37), the mythologem's ability to give 'birth to a dialectic whose aim is not synthesis, but a never-ending juggling of thesis and antithesis'. We might call this kind of understanding 'dialogical' rather than 'dialectical' because, as Rowland (2005) argues of Jung's construction of the psyche, 'the most fundamental relationships Jung encounters are not *resolvable* through dialectical synthesis, mainly because they consist of polarities within a multiplicitous field . . . "dialogical" . . . suggests something more flexible, adaptable and plural for Jung's psyche' (Rowland 2005: 85, original emphasis). Her application of the more complex term 'dialogical' to describe Jung's thinking, certainly relates to trickster, especially if we see it as one of, if not *the* governing paradigm of his theoretical framework.

The sense of meaningfulness in Leonard's cyclic search is, like the structure of *Mulholland Drive*, only clear when viewing the vignettes of his life as fragments of an overarching whole. From this perspective, the binaries of reality/fantasy, truth/deception, past/present and life/death converge to offer Nolan's (and Lynch's) audience a tricksterish experience. Walking a line between the tension of opposites allows us to see both sides of the margin and the organizing structure of the Self in which these stresses lie: 'It seems closer to the truth', says Pelton, 'to say that trickster is a symbol of the liminal state itself and of its permanent accessibility as a source of recreative power' (1980: 35). Like Lynch's play with the chronology of events, Nolan's structural blurring of time margins reflects his central subject's psychological struggle to reconcile the more flexible nature of the external with the immediate nature of memory and imagination. The film articulates how memory in its elasticity, subjectivity, and embrace of reality and fantasy, is in itself a manifestation of the trickster archetype central to the formation of identity.

While Leonard is of course a fictional subject for the spectator rather than the analyst's scrutiny, he nevertheless provides an opportunity to reflect on the tricksterish machinations of memory function and the deceptive nature of this process. Guy Pearce (Leonard) spoke with host Andrew Denton on the Australian television chat show *Enough Rope* about how *Memento* forced him to question the objective nature of his own memories. The following quote relates to an incident shortly after the death of his father when Pearce was still a child:

> I did this film about memory once called 'Memento' and it made me question my memory and my ability to remember things. So every time I say anything about my past or my childhood, I have this slight voice in the back of my head that says, 'I'm not sure if that's true or not, if I've projected something.' But I feel I have this memory of my mother saying to me . . . 'You have to be responsible, you have to be the father of the family, you have to help me look after your sister.' She never did that. She said, 'It's so wonderful you're so responsible.'
>
> (Denton 2003)

This admission, a common instance of how past experiences can be embellished and misread, also suggests that the fantasy/reality aspect of memory shapes identity by providing a context for the roles and behaviours we adopt. One of the key themes of *Memento*, echoed so poignantly in Pearce's story, is the question of whether accumulated reminiscences form identity, or whether memories are selected and filtered to support a self image we find necessary to establish. As a colleague commented in relation to this kind of misremembering, 'Ah, the superego!'

Although structuring an identity that suits an ideal, as in Leonard's case, might appear to figure significantly in our development, Jung sees it as a mere casing, a persona, that shouldn't be mistaken for the more complex and constantly maturing self that lies beneath it. By refusing to confront uncomfortable parts of his life, Leonard lives in a self-imposed paralysis, never able to concretely locate the core beneath the stuck mask of avenging warrior. This confining psychological groove also exemplifies the necessity of being in charge of the persona so that it can be modified and shifted. Because Leonard can never remember the context of any given situation he's in, he is unable to construct and apply a persona to that situation in order to both relate to, and protect himself from, others. He therefore remains dependent on a stereotypical form of heroism to maneuver through each physical and emotional interaction.

Through vigorous note-taking he tries to defy the void-like nature of his disability where there is no concept of an immediate past or future, just the stark confrontation of an ever-present now: 'How am I supposed to heal if I can't feel time', he says. He takes polaroids of places and faces significant to his investigation and 'writes' the most important 'facts' on his body as if anchoring them in his skin as a sensual, lived experience. Although he exists in the confining prism of the present, his memories before the accident and his sense of purpose (the hope of tracking down his prey) provide an artificial sense of 'normal' time dimensions necessary for the framing of personal and collective development. His collection of images and words, in the form of documents and tattoos, as well as providing clues, are also useful as concrete traces of an immediate past that he must otherwise take on faith. In this way he tricks himself (much like the replicants of Ridley Scott's *Blade Runner*, 1982) into having a clear history through which to negotiate the future. But like memory itself, Leonard's words and images are open to interpretations predictably coloured by his ultimate objective.

A creature of language

While Leonard uses written words as navigational tools, they are also the very things that consciously and unconsciously ensure he will remain in a perpetual state of searching for, never reaching, conclusions. The very nature of the instructions, phrases, initials, names and numbered 'facts' that he wears on his skin serve his dual aims: to cyclically lead him to dead ends which ensure that his life *always* has meaning, and to create the illusion that he is more than adequately able to manage his memory loss. If, as Pelton (1980: 223) suggests, 'words are what he [trickster] juggles best', then Leonard, like his fellow mythic tricksters, can be seen to use words not only as a means of shape-shifting realities, but also as a way of elevating himself to what he imagines is a position of control. 'Do I lie to myself to be happy?' he says in voice-over at the end of the film, 'I have to believe in a world outside my own mind. I have to believe that my actions still have meaning, even if I can't remember them'. If Leonard is able to manipulate himself through a sheath of elusive and ambiguous words, he is clearly able to ensure some kind of future even if he is not sure of the direction it will take:

> To have all sacred words is to be capable of all sacred moves; the trickster can change forms as easily as he can tell lies. To pin him to one meaning is to annul his power to link the many levels of experience and to destroy the imaginative irony that he incarnates.
>
> (Pelton 1980: 224)

In Jung's rationale of the relationship between symbols and signs (see Chapter 1), the universal, a priori nature of symbol imagery is beyond conscious manipulation and represents an archetypal energy. The sign, however, as both manufactured image and word, is a socially constructed means of representation. Because of the fabricated and variable import of words, trickster is easily able to use and misuse language as a way of slipping and sliding through the cultural environment. As Derrida argues in relation to the act of writing, itself a tricksterish play with orality, 'It is the moment at which we must *decide* whether we will engrave what we hear. And whether engraving preserves or betrays speech' (Derrida 2001: 9).

Leonard's body is a string of signifiers with no fixed signifieds. His story exemplifies the arbitrary nature of the linguistic sign – trickster's plaything. Without history, memory or context, words are ultimately empty. With each new reading their meaning must be renewed. This is what Leonard, in trickster mode, both fails to understand and cunningly depends upon. When thinking of his wife, before the accident, he says he remembers the *feel* of her in varying moments that were never put into words. In these flashback scenes his driven logos (rationality) abruptly surrenders to a form of relatedness, otherwise inaccessible to him. This notion that the *feel* of a person gives a stronger sense of connection than words or images, is the only surety he appears to trust. Throughout the film his wife's words are remembered in sketchy, romantic grabs. Not surprising, since her verbal instructions were the only cues he needed to kill her.

In trying to shape-shift his reality, make it whatever he wants in moments when he is reminded of the need to be purposeful (when purpose is in doubt), Leonard is very conscious of his ability to play the trickster. But when looked at from another perspective, it is as if in releasing the archetypal energy, he is unable to direct its impact. For if an archetypal component of the unconscious is tripping one up in order to intensify self-awareness, then its force cannot be consciously controlled. If the trickster figure, guided by this energy, is, as Radin (1972: xxiii) theorizes, 'he who dupes others and who is always duped himself', then the motif can operate on a conscious and unconscious level, so that the deceptions practiced on one's self or others, merely reflect the tricks that the archetype plays on the ego. Leonard might think that he is cheating his condition through his manipulation of the words and images he chooses to record, but his more authentic trickster aspect ultimately undermines these efforts by revealing the futility of such defiance.

Does *Memento* ultimately reveal that it is meaningful to accept the possibility of meaninglessness, a throwback to Jung's often quoted assumption that trickster transforms the 'meaningless into the meaningful' (*CW* 9i, para. 458), or can it also be read as a parable of how trickster returns in different guises to confront and challenge? The film leaves open the possibility that Leonard might either come to understand his self-deception through the perseverance of his own internal trickster and therefore eventually accept his wife's murder, or (more likely) perpetually circumvent any external reality that conflicts with his 'meaningful' mission of revenge and continue to maintain the illusory memory of his wife that had no words – the beautiful, silenced, wrapped-in-plastic guarantor of his sanity.

Memento reminds us that memory, whether channeled through the imagination or the bodily senses, is deceptive and shape-shifting, in itself tricksterish. The Puck-like Leonard, who creates chaos through illusion, is an unreliable, yet apt conduit for this aid to self-awareness and self-deception. In the canon of mythic tricksters before him, he remains in perpetual movement from one ruse to another, playing the amoral hero and fool. Unlike *Mulholland Drive*'s Diane, Leonard resists confronting his demons and accepting responsibility. Perhaps to do this is to risk Diane's self-annihilation. While dreams take her to the underworld/unconscious, she is unable to make a bridge from one state to the other and so falls between the cracks. Leonard, though, refuses to even acknowledge any subterranean site of dissonance. When it rises to challenge him, he contrives to forget the conflict, and the ruthless energy of both the conscious and unconscious trickster is set in competition once again. The conductor of souls function has been stifled and the opportunity for internal dialogue between points of opposition is not allowed to take place.

The following chapter concentrates on this psychopomp aspect in a much more literal way than *Memento* or Lynch's work, by focusing on the undead, their holding pattern in purgatory/limbo/bardo, and their eventual transit to the underworld via the trickster paradigm. Through the metaphor of the dead and the living, we are able to see the full trajectory to awareness via the painful crossing from unconscious to conscious realities. Leonard though remains in purgatory, unwilling to atone for the past, unable to cope with who he is, and therefore seemingly incapable of accessing his potential Self – a fool who refuses to peep.

Chapter 5

The undead, psychopomps and filicide

The Others

> 'Of course we have the others.'
> 'We have the others – we indeed have the others,' I concurred.
> 'Yet even though we have them,' he returned, still with his hands in his pockets and planted there in front of me, 'they don't much count, do they?'
> I made the best of it, but I felt wan. 'It depends on what you call "much"!'
> Henry James, *The Turn of the Screw* (1991: 80)

Chapters 3 and 4 explored the capacity of trickster to buoy up fragile and floundering egos. As we saw in *Mulholland Drive* this survival mechanism isn't always successful. In the case of *Memento*, even though the trickster's success or failure remained open-ended, the film allowed us to understand the archetype as a persistent and resilient energy that pushes us to self-examination no matter how desperately the ego tries to resist. In this reading of Alejandro Amenábar's film *The Others* (2001), I'm going to open up this 'therapeutic' aspect of trickster further by exploring its 'conductor of souls' or *psychopomp* function (*psyche*/soul and *pomp*/guide).

The connection between more run-of-the-mill mythic trickster figures and underworld guides is embodied in Jung's pet saviour Hermes/Mercury/Mecurius, 'the god of revelation, lord of thought and sovereign psychopomp' (*CW* 12, para. 404) who not only ferries souls to the underworld, but also redirects the souls of the living to a new, and ultimately more liberating awareness. This association of trickster with the life/death motif and its role as divine orchestrator of underworld/upperworld appropriateness, is also clearly evoked in Radin's (1972) anthropological studies. The Hare trickster figure, for instance, divides the living from the dead by pushing evil spirits underground and tossing attacking birds toward heaven so that humans can live peacefully in between (Radin 1972: 87). *The Others* offers us a contemporary reworking of this trickster dimension.

The film takes us to lost souls and temporal ambiguity where the dead encroach on the living, psychological projections and realities blur, the knowing child inhabits the same space as the naive adult, and guilt parallels innocence. While on the surface Amenábar has created a ghost narrative about the undead seeking identity, his work exposes the necessity of coming to terms with the self as a preliminary step toward accessing 'a bigger picture'. In this story of loss, conscious and unconscious fields interlink through a tricksterish play with various framings of time and space. As the central character, Grace (Nicole Kidman), eventually relinquishes her armored persona and frees herself to straddle the margins of these energies, we are again exposed to an unconsciously surging want for more than the ego can offer.

Amenábar's thriller *Open your Eyes* (1997) and his commentary on euthanasia, *The Sea Inside* (2004), also deal with the theme of fear, renunciation, and eventual acceptance of the life/death paradigm. In *The Others* these three phases are charted by intertextually fusing mythic and screen/literature fictions of the ghostly and paranormal. Through the haunted-house-as-haunted-psyche formula, Amenábar cleverly reworks the narrative device of 'repression'; that old Freudian signifier of 'disturbance' that as we saw in the previous chapter, has become increasingly relegated to fiction. As a reworked myth of the pathology of denial, *The Others* allows us the luxury and thrill of imagining repression at its most extreme – the disavowal of death. This chapter not only looks at the amoral trickster as psychological psychopomp, but also tackles three key themes woven into the text: the cultural discrimination of mothers perceived to lack maternal feelings; the parallel between Catholicism's *limbo* and *purgatory* states and Tibetan Buddhism's *bardo* realm; and the psychological import of 'the undead' and paranormal. Amenábar's film is more than a simple ghost thriller. What opens up before us is a complex twist of issues, prejudices, ideas and archetypal presences.

Returning the screw

The Others sacrifices seductive digital technology that allows *everything* to be exposed, for a more menacing effect where the audience realizes the multiple identities of what is 'other' only through the eyes of the central characters. This allows for the kind of physical/psychological ambiguity that Henry James so skillfully worked into his classic novella *Turn of the Screw* (1898), a story of phantoms who haunt little Miles, his sister Flora, and their emotionally fragile governess. Amenábar's opening sequence begins with the motherly narration of a child's version of genesis, punctuated by a series of sepia, Victorian styled picture-book illustrations. As the credits begin to appear the imagery switches to similarly styled sketches of another narrative, clearly echoing James' brand of gothic fiction where childhood and the spectral fuse.

This newly introduced story unravels in the following way: two small children crouch on an upper level of a large staircase; a woman is seated between a standing girl and boy playing with his train set; an adult female holds a candle in one hand, and a large key in the other; the same woman carrying the candle talks to a frightened girl on the staircase as she points to a space off screen; an elderly woman's hand manipulates the puppet of a young boy-angel, his limbs askew; and finally, a drawing of an isolated mansion morphs into a long shot that transports us to the moving image. While not exactly reproducing James' work, Amenábar unambiguously pays homage to the psychological shadow of parental love that marks *Turn of the Screw*.

The threat of annihilation often takes the form of a dreaded other to whom we are disturbingly vulnerable. This other often manifests as a projection of disavowed emotions onto a specific person/persons or actual paranormal phenomena. *The Others* relies on a combination of both. The film maintains a tension between disturbances of the psyche and the outer world through the leakage of material ordinarily held within the container of 'reason'. The ghostly others living outside the margins can be read as eruptions of the objective psyche that, as Jung argued, function outside time, place and rationality.

The film follows a collection of ghost-like characters divided into two factions; those who know they are ghosts (the servants), and those who are unable to accept their death (the family of the house): Grace and her two children Anne (Alakina Mann) and Nicholas (James Bentley). In their role as psychopomps, the first group guide the second to the underworld. Unaware of what they are, the family inhabits an eerie undead state, fraught with anxiety and fear of 'the others' who haunt their lives. For Grace, these others are disturbed spirits who cease their torment only when she is able to acknowledge killing both her children and herself. Grace is indeed dead; she just doesn't know it. The others haunting her and the children are not fellow phantoms, but a 'living' family who now occupy the house and in turn, 'other' Grace, Anne and Douglas as ghostly presences.

In refusing to acknowledge her past, Grace (and her children as a consequence) are locked in psychological limbo or purgatory. This plateau haunted by terror, repression and illusion is a veritable playground for trickster energy. The archetype can be seen as the most likely driver behind Grace's burgeoning awareness. In its disrespect for borders and boundaries, trickster signifies the mediation between the polarities of mortality/immortality, life/death, reality/fantasy, and consciousness/the unconscious. The wily methods it employs to activate transformation in each lost soul and so ferry them to the afterlife, clearly show us trickster's skill in maintaining boundaries. While the motif provokes disorder and psychological chaos, the insight that results from this agitation can lead to a sense of equilibrium and a re-establishment of order. The servants as trickster-psychopomps who guide, classify and stabilize, generate a forceful energy between themselves and the psychokinetic oscillations of the living (the inhabiting family) and the dead (Grace, Anne and Nicholas). Before looking in detail at trickster as psychopomp, the inherent role this function plays in *The Others*, and the import of the film's hauntings as both physical realities and the product of psychological trauma, we have to go back to Grace and the vexed concept of 'mother'.

Motherhood and filicide

The 'mother' archetype (I'll now refer to as simply *mother* in this chapter) has been variously popularized in myth as Demeter (Greek), Diana (Italian), Mary Immaculate (European), Isis (Egyptian), Inanna (Sumerian) and Ishtar (Babylonian), but the multiple faces of *mother* (entwined with other diverse archetypal patterns) are not necessarily linked to notions of motherly nurture. Mythic motherly nurture, in turn, is not always connected to birth mothers or women. As far back as the 1970s with Nancy Chodorow's (1978) research, the maternal was acknowledged as a dynamic able to transcend biological parenthood and more specifically, the birth mother, to male figures, adoptive parents and guardians. The governess of gothic fiction often embraces the *mother* paradigm. Motherly without giving birth, she functions to highlight the underlying tension between an assumed female predisposition to the maternal and the possible antithesis of this 'instinct'.

The film *Evil Angels* (a.k.a. *A Cry in the Dark*, 1988) fictionalized Lindy Chamberlain's trial for supposed infanticide and exemplified the venom directed at mothers who fail to show sufficient signs of nurture. Although she claimed that her 10-week-old daughter Azaria was taken by a dingo at Uluru (Ayers Rock, Australia), Chamberlain was nevertheless convicted for murder and eventually pardoned through misleading evidence. Unfortunately she wasn't particularly media savvy. Her refusal to play along with popularly established codes of appropriate grief and suffering while in court and in front of the media significantly contributed to her assumed guilt and incarceration. *The Others* capitalizes on the discomfort of this kind of containment, more often than not read as an 'unholy' and/or 'unnatural' renunciation of the maternal.

The kind of moral conflict that the denials of perceived motherly 'instinct' stir up is clearly woven into gothic fiction. Mary Shelley's *Frankenstein, or The Modern Prometheus* (1818) is an obvious example: Victor abandons the monster-son he created and consequently suffers his 'child's' wrath. In keeping with this tradition, direct references are made to the night Grace 'went mad', her harsh (verging on abusive) treatment of the children, and Anne's wariness of this erratic behaviour. These 'hints', coupled with her excessively literal reading of the bible and fixation on sin, guilt and punishment, set up the expectation that Grace has done (or will do) something wicked.

In cinema where the unquiet souls of murdered children reach *from* and *to* the grave to right injustices (*The Changeling*, 1980; *The Shining*, 1980; *The Sixth Sense*) or seek revenge (*Ringu*, 1998; *Ju-on*, 2000), the killing of children is usually at the hand of the mother, surrogate mother, or father. The intense *affect* of the parental betrayal is often analogous to the intensity of the need for payback, or at least acknowledgement of the crime. It's not just the more brutal tricksterish transgression of betraying an assumed predisposition toward nurturing that allows us to be morally challenged by parental filicide and infanticide (whether fictional or actual), it's much more psychologically barbed than this. The various personifications of trickster have been linked to fertility, regeneration, birth and consequently mother (discussed in Chapters 2 and 11). Because the archetype isn't governed by conscience or morality, the child killings attributed to mythic trickster figures slip around ideas of guilt, evil and pathology.

In Radin's (1972) version of the Winnebago Trickster Cycle (part one), Wakdjunkaga the Winnebago trickster, already with a family of his own, has sex with a fox, jaybird and nit. This results in him giving birth to three male infants (Radin 1972: 22–23). Later in the story, after discarding his female persona, Wakdjunkaga baby-sits a large group of children, kills them, and on discovering they were really raccoons, boils and eats them (Radin 1972: 29). In the Asiniboine Trickster Cycle, Sitconski (one of the names for trickster) also shifts from male to female and dines on his roasted son (Radin 1972: 103). Not only is the notion of female reproduction in this cycle of mythology a flexible concept, but also the 'essential' nurturing qualities stereotypically associated with motherhood, and more generally parenthood, are mocked and contested. It is not the mother who is blamed for carrying out violence, or carelessly allowing various acts of violence to be committed against her children. The mother is merely a shell in which the amoral trickster plays. *It*, not *she*, is guilty, while *she* not *it* bears the burden of guilt. However, when trickster and the archetypal *mother* join forces (as in *The Others*), *mother*'s torn loving/terrible aspect and trickster's humorous/sinister aspect provide us with a much more complex and demanding psychological situation.

In the films mentioned earlier in this part of the book, the sinister mother undertone isn't dependent on the shock value of graphic allusions to conception, gestation or birth, but more closely related to the Greek tragedies of maternal filicide (Euripides' *Medea*, 431 BC, *The Hippolytus*, 428 BC, *The Bacchae*, 405 BC, for example) where a moral rule is broken so that it might be more potently reinstated. In keeping with Aristotelian theory, this genre often arouses a simultaneous sense of fear and pity (Aristotle 1967: 45). *The Others*, too, belongs in this canon of filicide texts that lend themselves more to tragedy than horror. In the final 'healing' scene where Grace confesses to her children as she pulls them tightly to her body in a demonstratively maternal embrace, the rule of mother/nurture is reinstated:

> At first I couldn't understand what the pillow was doing in my hand, why you didn't move, but then I knew it had happened, I'd killed my children. I got the rifle and put it to my forehead and I pulled the trigger, nothing. Then I heard your laughter in the bedroom, you were playing with the

> pillows as if nothing had happened and I thought the Lord in his great mercy was giving me another chance, telling me, don't give up, be strong, be a good mother.

Grace's confusion and paranoia dissipates with an acceptance of her crimes. As she humbles herself before her children and reveals the shame of failing to be a 'good mother', she strengthens her resolve to remain eternally bound to Anne and Douglas and so fulfill the cultural expectations of mother as a ubiquitously nurturing presence. Until these scenes, Grace remains in shadows, unrealized in terms of both s/Self. If, as Jung writes, 'the magic circle or mandala can be a form of mother archetype' (*CW* 9i, para. 156), then Grace's fragmentation, that little by little gives way to a more complete awareness, can be imaged as an incomplete uroboros; a circular snake that has not yet joined its tail to its mouth in an act of cyclical eternity.

In *Memories, Dreams, Reflections* (1963) Jung wrote of his own mystically inclined mother (Emilie Preswick) in tones that echo Anne and Douglas's bewildered and distrustful relationship to Grace. The upshot of his suspicions about her character led him, 'to divide everything my mother said in two. My confidence in her was strictly limited, and that was what prevented me from ever telling her about my deeper preoccupations' (Jung 1963: 70). Jung had anxiety fantasies about Emilie, once dreaming that she presided over a particular room in a haunted house where beds in hanging pavilions were provided for visiting dead spirits (Jung 1963: 240):

> I was sure she consisted of two personalities, one innocuous and human, the other uncanny. This other emerged only now and then, but each time, it was unexpected and frightening. She would then speak as if talking to herself, but what she said was aimed at me and usually struck to the core of my being, so that I was stunned to silence.
>
> (Jung 1963: 60)

His more idealized, theoretical, depersonalized versions of *mother* are predictably balanced with allusions to darker, shadow manifestations, clearly marked for example in the Hindu deity Kali. Jung sees the ambivalent *mother* surfacing in the forms of fate goddesses Moira, Graeae and Norns, and the negative or evil aspect of the archetype in 'the dragon (or any devouring and entwining animal, such as a large fish or a serpent), the grave, the sarcophagus, deep water, death, nightmares and bogies (Empusa, Lilith, etc.)' (*CW* 9i, para. 157).

In a similar sentiment to Amenábar and Kidman's formation of Grace as both loving and terrible, Jung further associates the negative aspect of the *mother* energy with, 'anything secret, hidden, dark; the abyss, the world of the dead, anything that devours, seduces and poisons, that is terrifying and inescapable like fate' (*CW* 9i, para. 158). The association of 'lamias', child-eating women, is another mythic image he uses to describe the proliferation of the negative *mother* as a dominant cultural motif:

> The original legend is that Lamia seduced Zeus, but the jealous Hera caused her to bring only dead children into the world. Ever since then, the raging Lamia has persecuted children, whom she destroys whenever she can. This motif is a recurrent one in fairytales, where the mother often appears as a murderess or eater of human flesh; a well-known German paradigm is the story of Hansel and Gretel.
>
> (*CW* 5, para. 369)

The Others reads as one more screen retelling of the mythic narratives Jung cites to illustrate the potency of mother's shadow. Dark and menacing to her children, Grace encapsulates the fear of the lamia, the grave, the sarcophagus, nightmares, the abyss and of course, the world of the dead.

The specter of the mother as sign of the life/death nexus – Freud's (1905) castrated other, Bakhtin's (1984) grotesque, Kristeva's (1982) abject, Jung's *mother* (*CW* 9i) – is, like Grace, a force to be reckoned with beyond the grave. She is fixed in the roots of both analytical psychology and psychoanalysis as the ghost against which identity is forged. Mother is always haunting the liminal spaces of being and non-being as an actual mother; religious creation deity; a concept from which various psychological disturbances are attributed (Oedipus complex, castration complex, Don Juanism, attachment disorder); and a multidimensional archetypal energy of the objective psyche. Grace represents this intrusive 'all-seeing-eye' expression of mother. She is the intangible ghostly other shifting between action, thought and reaction. She is as real as she is imaginary. By epitomizing the haunting specter of the *mother* archetype, Grace also embodies the ghostly, liminal and atemporal nature of the film itself. She is, in an intricate series of psychological twists, a site of the uncanny.

Reworking of the haunted house cliché

In 1919 Freud theorized the uncanny as both familiar and strangely displaced. He understood the German word *unheimlich* (uncanny/unhomely/forbidding) and its antonym *heimlich-heimisch* (homely/native/familiar) as providing the tension that could trigger the condition of an uncanny experience: a return of the repressed. And yet, in an echo of Jung's construction of the unconscious as collective and atemporal, he cautioned that only specific sensations that fell into this *unheimlich/heimlich* synergy evoked a sense of displacement and wariness: 'not everything that recalls repressed desires and surmounted modes of thinking belonging to the prehistory of the individual and of the race – is on that account uncanny' (Freud 1955: 245). The abject signs of mother in horror are often based on an imagined repressed memory of separation, becoming, and the lure of return and death. Grace's children see her as an uncomfortable sight of something familiar and frightening (mother and murderer) that they cannot fully remember. Because of this surfacing yet still buried memory, she becomes a threatening force in their imagination as a sign of separation.

The notion of the house or home, integral to Freud's etymological understanding of the uncanny also plays a significant role in *The Others* as the place where Grace tries to stifle her emerging memories and contain the paranormal energies that work against her disavowal. Like the clichéd haunted house of the horror genre, Grace's home becomes the nerve center for the action in the film. It develops into a receptacle for what is, and refuses to be acknowledged. The final sepia sketch in the opening sequence shows a distant image of a large mansion reflected in water to the foreground of the frame. The drawing then morphs into an identical filmed image of the house with print in the lower left hand corner to set the scene – 'Jersey, The Channel Islands 1945'. The landscape, like the building itself, is bleak. The large expanses of lawn fringing the house are reduced to patches of grass amidst grainy barren soil. The exterior shots are muted in a grayish-blue haze that gives the impression of an enveloping mist. This imagery of sterile land hemmed in by fog is not too dissimilar to early-twentieth-century film reels and photographic stills of battlefields.

These initial shots establish an uninviting atmosphere that is isolated and, despite the inserted date and allusions to the final bloody year of the Second World War, timeless. As an allusion to the psyche, the house lends itself more to Freud's id (that dark repository for the repressed), than Jung's up-beat version of the unconscious. The fog encircling the house/psyche hints at entrapment, but because fog is transitory and elemental, there is some indication already that secrets will be revealed. The servants' arrival and entry into the house, via Grace's invitation, provides a key metaphor for the rest of the text. If these characters can be understood as the projections of the archetypal trickster as psychopomp within the house as psyche, then their admission suggests a more Jungian framework than the initial Freudian one so easily applicable to much 'haunted-house' cinema: *The Uninvited* (1944), *The House on Haunted Hill* (1959), *The Haunting* (1963), *Amityville Horror* (1979), *The Shining Poltergeist* (1982), *Haunted* (1995).

The interiors of Grace's house reflect the external images to create an effect of inner/outer exchange and fusion. The sets of austere furniture echo the barren landscape that surrounds the house; the muted bluish-gray colouring of the rooms is relieved only by intermittent splashes of colour, and there are few personal adornments to clue us into the owner's character. The wooden staircase so prominent in the sketched introductory images, and the many large and closed doors, highlight the darkness of the building. Grace's need to block out the daylight, so that she can protect the children who she believes have a life-threatening, 'photosensitive' allergy to light, is another device to maintain sense of shadowy menace. Again, as with the mist, there's the suggestion that this 'blockage' can be shifted.

Unlike the traditional haunted-house narrative, the building is not by its nature dark or cavernous, and the action doesn't take place at night. Grace maintains the darkness. If light can be shut out, it can be introduced. It's not such a leap to equate Grace's envelopment in darkness and fog as a metaphor for her inability or unwillingness to bring to light the hidden psychic material perched on rim of consciousness. As well as the house and the rumblings within it representing Grace's psychological confusion, they're also uncanny signifiers of her unacknowledged acts. 'You'll find there are times', she warns the newly arrived servants, 'when this house is not an ideal home'. As id-like as this initial setup appears, the Jungian framework of an unconscious able to move consciousness forward though the activation of archetypal energies, is ultimately the more appropriate hook for this mythic text where the trickster function ruptures and unblocks the shadowy half understood past that drives the narrative.

Jung also used the term uncanny to describe a situation where complexes arise from the objective psyche. He argued that during an uncanny sensation:

> the conscious mind falls under its [the complex's] spell, either feeling it as something pathological, or else being alienated by it from normal life. The association of a collective content with the ego always produces a state of alienation, because something is added to the individual's consciousness, which ought really to remain unconscious, that is separated from the ego. If the content can be removed from consciousness again, the patient will feel relieved and more normal.
>
> (*CW* 8, para. 590)

Grace uses fifteen keys to lock each of the fifty doors of the house before and after entering each room on the pretext that light must be blocked from the children. This obsessive behaviour can also be seen as a way of removing the complex (an archetypal fusion of material from the personal unconscious). She literally tries to shut out any disturbances or archetypal motifs that arise to shift her consciousness and draw her toward the terror of her surfacing memories. By attempting to control the house in this way, she is trying to control her psyche. No wonder she fails.

After 1950, Jung was more clearly interested in, as Charet (1993: 234) writes, 'developing a clearly psychological view of spiritualistic phenomena'. Prior to this, he was open to the possibility of 'spirits' while still championing the psychological aspects of external 'specters'. In a letter to A. D. Cornell (9 February 1960) Jung more confidently came to believe that paranormal activity usually occurred during periods of heightened emotional states or alternately when the subject experiencing the phenomena has a personality disorder where the conscious/unconscious margin is unusually porous

(Jung 1976: 537–543). In relation to acts of meaningful coincidence, or *synchronicity,* where two events occur simultaneously beyond reasonable chance, the import of a paranormal experience, as Jung understood it, is driven by an underlying archetype that responds to a psychological upheaval (Main 1997: 9).

In 1920 while visiting London, Jung's friend 'Dr X' arranged for him to stay in a Buckinghamshire farmhouse. It was here that Jung once again found evidence of 'hauntings'. Over a number of nights he began to experience the sickly smell of an open carcinoma, a dripping tap, rustling sounds, knocking, and then climactically, the head of an old woman beside him on the pillow. Dr X, who at first contested the idea of ghosts, also slept in the farmhouse at Jung's challenge and witnessed similar hauntings. The house was subsequently pulled down (*CW* 18, paras. 764–777). Although this experience appears to be one of the instances where the apparition was not connected to the subject in particular, but acted more or less as an independent presence, on later reflection Jung reasoned that the 'unconscious, which possesses very much more subtle powers of perception and reconstruction than our conscious minds, could . . . project a visionary picture [ghost image] of the psychic situation that excited it' (*CW* 18, para. 781). He also posited that spirits, 'viewed from the psychological angle, are unconscious autonomous complexes which appear as projections because they have no direct association with the ego' (*CW* 8, para. 585). Although these 'spirits' surfacing from the collective unconscious and 'souls', (which he defined as the autonomous complexes of the personal unconscious *CW* 8, para. 591) worked through the container of the medium at séances and appeared in dreams and visions, Jung also saw them as exteriorized apparitions, 'a real outer object which behaves as if it were motivated or evoked by, or as if it were expressing, a thought corresponding to the archetype' (1976: 537–543).

Trickster psychopomps – archetypal phantasms

The first character we see is Grace screaming as if awaking from a nightmare. The scene then switches to an exterior shot of the servants, Mrs. Mills (Finial Flanagan), Mr. Tuttle (Eric Sykes) and Lydia (Elaine Cassidy), walking toward the house as they chuckle about 'the dead' they've known. In hindsight, all three are set up as trickster figures from the moment they appear claiming to be looking for work 'on the off chance'. Their arrival mysteriously occurs after the fleeing, for no apparent reason, of Grace's previous staff. The juxtaposition of the scream and the laughter establishes an uneasy relationship between the internal and external elements of the house/psyche personified by Grace and the servants who, as the film develops, seem to have an unusually intimate knowledge of both the house and Grace's psychological state. It's later revealed that they all worked and died of typhoid in the house many years earlier. Their arrival quickly follows Grace's crimes, denial of them, and consequent 'holding position' in purgatory. They clearly filter psychopomp energy in their function as soul guides responsible for directing Grace, Anne and Nicholas to the underworld.

Servants of classical and popular fiction are often marginal figures who tentatively straddle the borders of home and workplace, participation and alienation, familiarity and formality, commitment and indifference. They are keepers of homes they neither own, have freedom of movement in, nor any right to occupy without their employers' permission. Not only do the three new arrivals embody what is semiotically understood as servant material, but also they appear to play on their marginality to the point of being other worldly to Grace and her family: 'the others' as they are called by Anne. This state of fluidity is very much a trickster function according to Spinks (1991: 177), who classifies trickster as 'always the border creature who plays at the margins of self, symbol and culture and who echoes the epigenetic ambivalences of any line of demarcation'.

The servants are unable to claim a relationship to the family or the house in any formal sense, but from the first few scenes it becomes apparent that they have control over both. As 'free agents' untied to place or time, they are not intimidated or beholden to cultural, ideological and psychological boundaries as is the tightly repressed and religiously sanctimonious Grace. Her wariness of them and her tendency to blame them for each occurrence in the house beyond her control, suggests that on some unrealized level she 'knows' they have an understanding of what is happening to her and her family. The servants can of course also be interpreted as projections of the trickster motif generated by Grace. Jung talks about fictional figures in mythology functioning in the same way for the reader. He argues that the mythological figure secretly 'participates in the observer's psyche and appears as its reflection, though it is not recognized as such. It is split off from consciousness and consequently behaves like an autonomous personality' (*CW* 9i, para. 484).

In keeping with Jung's cross-cultural and atemporal understanding of the unconscious, the psychopomp has adopted a variety of mythological identities: Charon, Persephone (Greek); Agni (Hindu); St. Peter (Christian); Anubis, Neith, Thoth (Egyptian); Odin, Valkaries (Norse); and Don (Celtic). As assorted as these figures are, none directly merge with the trickster function as powerfully as the Hermes/Mercury figures popularized by Jung, although many embodied aspects of trickster in their shape-shifting and dual existences among the living and the dead. The servants of *The Others* contemporize the mythic trickster-psychopomp in their primary function as guides able to filter through the dimensions of time, form, consciousness and the unconscious to channel the lost to their appropriate destination. Unlike the fluid movements of the servants from one state to another, Grace and her children are trapped in the fog of limbo or purgatory. It is from this psychological plane, that Mrs. Mills, Mr. Tuttle and Lydia must shift her awareness.

Limbo, purgatory, bardo

The indeterminate state between life and death where Grace and her family are caught is hinted at early in the film. During the children's biblical reading lesson, Anne, with Nicholas giggling in agreement, admits that she would have denied Christ publicly to save herself, although inwardly believed in him. This act is equal to the thrice denial of St. Peter, the Christian psychopomp. Grace then asks Nicholas to list the four hells in a response calculated to point out the consequences of lying. 'There's the hell where the damned go', he says, 'then there's purgatory and the bosom of Abraham where the just go and limbo where children go'. Grace's response is a telling displacement of her own guilt at renouncing (via her acts of filicide) the moral and ethic tenets of Christianity: 'At the center of the earth where it's very, very hot. That's where children go who tell lies but they don't just go there for a few days. Oh no. No they're damned. Forever.' In her rebuke Grace self-righteously justifies her unremitting claim that Anne and Nicholas are prone to lie. The children's 'lying' or 'story-telling', as we see throughout the film, are merely accounts of their half-remembered murders and experiences of ghostly visitations by the living.

Within the house the notion of the ghost is realized in terms of a parallel universe. As mentioned earlier, the family and the servants are revealed to be dead at the end of the film, but they experience ghostly visitations throughout. These spectral experiences become known as the actions of the living family who now inhabit the house. Their spectral experiences, in turn, are the actions of the undead Grace, Anne and Nicholas. Each family is invisible to 'the other'. Anne, though, has a more acute grip on the situation and sees the living family as another tangible reality. She draws them and lists the number of times they appear to her. She and Nicholas become particularly drawn to the boy Victor (Alexander Vince) with whom they share a bond of fear and familiarity. One can argue that the Grace, Anne and Nicholas are the pivot to this parallel phenomenon. Because they straddle the planes of life and death, they're able to access both and yet belong to neither. The living family, however, have no access to the world of the dead except via a 'medium' they recruit to help flush out their 'others' – Grace and her children who unwillingly flail against the margins of the upper and under worlds.

In Catholic doctrine *purgatory* is a purifying plane of existence where the sins of the dead have the opportunity to be purged. Although not specifically acknowledged in the Bible, the Catholic Church legitimizes the state of purgatory. *Limbo*, however, remains a less officially recognized 'holding pattern' where the souls of unbaptised children, or children who have not 'sinned', remain suspended for an indeterminate period. One could argue that while Grace sits in purgatory, Anne and Nicholas, the innocent victims of her psychotic lashing out, hover in a state of limbo. Grace is caged until she repents. For this she needs to admit guilt.

The Buddhist tradition also incorporates a state of 'passage' and holding before one enters either the afterlife of nirvana or rebirth through reincarnation. This transitional plane where one's karma must be dealt with before re-entering the womb, or finding enlightenment, is called the *bardo*, and can, along with purgatory, also be applied to the situation in which Grace finds herself:

> Freedom is the attainment of the Supreme State called the Void, *Nirvana*, and by other names. They [Brahmanism and Buddhism] deny that there is only one universe, with one life for each of its human units, and then a division of men for all eternity into those who are saved in Heaven or are in Limbo and those who are lost in Hell.
>
> (Woodroffe 2000: lxvii–lxviii)

Bardo can take the form of six states of existence: intrauterine; dreaming; the 'ecstatic equilibrium' of meditation; point of death; intermediate post-death period; and the realm of *sangsara* where the reincarnation cycle is played out (Evans-Wentz 2000: 102). The *sangsaric* existence can briefly be understood as the phenomenal (worldly existence) aspect of death/rebirth phase and stands in direct opposition to the concept of the nirvana, or ultimate enlightenment (Evans-Wentz 2000: 12). The bardo realm after death is said to last for 49 days and instructions for each day are detailed in the *Tibetan Book of the Dead* or *Bardo Thödol*, originally compiled in the eighth century as a detailed Buddhist 'manual' for guiding the dead to their next incarnation.

In Jung's passionate commentary to Evans-Wentz's (1927) translation (that he refers to as his 'constant companion'), he writes of the psychological stages documented in the interim period before rebirth where each soul (unless to the point of enlightenment) encounters their multidimensional karmic shadows, as analogous to the concepts of unconscious collectivity and archetypal projection. *The Others* is interesting in the light of the bardo state. It can be understood to take place in this post-death plane where Grace is confronted with her shadows before she can shift into a new stage of the rebirth cycle. The encounters with various forms of light, evil, brilliance etc. mentioned in the *Bardo Thödol* as Jung reads it, are largely psychological projections of potent archetypal motifs that allow the subject to understand, confront, recognize, and accept responsibility for problematic aspects of their former life.

The concentration of light throughout the film, its negation, and the moment when it streams into the rooms of the house, can also be looked at in terms of the significance of light during the bardo stage. On the third day after death, the doctrine talks of an encounter with a brilliant 'yellow light' that evokes fear, and a 'dull bluish-yellow' light coming from the human plane that becomes more alluring:

> do not fear that bright, dazzling-yellow, transparent light, but know it to be Wisdom; in that state, keeping thy mind resigned, trust in it earnestly and humbly. If thou knowest it to be the radiance of thine own intellect – although thou exertest not thy humility and faith and prayer to it – the Divine Body and Light will merge into thee inseparably, and thou wilt obtain Buddhahood.
>
> (Evans-Wentz 2000: 111)

Grace's vampiric desire to keep out the light for fear of death suggests a need to remain tied to the human world. Acknowledging her filicide and suicide would be to also acknowledge her death. Grace stifles any opposition that threatens the compensatory 'good maternal mother' persona she vehemently adopts, so her insistence that the children be constantly kept-in-the-dark, is an overly literal metaphor for refusing them access to former memories, assumptions, intuitions, and truths about their lives and deaths. The final revelatory scenes of the film that lead to a confrontation of the living and the dead, explore in more detail the power of this light/dark synergy. When the living family remove the drapes from each window of the house and light floods the rooms without affecting either Anne or Nicholas, we understand that Grace has imagined the children's photosensitivity. It is at this point that all three gradually become aware of their disposition.

As Evans-Wentz explains in a footnote to the *Bardo Thödol*, Buddhists also talk about an initial passage of 'clear light' where the newly dead initially experience a sense of perfect equilibrium. This 'egoless' experience is so unfamiliar, though that most will not be able to remain in this state, because '*karmic* propensities becloud the consciousness-principle with thoughts of personality, of individualized being, of dualism and, losing equilibrium, the consciousness-principle falls away from the Clear Light' (Evans-Wentz 2000: 97). Too fixed in a maze of self-deception, Grace is so psychologically attached to illusory ideas of what and who she constructs herself as, that a state of 'non-ego' or equilibrium seems impossible. In refusing to examine and release her earthy identity she is able to maintain a self-righteous innocence.

The *Bardo Thödol*'s concentration on states of lightness and darkness, standard metaphors for positive/negative or conscious/unconscious dualities mentioned earlier, also includes references to shades of greyish light. The fog that envelops Grace's cinematically clichéd 'haunted house' hints at 'the dull, smoke-coloured light from Hell' that Tibetan Buddhists understand to be that which must be avoided because it is 'the path which openeth out to receive thee because of the power of accumulated evil *karma* from violent anger' (Evans-Wentz 2000: 109). This signifier of 'the Hell-Worlds' outlined in the *Bardo Thödol* is aptly situated *around* Grace, Anne and Nicholas. The fog never entirely engulfs or shifts these characters to another plane, it only threatens to do so in its function as the diaphanous margin that separates the bardo/purgatory/limbo state from either the living/conscious or unliving/unconscious sphere. As Grace attempts to leave the grounds of the house to find the local minister, she becomes disoriented in the fog, losing her bearings with each landmark that gets swallowed by the enveloping mist. In her confusion the figure of her soldier husband Charles (Christopher Eccleston), who we are told never made it back from 'the front', emerges to join her and the children.

It is apparent during the scenes where Charles returns to the house and learns of Grace's crimes through Anne, that he is also merely wandering in the vacuum of the post-death bardo; as Mrs. Mills tells Mr. Tuttle, 'He doesn't know where he is'. After appeasing his need to find out what happened to his family, Charles returns to 'the front', seemingly unaware that he is dead, which in *Bardo Thödol* informed reading suggests that he is caught in the *sangsara* death–rebirth cycle and still bound to his former life. Alternately, his return to the fog might indicate that he could be heading toward the Hell-Worlds; similar in ferocity to the war he came from. Charles' appearance prompts a veiled confession from Grace. When he leaves, this awareness acts as a catalyst for the gradual unfolding of her story that is not yet conscious, but no longer fixed in the unconscious either.

The undead and the paranormal

After a number of viewings of the film, some ambiguity creeps into the question of whether or not Grace knows what she has done. Her final confessional speech to the children, allows for the possibility that to some degree, she has always been conscious of her actions. The repeated discouragement of the children's 'story-telling' and fantasies, or 'lies' as she calls them, serves to suppress any involuntarily sparking, and speaking of the memories they might arouse. The scream at the beginning of the film that introduces us to Grace, alludes to the nightmare she believes she has awoken from. But as we learn, this scream might in fact be the transition point from one reality (suicide) to another (purgatory). Perhaps she does remember killing her children, but because they are heard 'playing with pillows as if nothing had happened' she is able to relegate the memory/nightmare to fantasy or repress it. The only certainty throughout *The Others*, similar to the themes of *The Sixth Sense* and *Jacob's Ladder* (1990), is that the central characters, unaware that they are dead or dying, inhabit a bardo-like realm.

John Woodroffe's introductory paper to Evans-Wentz's translation makes explicit the suggestion in the *Bardo Thödol*, that the dead are initially often not aware that they have died. The following passage from Woodroffe's commentary illuminates Grace's dilemma:

> as he carries over with him the recollection of his past life, he, at first still thinks that he has such a physical body as he had before. It is, in fact, a

> dream-body, such as that of persons seen in dreams. It is an imagined body, which, as the Text [*Bardo Thödol*] says, is neither reflected in a mirror nor casts a shadow, and which can do such wonders as passing through mountains and the like, since Imagination is the greatest of magicians.
>
> (Woodroffe 2000: lxxvi)

On a collectively unconscious level anyway, the *Bardo Thödol* offers a narrative framework for *The Others* and also acts as an inspirational guide for the classic ghost and horror genre that draws on notions of the oblivious or vengeful undead hovering in an ethereal bardo zone. Jung argues that this relationship between the eighth century writings in the *Bardo Thödol* where the dead are unaware of their condition, and the Western writings on the spiritualism of his day, testifies to the concept of pre-existent archetypes: 'It is a primordial, universal idea that the dead simply continue their earthly existence and do not know that they are disembodied spirits – an archetypal idea which enters into immediate, visible manifestation whenever anyone sees a ghost' (*CW* 11, para. 845).

In ' "Something Tremendous, Something Elemental": On the Ghostly Origins of Psychoanalysis' (1999), Roger Luckhurst draws on James' fiction to illustrate the notion that the undead are often located at access points from one space to another. Doors, windows or staircases haunted by entities that either allow or refuse admission, also act as effective signs for the psychological and physical margins that these entities manipulate: 'Monitoring borders, the ghost also breaches boundaries (life versus death, presence versus virtuality), thus necessitating an anxious restatement of the border with each passage' (Luckhurst 1999: 52). This reading of the ghost ties in with trickster's physical, psychological and moral border straddling and its ability to restore borders. The sequences in *The Others* where hauntings occur usually happen at doors and windows or other sites of entry and exit.

As mentioned earlier, throughout the film there's a constant tussle with light and darkness (conscious/unconscious states) as it relates to the living and the dead of the house. This is played out in the drawing (by the dead) and opening (by the living) of drapes to obscure, or expose, light. The first time a haunting occurs, the living child Victor, opens the drapes across the large window in Anne and Nicholas's room. There is also a poignant shot of Grace's reflection in the glass as she stares out of the window looking at Mr. Tuttle raking leaves on the lawn. In this briefly held image she seems captured by the glass, unable to move through it or beyond it (an apt metaphor for her psychological entrapment), unlike the ghosts of Mr. Tuttle, Mrs. Mills and Lydia who in the final sequences of the film, permeate inner/outer spaces. Doorways that mysteriously close, open, and as in one scene, slam, throwing Grace to the floor, are also significant. Although she tries to combat the mysterious movements of the doors by locking each as she enters and leaves a room, she is unable to maintain any sense of boundary within the house.

The fog also serves as an entry/exit point as it produces and reclaims both Grace's husband Charles and the servants. It signifies a bridge or gateway to the underworld and acts as a barrier to contain Grace in the bardo/purgatory state. The chaos trickster creates by tapping into leaky margins and disturbing equilibrium, gives way to the re-establishment of stronger boundaries that work to secure a more authentic sense of self. As Radin (1972: 134) writes of the ancient trickster cycle, the act of being 'frightened is, in Winnebago symbolism, generally the indication of an awakening consciousness and sense of reality, indeed, the beginning of a conscience'. All assumed 'sureties' must necessarily be challenged for a more advanced level of awareness to emerge.

Jung's brushes with the paranormal

Jung was interested in the supernatural since childhood and became a member of the Society for Psychical Research (established in 1882 by Frederick Myers) along with Freud and William James (brother of Henry and president of the society in 1894–1895). He frequently experienced paranormal phenomena, like the frequently cited inexplicable splitting in four of a steel knife that lay in a drawer of his kitchen dresser (Jung 1963: 126). As a child he attended séances with his mother and later in early adulthood (1895–1900) these events, becoming ever more private, centered on the medium Helene Preiswerk, Jung's thirteen-and-a-half year old cousin in love with him at the time (Charet 1993: 155). Although Helene was exposed as a fraud by Jung's fellow students from Basel university, he nevertheless drew on his experiences of these séances and the appearance, via hypnotism, of her secondary personality 'Ivenes' for his 1902 doctoral dissertation *On the Psychology and Pathology of So-Called Occult Phenomena*. It's here that he rather ruthlessly diagnosed Helene (under the pseudonym S.W.) with an adolescent hysteria specifically related to her burgeoning sexuality. This served his argument that spiritualism and the paranormal were psychologically generated.

Like Jung's mother Emilie Preiswerk, Ivenes can also be tied to the *mother* motif filtering through *The Others*. Jung writes of her as a sophisticated, mature aspect of Helene's psyche, able to access great expanses of fantastically interwoven histories and personalities as well as also being a 'direct continuation of her [Helene's] everyday ego' (*CW* 1, para. 114). He describes the change in Helene's manner and maturity when she 'channels' the more worldly Ivenes, an ancestral mother figure to an enormous and complicated family tree. She became mournful, effected a persona of 'suffering resignation', and alluded to a 'mysterious fate' to fully capitalize on the fascination of her audience (*CW* 1, para. 116) As well as being mother to a multitude of historical figures, Ivenes was also Jung's mother in another life, burnt at the stake for witchcraft (*CW* 1, para. 63). Mother for Jung is once again uncanny and shrouded in mysticism. The attraction Helene felt for Jung was clearly underpinning these somnambulistic fantasies, particularly when she linked herself to him through the intimacy of motherhood.

Jung also acknowledged his own psychological presences 'Salome' and 'Elijah'. From Elijah the more potent inner guide of 'Philemon' surfaced to represent 'superior insight' (Jung 1963: 208). After compiling a collection of unconventional thoughts on ghosts in his *Septem Sermones ad Mortuos* (*Seven Sermons to the Dead*, 1916), Jung's house become the repository for poltergeist activity witnessed by himself, his family and staff (Jung 1963: 215–216). As Roderick Main (1997) notes, many commentators have pointed out that the 'eccentric' *Septem Sermones* in fact 'express in germinal form almost all of Jung's developed ideas: the nature of the unconscious, individuation, the problem of opposites, the archetypes, and the self' (Main 1997: 6).

In his commentary to Radin's (1972) study of trickster mythology, Jung once again discussed his belief that apparitions were ultimately associated with archetypal motifs. He felt that the global experience of the anarchic, malevolent and shape-shifting nature of the 'poltergeist phenomena' intimately connected to pre-pubescent children, corresponded to the mythological documentation of trickster in its primitive, infantile form (*CW* 9i, para. 457). In a letter to J. B. Rhine he talked about the atemporal nature of the psyche and his belief in the capability of the unconscious to 'influence matter detached from bodily contact and to assemble matter beyond the reach of the body to such a degree that it appears as a physical body perceptible to our senses as well as to the photographic plate' (Jung 1973: 394). Not only can trickster in its various evolving phases operate as a dominant energy surfacing from the unconscious, as in *The Others* and films dealing specifically with poltergeist behaviour (*Poltergeist*, 1982; *Ringu 2*, 1999; *The Exorcist*, 1973), but following Jung's reasoning it can also take a material ghostly form. If Grace, Anne and Nicholas are in fact generating the trickster pattern from their psychological confusion and anxiety, as mentioned earlier, they may also be generating the phantom forms of Mrs. Mills, Mr. Tuttle and Lydia in trickster's psychopomp aspect.

The problem in trying to fathom the characters and the psychological concepts they inspire in this way, is tied up in notions of the temporal and spatial. The Buddhist belief in reincarnation outlined in the *Bardo Thödol* and its concentration on the continuous nature of both consciousness and the unconscious helps to put the dual living/dead realities of the characters in the film into some sort of context. Jung's fascination with Eastern religion and the psychological import of the *Bardo Thödol* feeds into this idea of psychic atemporality. He often talked of the psyche as an element of the human condition that stood outside the precincts of time and space (*CW* 8, paras. 814, 996) and went as far as to pose the possibility of a fourth dimension (Jung 1973: 379). As he was nearing his own death, he reasoned that: 'We lack concrete proof that anything of us is preserved for eternity. At most we can say that there is some probability that something of our psyche continues beyond physical death' (Jung 1963: 354). Jung's writing on the supernatural might seem implausible and absurd to detractors, but the questions about time, space and the possibilities of the unconscious that he poses are regurgitated in contemporary screen culture; rapt as it has been (particularly since the 1970s) in narratives of myth and the paranormal.

Finally claiming 'the house'

In its focus on the possibility of a psyche that inhabits frames outside the linear canon of rationality (bardo, limbo, purgatory), *The Others* is a myth retold in contemporary form. In our current scientific logic of organizing time and space, death is perhaps one of the last frontiers. At least Jung was willing to go to the edges of that outpost when he wrote:

> the possibility of an other-valued reality behind the phenomenal world becomes an inescapable problem, and we must face the fact that our world, with its time, space, and causality, relates to another order of things lying behind it, in which neither 'here and there' nor 'earlier and later' are of importance.
>
> (Jung 1963: 336)

The denial of another existence beyond our rational (logos) ways of seeing is the very thing that keeps Grace tied to her form of purgatory.

Although ego bound and unable to acknowledge death, it can be argued that in her chaos, Grace's psyche (in the guise of the house) generated trickster psychopompos; an energy able to cross the boundaries of the living and filter through the phantasms of the servants. In keeping with Jung's estimation of trickster as saviour, these spectres of the unconscious inevitably served to liberate:

> If, at the end of the trickster myth, the saviour is hinted at, this comforting premonition or hope means that some calamity or other has happened and been consciously understood. Only out of disaster can the longing for the saviour arise – in other words, the recognition and unavoidable integration of the shadow creates such a harrowing situation that nobody but a saviour can undo the tangled web of fate.
>
> (*CW* 9i, para. 487)

The Others is an allegory of the potential muscle of trickster in its capacity as guide to self-awareness. As Grace says in her final words to the children huddled close to her side, in what seems to be code for her now stabilized psychological state, 'this is our house. No-one can make us leave this house.'

In keeping with the aims of classical analytical psychology, Amenábar's text seems driven by a need to accept the moral complexity and atemporal nature of that which is beyond the culturally bound strictures of the ego – the big 'S' Self perhaps. The idea of discovering identity, playing with 'the truth', and therefore coming some way toward imagining the possibility of 'a bigger picture', continues in the next chapter. *The X-Files* television series and its central characters 'Scully and Mulder' pick up and parody many of the ideas presented in this section of work. Grace's process of 'finding herself' may well have been one of the more poignant 'Scully and Mulder' episodes set up to parallel the couple's identity crisis. Instead of a haunted house on a remote and desolate estate as a sign of the psyche in process, Scully has Catholicism and Mulder has his UFOs, or in Jung's terminology 'flying saucers' – yes, he had something to say about them too.

What Grace lacks in self-reflection, Scully and Mulder as the ultimate navel gazers of the 1990s, have in spades. Still as we will see, their search for Self only ever manifests as an illusive desire. In plumbing the paranormal yet again, but with a more tongue-in-cheek lightness, it's impossible to avoid the saviour paradigm. *The X-Files* offers this to us in the form of 'special children' who act as guides and redeemers. Although lesser trickster figures than Amenábar's phantasms, they're equally divine signs of potential.

Part III

Redeemers, bad dads and matricide

Chapter 6

Dana immaculate and divine children

The X-Files

> In Ireland we don't need aliens; we already have a race of higher beings with strange powers who gaze deep into our eyes and force us to have babies against our will. We call them priests.
>
> Anne Enright, 'Diary' (1995: 25)

If U.S.-dominated 1980s television mirrored the cultural excesses of wealth, power and yuppiedom – *Dallas* (1978–1991), *Dynasty* (1981–1989) and *LA Law* (1986–1994) – then the 1990s, by way of apology or novelty, was excessively numinous. The Fox Network's *The X-Files* (1993–2002), one in a stream of small screen spins on myth, spirituality and pop-psychology, took the Jungian road less traveled by milking the analogy between the search for UFOs and the search for the divine. Wanting was no longer about material avarice. Although creator Chris Carter used the hunt for extraterrestrials as a device to play with unconscious drives and eruptions, his most deep-rooted hook into the psyche revolved around variations of the *divine child* motif; the more potent allusion to the Self throughout the series.

Sandwiched between two Gulf wars (1991 and 2003) and two Bush presidencies (1989–1993 and 2000–), *The X-Files* is now immortalized in nine collector's DVD packs as one of the classic tributes to the pre-millennial decade. Just as the influential names of the turning nineteenth century – Jung, Freud, William James, Sandor Ferenczi, Henri Bergson and fellow members of the Society for Psychical Research (1882) – reflected the popular penchant for séances, mediumship and the occult (Luckhurst 1999: 55; Noyes 1999: 245), twentieth-century cultural commentators and artists also steeped themselves in the buzz of the bizarre. Alien abductions, conspiracy theories, millennium bugs, and yet again, the occult and cultism, were fodder for research, cultural analysis and television ratings. With the advent of 2000, George Bush's invasive foray into the Middle East and the 'be alert not alarmed' campaigns supposed to buoy us against global terrorism, the magical consciousness of the 1990s has (somewhat) taken flight. The small screen landscape is more serious now – an open war sore. Even television fictions reflect the contained weekly narratives of hard and fast paced procedural drama where closure, justice and morality are synonymously peddled. One hundred years after Jung's PhD, *On the Psychology and Pathology of So-Called Occult Phenomena*, the last X was filed. Both were works of their time: reflections in their own way of a social and psychological climate in the throes of change.

Intertextual references to the horror, slice-and-dice, sci-fi, supernatural and detective genres established *The X-Files* as a fusion of much screen vocabulary of the last century. The series reads like a time-capsule of the postmodern 1990s, with writing contributions from pop culture/cyberpunk aficionados William Gibson and Tom Maddox ('Kill Switch' 5×11) and cross-genre homages to directors Wes Craven/Tobe Hooper ('Home' 4×3), Steven Soderbergh ('John Doe' 9×7), James Whale ('Post Modern Prometheus' 5×6) and David Lynch ('Via Negativa' 8×7). But it was primarily the plays on John Mack's controversial 1994 research on abductees, mythology, cultism, Gnosticism and Catholicism that gave *The X-Files* an edge. In its day, the series stood as an exemplar of the West's quasi-religious underbelly; a work bred out of the spiritually wanting, entrepreneurial, cashed-up-crashed-down 1980s.

In a climax that manipulated the series' pretensions for empirical and spiritual truths that would ensure salvation, the final episodes, confirmed previous rumblings of governmental conspiracies and an impending alien invasion that would either destroy or change the world. Plays on the anxieties associated with the Mayan calendar (11 August 3114 BCE – 21 December 2012 CE) said to predict global upheaval through a shift in solar conditions (Kremer 2000: 24) were made explicit in the final episode 'The Truth' (9×19/20). Although the energies of the divine child were in place from the beginning of the series, in the final two years the archetype was most fully realized with the arrival of an ultimate alien/human hybrid and possible saviour. Though the twists and open-ended nature of *The X-Files* left many questions unanswered, the program can be read as a redemptive myth. The overarching themes of death and renewal (the very cycle of maturation), culminated in hints that humanity, personified in heroes Mulder and Scully, was about to be put to the test, but would survive the battle thanks to their progeny *William the divine*.

Disciples of truths

FBI partners, the scientifically constipated Dana Scully (Gillian Anderson) and the more psychically receptive Fox 'Spooky' Mulder (David Duchovny), coupled up as the focus of each hour episode. In the final two seasons, their FBI co-workers and sometime surrogates John Doggett (Robert Patrick) and Monica Reyes (Annabeth Gish) were introduced to pick up the slack left by Duchovny's reluctance to remain a main cast player. In conflict with their bureau superiors, government conspirators and sundry genetically mutated villains-cum-victims, all four never wavered in their loyalty to each other and the ambiguous much hyped 'truth'.

Familiar ancillary characters were regularly introduced to thwart, facilitate, or merely stifle their necessarily clandestine missions. The most central of these adjuncts included: Special Agent Walter Skinner (Mitch Pileggi), Scully and Mulder's supervisor; Alex 'rat boy' Krycek (Nicholas Lea), the double agent/Judas nemesis bent on frustrating Mulder's Christ-like calling; The Lone Gunmen, Frohike (Tom Braidwood), Langley (Dean Haglund) and Byers (Bruce Harwood), Mulder's conspiracy fixated hacker friends; and Cigarette Smoking Man (CSM) a.k.a. Cancer Man or 'that cigarette smoking son of a bitch' (William B. Davis), the irrepressible quasi-government, all-round bad guy. As we're told in the episode 'Musings of a Cigarette Smoking Man' (4×7) CSM framed Lee Harvey Oswald, murdered John F. Kennedy (JFK) and Martin Luther King, and rigged baseball games. His most endearing quality, though, was a passion for writing boys-own-adventure stories, only one of which he managed to get published in a tabloid magazine.

The superficially marked similarities between the early Dana Scully in the pilot episode and tenacious FBI recruit Clarice Starling (Jodi Foster) of Jonathan Demme's *Silence of the Lambs* (1991) gave way as Scully, graduating from off-the-rack to designer pantsuits, became a feminist icon in her own right. Initially assigned to the FBI's X-Files section (reserved for unsolved cases) to spy on Mulder's activities, Scully played out the role of his 'perfect other', the rational voice to his gut feelings. The most scientifically flexible character on prime time, with her vast expertise in all disciplines of medicine and science, specifically forensic pathology, she managed to fuse a convincing kick-arse attitude with an evolving Catholic spiritualism. Although a sexual history was fleetingly hinted at, the impression is one of self-imposed celibacy in the service of higher things. The satirical yet reverential 1990s fansite, *The Order of the Blessed St. Scully the Enigmatic* (http://www.obsse.com), paid tribute to Scully's beatific rise as the series progressed, with contributors/nuns deferring to her as 'The Sainted One', 'Our Lady of the Latex' and 'She whose Eyebrows Arch Like the Vaults of Heaven'. Sarah R. Wakefield's (2001) study of 'the order', 'Your Sister in St. Scully: An Electronic Community of Female Fans of the *X-Files*', discusses the techniques used by members to poach what they saw as the triple saint/everywoman/sexpot aspects of Scully to explore their own relationships and creativity.

Fox Mulder, the angst-ridden UFO/conspiracy believer and founder of the X-Files, whose first words as an infant were 'JFK' and whose biological father in a Darth Vaderish twist turned out to be CSM, was established as a serial killer profiler with an interest in the paranormal and an aversion to Freud. He was also an object for both the male and female gaze with his impressive genetic credentials often verbally and visually flashed in juxtaposition to the genetically defective mutants he frequently encountered. His early status as *The X-Files* chief protagonist eased up when Scully began to be written as a more complex and independent character. The relationship between the pair was constructed as a plutonic union of trust with an underlying teaser of unresolved sexual tension, until the final two seasons when their much acknowledged understanding that they had found 'the other' in each other, was consummated and personified in their miracle child William (despite his parentage being tainted with alien DNA). Latecomers Dogget and Reyes were never allowed the luxury of extended character development and consequently remained as aides to the complex story arcs rapidly working toward closure after William's birth.

UFO spotting and the numinous

In interviews and DVD featurettes, the key crew of *The X-Files*, Chris Carter (creator/director/writer), Frank Spotnitz (writer/director/ producer) and Kim Manners (director), often refer to the program's internal mythology as distinct from the episodes infused with the occult and paranormal. The mythology episodes in each season developed a distinct narrative built around Mulder's search for extraterrestrial life, abductions, implantations, fertility experiments, and conspiracies bent on subjecting humanity to *and* saving it from, an impending alien invasion. The search for UFOs and the search for god were analogous missions central to the increasingly convoluted nine year myth. The parallels Jung drew between mandala-like images and UFOs in the short 1959 work *Flying Saucers, a Modern Myth of Things Seen in the Sky* (*CW* 10), specifically details the relationship between 'flying saucers' and the desire for the Self. He argued that the cigar and disc-like shapes commonly cited in UFO reportage could be interpreted as archetypal mandala symbols that periodically and cross-culturally surface in a variety of forms (sun-wheel, a magic circle, or uroborus etc.) as an expression of wholeness (*CW* 10, para. 619).

For Jung these visions and unexplained specters of the fantastic arose through:

> a split between the conscious attitude and the unconscious contents opposed to it . . . these contents cannot be integrated directly but seek to express themselves indirectly, thus giving rise to unexpected and apparently inexplicable opinions, beliefs, illusions, visions, and so forth.
>
> (*CW* 10, para. 608)

From this perspective it can be argued that the concept of psychic wholeness is the holy grail that Mulder and Scully seek in disguised form through their joint encounters with the surreal and their individual quests – Mulder's search for alien intelligence, conspiracies and the supernatural, and Scully's need to turn to, and in some cases, function as a catalyst for, the evocation of Christian and Gnostic doctrine ('All Souls' 5×17; 'Milegro' 6×18). These events and desires present themselves as outward expressions of inner conflicts or 'psychic dissociations' (*CW* 10, para. 608). Scully and Mulder's thwarted pursuits therefore suggest a desire for the oceanic rapture of an unrepresentable, unknowable and (as they discover) impossible psychic unity.

In trying to make sense of the way spirituality can function as a healing agent, Jung argued that 'in religious experience man comes face to face with a psychically overwhelming Other' (*CW* 10, para. 655). Experiencing *The X-Files*' parade of 'psychically overwhelming Others' may well be the prime-time equivalent of a religious happening, and if not for audiences, then almost certainly for Mulder and Scully, who crave these 'others' to heal their wounds and facilitate their individuation. The likening of external phenomena (UFOs) to the experience of being overcome by a greater force (the divine) takes a tangible turn in the episode 'The Sixth Extinction' (7×3). Scully discovers that patterned inscriptions etched on the surface of a partially exposed UFO on West Africa's Ivory Coast are a map of the human genome and a coded cocktail of religious scripture from the Bible, the Koran and religions of Samaria: 'science and mysticism conjoined', she says in a self-referential play on her own dual drives.

The mandala symbolism of the UFO and the doctrine adorning it is a not so subtle climax for Carter's UFO/religious trajectory as well as an analogy for what Jung believed the UFO experience to be, a projection of the numinous – God and Self: 'The symbols of divinity coincide with those of the self: what, on the one side, appears as a psychological experience signifying psychic wholeness, expresses on the other side the idea of God' (*CW* 10, para. 644). Scully's voiced thoughts that the inscriptions on the craft are 'more than words, they are somehow imbued with power', are later reinforced by her colleague who sees the complex communication as 'the word of god'.

In *Hystories: Hysterical Epidemics and Modern Culture*, Elaine Showalter (1997: 194) argues that reported alien abductions are a contemporary form of hysteria, but her take on the phenomena isn't shared by researchers in the area. They acknowledge that many who identify themselves as abductees or 'experiencers' report an elevated sense of the religious or spiritual when they return. Brenda Denzler's (2001) sympathetic analysis of UFO/abductee accounts, *Lure of the Edge: Scientific Passions, Religious Beliefs, and the Pursuit of UFOs*, details the belief of some abductees who felt that although their captors exuded a sense of the divine and embraced a concept of god, they strongly disapproved of organized religion (Denzler 2001: 137). Harvard professor of psychiatry and 1977 Pulitzer prize winner John Mack's (1994) controversial study, *Abduction: Human Encounters with Aliens*, similarly talks of the 'spiritually transformative' accounts of his abducted patients who return with the belief that the cosmos is sacred and that aliens are 'emissaries from God' or 'a split-off part of the abductee's soul or Self' (Mack 1994: 407–408). In his assessment of abductees, McNally (2003: 232–234) argues that prior to their episode, many subjects had a history of alternative spiritual practices or leanings, but all shared an enriched sense of the spiritual upon their return. Keeping in mind Jung's concept of 'psychic dissociation' where unconscious eruptions conflict with the realities of consciousness and are therefore outwardly projected, the above accounts similarly suggest (in line with Showalter's thinking), a desire to transcend and/or displace a conflicted (personal) self via an experience of jouissance often akin to religious ecstasy.

Katherine J. Holden and Christopher C. French's (2002) study, 'Alien Abduction Experiences', adds that evidence exists:

> to suggest that many of the features said to characterize abductees (tendency to dissociate, difficulty distinguishing fantasy from reality, etc.; see French, 2001) are precisely those that would indeed lead to heightened susceptibility to false memories.
>
> (Holden and French 2002: 171)

This not uncommon assumption forms the basis of the episode 'Jose Chung's from Outer Space' (3×20), a spoof on alien abduction scenarios, repressed memory, psychic dissociation, cultism, and *The X-Files* itself. Here abduction claims are exposed as outward projections of assorted desires for love, sexual fulfillment, religious enlightenment and an escape from the mundane. As the character Blaine Faulkner, UFO wanna-be experiencer and avid 'Dungeons and Dragons' enthusiast, says of his desire to be whisked off by alien grays, 'I just want to be taken away to some place where I don't have to worry about finding a job.'

In addition to reading *The X-Files* as an allegory of the search for truth/god/Self, Carter's mythology can be variously understood as plays on technological and biological/genetic advances: fear of globalization and loss of nationhood/identity; imagined threats of immigration invasions; the suspicion of being constantly under surveillance; skepticism about the ability of governments to effectively ensure our safety; global warming; Chernobyl-esque nuclear mishaps; virulent viral infections like AIDS, the rarer but more grisly Ebola, and germ warfare; as well as a distrust of rapidly evolving information technology (Lavery et al. 1996; Dean 1997; Aden 1999; Delasara 2000; Izod 2001; Kellner 2002).

Back in the 1950s, Jung also suggested that the flying saucer phenomena could be viewed as an expression of national border expansion fears and our inability to imagine curbing global overpopulation without the help of forces from beyond (*CW* 10, para. 615). Carter's mythology, though, much more overtly fed into the 1990s proliferation of conspiracy theories via the increasing sophistication of computer/internet technology. The final double episode that attempted to explain the rationale behind the alien-abduction-fertility-syndicate-invasion thrust of the series, accords almost exactly with the more common principles of conspiracy theories, particularly those that Brian Keeley (1999) in 'Of Conspiracy Theories' calls 'unwarranted conspiracy theories' (UCTs): an explanation that contradicts the official line; the amoral intent of conspirators; unrelated events cleanly drawn to a conclusion; necessary secrecy; close knit groups of high ranking conspirators; and errant data, or unaccounted for information. But alongside the sociological underpinnings of *The X-Files*, its most enduring theme of selves in search of Self, is expressed through recurring mandala imagery and more potently, the energy of the divine child.

The divine children of *The X-Files*

The underlying intensity of the series revolved around the consequent births and deaths of Scully's covert fertility procedures, the abduction of Mulder's sister Samantha and the unresolved murder of Doggett's son Luke. Each child constituted a lost jigsaw piece that motivated the lead characters, connected them to each other, and ensured their ongoing emotional struggles and quests for wholeness. In this respect even the most mortal of these children had a divine function. The spiritual theme is given more mythic significance with the arrival of Scully's second alien/human hybrid child 'William' who, with all the religious overtones of past 'boy saviours', was ambiguously destined for great things despite being inevitably 'coveted by the forces of good and evil' ('Providence' 9×11). The concluding mythology episodes intimating impending global devastation along the lines of the Mayan prophesies, were also supported by the overarching themes of death and renewal throughout the series. This suggested that despite the threat of annihilation, the battle for supremacy would be won thanks to William the Astro Boy of the new millennium.

The divine child archetype is a distinguishing feature of contemporary organized religious traditions: Christianity (Christ), Islam (Muhammad), Hinduism (Krishna) and Buddhism (Gautama Buddha), as well as the polytheistic religions of ancient Egyptian, Mayan, Norse, Sumarian, Greek, Roman and Vedic cultures. Each bases their mythologies around the motif of special, gifted, enlightened or supernatural child figures, or figures destined to divinity from childhood, who act as vehicles for redemption. It's not surprising that numerous film and television versions of the saviour myth proliferate in popular culture through texts like *Astro Boy* (1963), *Superman* (1978), *Little Buddha* (1993), *The Terminator* trilogy, *Buffy, The Sixth Sense, The Matrix* trilogy. These wunderkinder of twentieth- and twenty-first-century screen/comic culture are clear manifestations of past mythologies. But rather than diminishing the sacred or psychological properties of their earlier prototypes, these incarnations indicate a collective and ongoing need to project, incorporate, and reinforce the archetype as a signifier of future potential.

Jung argues that the divine child represents one of the most fundamental quests of the individual and the collective; the desire for individuation, and the concept of the Self (*CW* 14, para. 103). The archetype conjures the enormous possibilities of childhood and the sense of becoming it embodies. It signifies triumph over the prerequisite confrontations that lead up to adulthood and the recognition and consequent assimilation of disruptive unconscious material. In synthesizing conscious and unconscious personality traits, the divine child can be understood to have a unifying function within the psyche (*CW* 9i, para. 278).

The first season of *The X-Files* tried to make sense of the urgency behind Mulder's mission to uncover extraterrestrial life by setting up a traumatic past, where as a 13 year old he supposedly witnessed the alien abduction of his younger sister Samantha. This episode, repeatedly alluded to and shown in flashback throughout the first seven seasons, ensures that he will never be 'complete' till he finds her or learns the 'truth' of her disappearance. In the seventh season we discover that Samantha was taken by her father Bill Mulder, part of the syndicate along with CSM (Mulder's biological father), in a plot requiring each member to donate one of their family for experimentation to meet the aliens demands of creating a human/hybrid/ Aldous Huxley-esque Gamma caste. This compliance was undermined by the syndicate's covert plans to simultaneously develop a vaccine that would reverse the transmutation. Mulder traces his sister's disappearance through a case (with overtones of the 1996 JonBenet Ramsey murder) where a number of children are mysteriously abducted by 'walk-ins'; ghost-like entities who whisk them off to a twilight dimension when they sense that these children are about to be murdered ('Sein Und Zeit' 7×10; 'Closure' 7×11).

At this point in *The X-Files*' mythology, Scully has well and truly taken over from Samantha as Mulder's sister surrogate-cum-other. Their thwarted and enduring relationship mirrors Mulder's desire for Samantha, but it is only through Samantha's sacrificial death that Scully is able to usurp her as Mulder's prime love-interest. For as is also often repeated, Scully and Mulder acknowledge each other as halves of an elusive whole. It's mythically predictable given that this brother/sister dyad is tainted by the celestial (each having been a 'vessel' for biological alien matter), that their child is the most divine of *The X-Files* brood. Throughout his writings on alchemy, Jung often cites the alchemists' obsession with brother/sister or Sol/Luna sexual trysts as representative of merging conscious and unconscious states in the coniunctio. For the alchemists this act gave rise to (as mentioned in previous chapters) the lapis philosophorum, the sun, gold, Mecurius or the divine child. All are symbolic of the Self (*CW* 9ii, para. 59).

In the last two seasons, with the gradual phasing out of Mulder as prime protagonist and the Samantha storyline resolved, Doggett and Reyes reignite the divine child theme. Although the motif doesn't run through the histories of these two characters with the supernatural zeal of the Mulder and Scully story arcs, the archetype is nevertheless an intrinsic element of their evolution when taking into consideration the onus Jung places on the archetype to represent 'the strongest, the most ineluctable urge in every human being, namely the urge to realize itself' (*CW* 9i, para. 289). Doggett, a former detective with the New York police department, is haunted by the unsolved disappearance and murder of his 8-year-old son Luke. The case is an unhealed wound that prevents him from developing intimate relationships, particularly with Reyes. Eventually the case is solved when Doggett learns that Luke was taken by a pedophile and murdered by one of his underworld associates ('Release' 9×16).

It's as if in providing Doggett with both emotional blocks and opportunities to 'evolve', Luke, like Samantha, was a necessary sacrifice to enable him to take on the parental/guardian responsibilities for William opened up through Mulder's disappearance in the last two seasons. In a twist on Robert Patrick's (Doggett) 1991 role as the robotic T-1000 liquid mercury cop sent back to the past to exterminate soon-to-be freedom fighter John Conner (JC) in James Cameron's Christ myth, *Terminator Two: Judgment Day* (1991), he now serves in the last gasps of *The X-Files* mythology as the macho minder of vulnerable little William. There is also a hint of the divine in Reyes, supposedly an adoptee of Mexican parents, born in Austin, Texas and raised in Mexico City. If the character had been given the chance to develop, there is some suggestion that her origins may have been 'other worldly' given her much lauded 'powers' of intuition.

Season six introduces the chess prodigy 12-year-old Gibson Praise, whose telepathic powers are the result of developed junk DNA. Praise becomes the first natural (untampered with) missing link between aliens and humans, the theory being that we're all capable of Praise's alien-like abilities if our junk DNA could be turned on. A more sophisticated version of alien-ness than Scully's first test-tube child Emily, and a precursor to William, Praise becomes the lab rat of the syndicate in their search for the secrets to alien/human hybridization. Another caste of hybrids with allusions to Himmler's S.S. (*Schutzstaffel*) are the supersoldiers, human subjects who have been bio-engineered by the military to be 'super' replacement alien combat units. However, these supersoldiers and Gibson Praise are imperfect creations. Only William is the flawless divine boy; the 'perfect human baby with no human frailties' ('Essence' 8×20).

In the opening sequence to 'Trust no1' (9×8), Scully's voice-over to William acts as a televisual letter of what seems to be both a coded apology for abandonment (a mythical must for divine children) and a reminder of his 'destiny'. It's eerily reminiscent of Jor-El (Marlin Brando) and Lara's (Susanna York) farewell launching speech to their infant Kal-El before he's jettisoned off to Earth in Richard Donner's *Superman* epic. As with Kal-El, William is one of a long line of divine children, who, as Jung writes, are predisposed to shoulder the gifts of advanced human development, the nefarious threats and challenges that accompany such a mantle, and the victories of each battle (*CW* 9i, para. 289).

Sexing the divine

One of the most problematic aspects of the divine child is its predominant maleness in contemporary organized religion and myth. Only one supersoldier is female (played by Lucy Lawless a.k.a. Xena of *Xena Warrior Princess*, 1995–2001) and even the politically correct Scully is unable to breed a divine female worthy of survival. In the fifth season, DNA tests confirmed Scully to be the biological mother of 3-year-old Emily, an adopted child whose parents are mysteriously murdered ('Christmas Carol' 5×5; 'Emily' 5×7). Given Scully's previously established infertility, this 'Immaculate Conception' was presumably the result of the intrusive government/military-led fertility procedures she underwent during her staged alien abduction ('One Breath' 2×8). With no male human contribution to Emily's biology, much is made of Scully's uncanny twinning/likeness to the child at the same age. But Emily is of course an alien/human hybrid experiment and therefore the subject of nondescript medical infusions that eventually take their toll. So the chance for a female saviour in screen myth is once again thwarted . . . that is until the advent of Joss Whedon's Buffy the 'chosen' vampire slayer. Even Bertolucci's female reincarnation of the Buddhist teacher, Lama Dorje in *Little Buddha*, must share her divinity with two boys because the monks are unable to distinguish which of three chosen children is the true incarnation.

Western readings of extraordinary children, more often than not, confer the heavy burden of divinity to boys/men, while women remain duty bound to conceive and nurture these personifications of the sacred. In an archetypal reading though, one can logically assume that if the unconscious is collective/objective, it should have no gender agenda. Jung understood this clearly enough when he claimed that the divine child could be symbolized through a myriad of religious and non-religious images: male and female children, animals, plants, eggs, designs within mandalas or quaternity formations (*CW* 9i, para. 270). Although he stresses that the concept is a symbol that takes many forms, he argued that when imaged as a child, it carries all the magical alien qualities of a mythical figure and should never be read literally as human. He sees 'its futurity' as the prime function of the archetype: the potential to psychologically evolve or individuate by integrating conflicting energies (*CW* 9i, para. 278). Jung not only interpreted the divine child as a facilitating motif in the service of individuation, but also theorized it as a kind of bookend that contained the human experience: 'the pre-conscious and the post-conscious essence of man. His pre-conscious essence is the unconscious state of the earliest childhood; his post-conscious essence is an anticipation by analogy of life after death' (*CW* 9i, para. 299). This Buddhist ideal envisages the divine child as a kernel of latent promise for the possibilities of life and the spiritual afterlife, concepts that run thick and fast through each season of *The X-Files*.

Virgin(ish) birth and separation

As briefly mentioned earlier, Jung refers to the divine child as a demi-god, half human and half supernatural/god-like, conceived and born under extraordinary circumstances to illustrate the struggle of psychological development:

> Since it is a psychic genesis, everything must happen non-empirically, e.g. by means of a virgin birth, or by miraculous conception, or by birth from unnatural organs. The motifs of 'insignificance,' exposure, abandonment, danger, etc. try to show how precarious is the psychic possibility of wholeness, that is the enormous difficulties to be met with in attaining the 'highest good'.
>
> (*CW* 9i, para. 282)

To test the power of the child's endurance and divinity, a number of obstacles complicate its birth and infancy. Parental abandonment is a prime hurdle. Usually only the birth mother features as primary nurturer, the father is often of indeterminate origin, although mythical male mother figures, like Zeus who bore Dionysos and Athena, are not entirely uncommon. Abandonment is usually a painful act made for the well-being of the child because of the 'dark' forces bent on destroying it. The divine child, as a symbol of psychic processes, intertwines with the hero archetype when combating the menacing aspects of the unconscious, presented in myth as monsters or human adversaries, so that a more individuated state of awareness is able to evolve (*CW* 9i, para. 282). Being divine, the adult version of the 'special' child has no 'attachment' issues, separation anxiety, or obvious mother angst, although it is rarely able to attach/commit itself to mere mortals for any length of time for fear of contamination or loss of power.

Jung's argument that ' "Child" means something towards independence. This it cannot do without detaching itself from its origins: abandonment is therefore a necessary condition, not just a concomitant symptom' (*CW* 9i, para. 287), and his belief that 'Identity does not make consciousness possible; it is only separation, detachment, and agonizing confrontation through opposition that produce consciousness and insight' (*CW* 9i, para. 289) is echoed in Julia Kristeva's (1982) work on the abject. In Lacanian theory, infants at approximately 6–18 months identify themselves as separate from mother via *the mirror phase*, where the mirror reflection marks the recognition of a unified self or 'I'. From this point infants begin to acquire language skills and understand themselves as subjects. Their entry into culture, law, knowledge, rationality (the *symbolic*) is achieved only through a painful severing from, and repression of, what Kristeva calls the *semiotic*; a state that exists through a symbiotic mother/child union or the *chora* (from Plato's *Timaeus* 48–53) (Kristeva 1982: 14).

In this formulation, drives facilitate the move to oedipalization, where mother is rejected, made abject, and positioned as 'the necessarily unspoken underside of social and psychic order' (Grosz 1989: 78) – an underside that might explain the dominant maleness of divine children. So although the divine child must disassociate itself from mother (aligned with the semiotic/unconscious) and make itself known in the conscious/cultural arena (symbolic), it is also strongly characterized in traditional myth as androgynous. Like the divine product of the coniunctio it bridges binary states (*CW* 9i, para. 295–296).

In Kristeva's (1982) *The Powers of Horror*, largely influenced by Mary Douglas' (1966) *Purity and Danger*, she argues that cleanliness rites and bodily wastes like shit, puss, vomit, blood, etc., 'what enters the mouth and nourishes, what goes out of the body, out of its pores and openings' (Kristeva 1982: 108), signify the becoming of the subject. As Grosz (1994) writes of the body's frightening 'permeability', where the inside's continual seeping to the outside signifies inevitable bodily collapse/death, the 'abject is what of the body falls away from it while remaining irreducible to the subject/object and inside/outside oppositions' (Grosz 1994: 192). It thus represents and 'preserves' the pre-symbolic and the violence associated with separating 'from another body in order to be' (Kristeva 1982: 10).

Only through the revulsion of that which is rendered abject, according to Kristeva, can separation and identity can take place. The confronting experience of taking pleasure in, and feeling disgust for, what one was and will return to, is an ambivalence that underlies the discourses of horror and its various subgenres (Creed 1993). The threat inherent in this repulsion/attraction lies in, as Kristeva (1982: 13) writes, 'the constant risk of falling back under the sway of a power as securing as it is stifling'. With all its associated 'violence of mourning for an "other" that has always already been lost' (Kristeva 1982: 15), the abject can never be erased from consciousness but remains a menacing reminder of both the subject's vulnerability and the fragility of the symbolic.

Twentieth-century myths of the divine child often incorporate the abject into the tensions of their narratives. While one of the defining features of these children was their susceptibility to a minor ailment, unsuspected betrayal, or physical characteristic like Achilles' and Krishna's heel, contemporary reinventions of the myth now include matter from the birthplace of the child that has the capacity to bring about its destruction. We can easily find examples of this in Superman's vulnerability to geological material from his birth planet Krypton, or magnetite for all *The X-Files*' aliens and hybrids who are magnetically pulled toward, then explode on contact with, the magnetic iron mineral.

According to the series' mythology, a meteor carrying the seeds of human life, as well as an alien virus, crashed to earth. Evolving humans who filtered the viral agent through their bodies died in the last Ice Age, but the virus lay dormant till the current geological age where it now thrives in petroleum deposits and has the ability to communicate with extraterrestrials. When it made contact with UFOs in 1947, the spacecrafts crashed because the underground viral deposits thrived/gestated in an area of New Mexico where magnetite flourished. It's the Roswell incident in a fictionalized nutshell. Magnetite, in its association with the prehistoric arrival and revival of the alien virus, can easily be read as a metaphor for the metaphor of 'mother'; going back to mother, the womb, the precursor to subjectivity that threatens the dissolution of identity. Krypton and magnetite are thus forms of shit; reminders of the body's frailty and death; the waste that 'drops so that I might live' (Kristeva 1982: 3).

Making the abject so conspicuous in the form of kryptonite or magnetite is also a method of sustaining the dominance of the 'normative' maleness of the divine child. The encoded message being that 'going back to mother/the semiotic will kill you.' Jung's belief that the divine child signifies a desire for unity that transcends consciousness alludes to a merging of symbolic and semiotic. *The X-Files* seems to play on this idea in its creation of William who not only draws a fragment of an alien/mothership to him kinetically, but also spins it in the air above his cot, metaphorically playing with the abject, embracing it, as if the sharp divide between semiotic and symbolic, consciousness and the unconscious did not exist.

In the ninth season William is injected with a form of magnetite by Mulder's half-brother Jeffrey Spender, now mutilated beyond recognition through biological experiments performed on him by the conspirators and led by his father CSM. Spender ambiguously tells Scully that by injecting William with magnetite to save his life, the child is somehow 'changed'. His cryptic punchline, that the aliens will 'always know what he was, they'll never accept what he is', leaves William's biological upgrading or downgrading unclear ('William' 9×17).

After prolonged threats on the child's life and Spender's intervention in his alien/human composition, Scully has William adopted by a childless Jonathan-and-Martha-Kent type couple who live on a large rural property. The reference to *Superman* is so blatant in this episode, that when we last see William in close-up, gurgling in his new cot and sporting a blue jumpsuit patterned with little UFOs surrounding a larger mothership, it appears that the infant's alien biology and divine disposition is still very much a going concern. The injection of magnetite, like childhood vaccines where a version of infectious matter is injected into the body to stimulate an immune response to infection, may have made William resistant to magnetite, thus superseding all other hybrids and pure aliens. In embracing the abject and being strengthened by this 'reunion', William personifies the psychic possibility of the Self.

Scully – 'Our Lady' of the hour (or 43–45 minutes without advertising)

The Mulder/Scully (Sol/Luna) coupling is also tainted with a considerable serve of Catholic and Gnostic mythology. Episodes 'Biogenesis' (6×22), 'The Sixth Extinction' (7×3) and 'The Sixth Extinction 11: Amor Fati' (7×4) explore the effects of Mulder's alien infection. Like Gibson Praise, it enabled him to read minds and perform telepathic feats at breakneck speed. Eager to transfer his son's newly acquired alien/human make-up and immunity to the alien viral apocalypse, CSM hooks himself up to Mulder, who is now imaged laying Christ-like on an operating table, his head fixed in a Budde-halo-type skull clamp (reminiscent of Christ's crown of thorns) while his body is being readied for the procedure.

Much is made of Mulder's martyrdom in these episodes, although previous allusions to his Christ-like disposition were a constant throughout the series. When considering that to Jung, 'Christ exemplifies the archetype of the self' (*CW* 9ii, para. 70), Mulder appears to be the most likely to contain this Christ/Self energy. But because of Carter's open-ended final episode, where Mulder is flushed of any alien-ness that might ensure his victory over the forces working against 'the truth', the mantle of Christ/Self may well have been passed to William. While Mulder aspires to holiness, Scully's association with religion, from early episodes to the birth of William, makes her an unambiguous fusion of pagan goddesses and Catholic pin-up girl Mary Immaculate. It is a moot point as to who suffers the most for the cause, but her memorable line to Mulder in 'Memento Moi' (4×15) 'If I can save you let me', gives some insight into the hero/martyr synthesis that is St. Scully.

Although her surname was Carter's homage to 'Vince Scully', broadcaster for the Los Angeles Dodgers, 'Dana' has very specific Celtic roots. Anu, Danu or Dana was commonly known as the mother goddess of Irish mythology and her divine children that made up the peoples of ancient Ireland were known as the Tuatha dé Danann. The similarly named Italian 'Diana' (Greek Artemis), derivative of the Egyptian Isis, was known as both huntress and mother deity. The Early Empire statue of Artemis of Ephesus in the Roman Villa Albani, highlights the maternal aspects of the goddess who is here adorned with multiple breasts and sacred, human breasted animals. Scully's associations with divine motherhood and her nine year hunt for the truth with Mulder can also be extended to include the persecution of supposed Diana cults in the Catholic sweep of Europe prior to and during the inquisition and witchcraft hunts of the late Middle Ages.

The tenth-century Canon Episcopi (*c.* 906), a Carolingian capitulary that served as a reference/regulation handbook for bishops, connected Diana with pagan devil worshipers:

> It is also not to be omitted that some wicked women perverted by the

> devil, seduced by illusions and phantasms of demons, believe and profess themselves, in the hours of the night to ride upon certain beasts with Diana, the goddess of the pagans, and an innumerable multitude of women, and in the silence of the dead of night to traverse great spaces of earth, and to obey her commands as of their mistress, and to be summoned to her service on certain nights.
>
> (cited in Russell 1972: 76)

The treatise later influenced inquisitors to believe in the existence of a 'sisterhood of Diana' where perverted women gathered at night to eat and revive dead animals and cast demonic spells in the service of Satan (Russell 1972: 76; Sallmann 1993: 453–454; Engels 1999: 141).

These attacks on women, aided by Heinrich Institoris' *Malleus Maleficarum* (*Hammer of Witches*, 1486) and legitimized by inquisitors, ecclesiastical judges and later secular courts (Sallmann 1993: 446), can be seen to parallel Scully's persecution by the syndicate and the military over the entire series. Throughout her work on the X-Files she is continually hunted, abducted, threatened, subjected to intrusive bodily experimentation, and tortured through the invasive cancer that resulted from removing an identification implant that was inserted into her body during various involuntary surgeries. In paralleling this activity with Christian witchcraft persecutions (not so much of a stretch) a great paradox or irony is opened up by her ardent Catholicism, or more pointedly, her gradual make-over by Carter as Catholicism's central (accepted) female force, the Madonna.

The problematic relationship that Scully has with Catholicism began to develop as a character possibility during the alien (government) abduction episodes ('Ascension' 2×6 and 'One Breath' 2×8) where her gold cross necklace, the only trace of her post-disappearance, became a significant key into the nexus between the search for UFOs and the search for god. 'If she was such a skeptic, why did she wear that?' Mulder says to Scully's mother in direct reference to the small gold cross he holds in his hand. In her study of female corporeality, Grosz (1994: 80) writes that objects coming, 'into contact with the surface of the body and remain there long enough will be incorporated into the body image – clothing, jewelry, other bodies, objects. They mark the body, its gait, posture, position, etc.' From here to the end of the series, the cross, a quaternity symbol *and* a Christian torture device, becomes a clear signifier not only for Scully herself, but also her association with redemption and suffering.

While the contradiction of science, to which Scully is also firmly marked, and her bourgeoning need for a belief system that incorporates an 'overwhelming other', is an intriguing character twist, her conversion to a religion bound by patriarchal traditions also reduces her status as a kick-arse, self-made, independent woman of considerable intellectual means. 'All Souls' (5×17) in particular, with its references to various religious 'fathers' (including a male God), draws on the forces of Christianity, Gnosticism and science to paradoxically fix her as both a devout medic/scientist and good virgin exemplar (Waddell 1998). An interesting character arc in light of Douglas Kellner's (2002) reading of *The X-Files* where he discusses the various plays on shady 'fathers', like Mulder's father Bill, birth father CSM, members of the syndicate, and a corrupt baby-boomer generation driven by male-dominated systems and institutions (the military and government administrations) that function through codes of control and power. As GenXers on the search for truths, Kellner (2002: 148) argues that Scully and Mulder 'are the representatives of virtue, professionalism, and positive values, whereas the previous generation of the fathers and their system of patriarchal authority, is shown to be highly flawed, and even evil'. It's then ironic that Carter subjects Scully to yet another male-driven belief system that often stifles female agency and has had a clear track record of injustices toward woman.

Scully's saintliness is a heaven-sent opportunity for the 'Order of the Blessed Saint Scully the Enigmatic' web fans. Luckily for them her religious calling gains momentum through the series. Her Madonna-like status is given an extra push when the little Scully/alien hybrid Emily is introduced. And just in case audiences didn't 'get' the Immaculate Conception allusion, Kim Manners (director of 'Emily' 5×7) merges a shot of Scully and Emily into an image of the Madonna and Child. The same reference to Scully's holiness is repeated in 'All Souls' where a shot of Scully dressed in pale lemon outside her church, is followed by a stained glass image of a blond saintly women in golden robes (Waddell 1998: 38). References to Catholicism particularly in relation to Scully are conspicuously threaded among the pagan myths, other organized religious traditions and cult practices marking each season. The dominance of Catholicism, though, makes this particular faith the pet religious fixation of *The X-Files*.

While there are only fleeting references to Scully's sexuality ('Never Again' 4×13, 'Milagro' 6×18, 'All Things' 7×17) she is by and large intellectually driven, except of course for her brief fling with Mulder (possibly 'All Things') where she 'maybe-did' or 'maybe-didn't' conceive William. In addition to her purity, Scully's divinity is enhanced by a number of references to her immortality. In 'Clyde Bruckman's Final Repose' (3×4) a reluctant clairvoyant able to visualize the death of those he comes in contact with, tells Scully that she won't die. Similarly in 'Tithonus' (6×9) she investigates photographer Alfred Fellig, who can predict the moment of death, but is unable to die because when once on his own deathbed, he refused to look the specter of death in the face. As the episode unfolds, Scully is shot, and closing her eyes to the approaching 'grim reaper', gives Fellig the opportunity to gaze at it, thus saving herself and allowing him the peace he wants. The intimation of course is that Scully now becomes immortal.

In 'Never Again', on a wild impulse and buoyed up by the radical experience of having 'a date', she has an ergot infused tattoo of a uroboros inked into her back. This pagan symbol of eternity, imaged as a circular snake or sometimes a dragon with its tail in its mouth, is frequently mentioned by Jung in his studies on alchemy. He refers to it as yet another symbol of the Self, again echoing the matter/spiritual tensions that Scully constantly seeks to integrate. This notion of eternity/wholeness, in relation to Scully and the snake, also alludes to the Christian fall narrative where Eve influenced by sin incarnated as a serpent, seduced Adam and begot the new race. Yet another reference to her union with Mulder and motherhood of William, the first perfect alien/human child. Not only does Scully wear her ubiquitous gold cross and the uroboros as quaternity/mandala symbols, but also in the mythology of *The X-Files*, she *becomes* a sign of the eternal.

Implantations and the little über-Scullies

'The Truth' makes it clear that Scully was experimented on by the military under the instruction of nefarious government forces. These initial abduction and fertility treatments in 'Ascension' and 'One Breath' (inspired by Gillian Anderson's pregnancy at the time) were staged as alien interventions. When the episodes aired, Scully as legit abductee, was the central thrust of the story arc. Although no baby resulted directly, the experiments and the chip inserted in her neck played a central role in crafting the more perfected William. Whether Mulder lent a hand (or a sperm) in William's conception is a moot point, confused by his insistence on being the father, our knowledge that William was the result of early fertility experiments, and our previous understanding that both Scully and Mulder at various stages filtered alien matter through their bodies.

In the episode 'Home', a homage to classic 1970s slice and dice cinema (Wes Craven's *The Hills have Eyes*, 1977, and Tobe Hooper's *Texas Chainsaw Massacre*, 1974), Oedipal taboos are taken to extremes when three inbred sons each attempt to impregnate their armless and legless mother (at her request) to ensure their ancestral line. When the murdered mutant offspring of one of these unions becomes a case for Mulder and Scully, we have yet another referent to Scully's impending motherhood. In the post-baby-autopsy scene Mulder jokes of her one day 'pumping out the little über-Scullies' as a preface to their more philosophical discussion of genetic defectiveness.

Catholicism has traditionally provided two career paths for women – nuns and mothers. But within the motherhood option, the paradox of maintaining one's purity while also being expected to breed (ordinarily perverse) is no problem for Scully, who manages to pull it off with the minimum of 'sin'. She thus maintains the 'dignity' that her ordained fathers would consider desirable in one of their female flock. Although Carter's mythology relentlessly played on the Scully-as-virgin-mother theme, he simultaneously linked this mythologem throughout the series with fertility procedures that mimicked documented accounts of abductees: 'e.g., collection of sperm or ova, implantation of alien-human hybrid embryos, removal of fetuses, sexual activity, and presentation of hybrid babies' (Holden and French 2002: 164).

Details of these kinds of invasive surgeries became more elaborate after the popularized abduction and consequent fertility sampling claims of New Hampshire couple Betty and Barney Hill. Their story went public in 1965, four years after they claimed to be abducted, and was fully published a year later in *The Interrupted Journey*. Details of the case were echoed in abduction reports that followed: late night traveling interrupted by 'missing time'; hypnotic recovery of lost abduction memories; enlightening conversations with small alien beings; examinations of a sexual nature; implants; and ongoing post-abduction trauma. Mack (1994: 417) discusses the fertility/abduction reports of his subjects in relation to a specific alien repopulation agenda based on a 'total environmental collapse' of the planet. It's a scenario that is suspiciously mirrored in the unfolding *X-Files* mythology since the publication of his contentious study.

Holden and French (2002: 172) document the high incidence of emotional distress, loneliness, childhood disturbances, and attempted suicides of those claiming to be abducted, but add the caveat that no 'serious pathologies at a higher rate than the general population' distinguish this particular group of people from others (Holden and French 2002: 174). These findings tend to support the more accepted explanations that the phenomena (or hysteria) of alien abduction scenarios could well be compensating fantasies/expressions of a sense of personal fragmentation.

When fertility procedures are added to the mix, not only is the compensation for any sense of incompleteness taken care of, but also the potential to become immortally melded to the 'overwhelming other' through hybridization takes the 'experience' to an entirely higher level. The maternal and divine nature of these abduction/fertility stories is suggestive of Kristeva's maternally connoted semiotic, the desired and feared precondition of subjectivity. The coexistence of self and other is made more tangible in her notion of love (Kristeva 1987: 7), which Lechte (1990: 170) summarizes as 'the embodiment of both the symbolic and the semiotic, language and affect, knowledge and joy'. This comes close to Jung's Self and the abductees' understanding of the mothership.

The nativity scene

The birth of William, while in keeping with the associated environmental symbolism and traditional birth conditions of his fellow divine incarnations, smacks most convincingly of the Christian nativity. In the double episodes 'Essence' and 'Existence' (8×21) a very pregnant Scully is pursued by abductee turned alien replacement/supersoldier 'Billy Miles' and a number of government/military conspirators determined to rid her of William (whose status as a harbinger of good or evil is still up in the air). Reyes whisks Scully out of

Washington to a small country town in Georgia where they find a deserted shop with 'Water from the Rock' and 'Exodus 7.16' (which should read 17:16 – possibly a continuity error) written on the window. This confusing verse must allude to the father–son (Mulder/William) cyclic defeat of 'evil' as an invading force: 'He said, "A hand upon the banner of the Lord! The Lord will have war with Amalek [archenemy of Israel] from generation to generation." ' The shop interior is dark, dilapidated and 'barn-like'. The gloom is punctuated only by a saintly figure in a tiny stained glass window. This lack of ambience compels Reyes to disinfect and decorate the space with candles so that the birth setting has a more appropriate 'spiritual glow'.

With the trepidation of Roman Polanski's 'Rosemary' (fearing that she might deliver the devil's/alien's spawn reminiscent of the 1968 thriller) Scully pumps out her little über-William, surrounded (of course) by aliens intent on abducting the child. These 'witnesses' mysteriously disband when, according to Mulder in a throwaway line, the baby 'wasn't what they thought he was.' If this tongue-in-cheek reference to the nativity scene isn't transparent enough, then the later scene of Scully and babe safely rescued and reinstalled in her Ikea-ish apartment by Mulder, in protective Joseph mode, should cement the allusion.

When met by Mulder outside Scully's bedroom door, the three Lone (wise) Gunmen, bearing gifts, ask him how he managed to find Scully in the wilds of Georgia – 'there was a light, I followed it', he says. Scully in a pale blue Mary-esque robe, Mulder, and perfect/miracle child (also dressed in blue) embrace in a symbolic tableau of the relationship between search for faith, UFOs and Self: a divine *coniunctio* akin to the Early Christian heralding of the kingdom of God which Christ predicted would come:

> when the two shall be one, and the outside as the inside, and the male with the female, neither male nor female. Now the two are one, when we speak of truth among ourselves, and in two bodies there shall be one soul without dissimulation.
>
> (Lightfoot et al. 1927: 194)

William's delivery is typical of divine births. It represents a movement out of primordial 'non-differentiation between subject and object' into consciousness (*CW* 9i, para. 290). 'As bringers of light, that is, enlargers of consciousness,' writes Jung 'they [divine children] overcome darkness, which is to say that they overcome the earlier unconscious state' (*CW* 9i, para. 288). Even though the divine child symbolizes the passage to subjectivity, it also embodies the unconscious 'original' psychological state from which it came: 'a wholeness which embraces the very depths of Nature' (*CW* 9i, para. 289). The relationship of the divine child to nature as symbolic of the (metaphorically) maternally connoted aspects of the unconscious is of prime importance to Jung who sees divine births as

> the precious fruit of Mother Nature herself, the most pregnant with the future, signifying a higher stage of self-realization. This is why Nature, the world of the instincts, takes the 'child' under its wing: it is nourished or protected by animals.
>
> (*CW* 9i, para. 286)

In its association with nature and the instincts, the divine child archetype personifies the possibility of bridging psychological binaries, a concept aligned with French feminisms, that as Rowland (2002: 123) writes, have some sympathy with Jung's devotion 'to the (impossible) task of thinking in the "other" '.

Christian nativity art also links the divine child with fecundity and nature through the recurring images of flora and fauna mingled between the child, Madonna and witnesses: David's *The Nativity* (*c.*1400), Schongauer's *The Nativity* (*c.*1470), Ghirlandaio's *Adoration of the Shepherds* (1482–1485) and Botticelli's *The Mystical Nativity* (*c.*1500). The concepts of darkness into light, illustrative of death and renewal, the movement from tribulation to prosperity, and unconsciousness to consciousness, are also clearly encoded in divine birth scenes through the contrasting dimness of the straw lined shelter and the radiance of the 'glowing' infant and/or guiding star, particularly in Renaissance versions of 'The Adoration of the Shepherds': El Greco 1596–1600, Rubens 1608, Rembrandt 1646, Le Brun 1686 and Maratti *c.*1690 (Neville 2004). Reyes and Scully's dark yet hospitable refuge, surrounded with witnesses and sparse yet visible flora (in juxtaposition to the brightness of Scully's conventionally tasteful inner city pad), mimics the allusions in nativity art to an emerging sense of 'futurity'. Highly appropriate when on the verge of an alien invasion.

In the nine-year build-up to *The X-Files* epilogue sequences, the binaries of rationality/consciousness and the irrational/unconsciousness dominating the show have metaphorically been working toward a flow of movement from one psychological position to the other. The divine child archetype in its embodiment of this integration provided a nucleus for the series from which the central characters were able to develop individually and collectively. Through self-sacrifice and the overcoming of dark forces set against them, *The X-Files* über-kids were essential to the trajectory of Carter's elaborate mythology.

While the parallel missions of the search for god and the search for UFOs offered a postmodern fusion of, as Scully says in relation to her tattooed African spacecraft, 'mysticism and science conjoined', the divine child theme was a skillful take on ancient allegories of the Self that transcended the series' more obvious sci-fi overtones. Although Carter played on abjection and the lethal nature of the abject in almost every episode, the brother/sister – Mulder/ Scully union ensured transcendence from these primal fears. William, the

Figure 2.1 Christian Bale as Patrick Bateman, *American Psycho*, Dir. Mary Harron, Lions Gate, 2000.

Figure 2.2 Hermes, Budapest.

Figure 3.1 Naomi Watts as Betty and Laura Harring as Rita, *Mulholland Drive*, Dir. David Lynch, Canal+, Touchstone, The Kibal Collection, 2001.

Figure 4.1 Guy Pearce as Leonard, *Memento*, Dir. Christopher Nolan, Summit Entertainment, The Kobal Collection, Danny Rothenberg, 2000.

Figure 4.2 Guy Pearce interviewed on *Enough Rope with Andrew Denton*, ABC TV, 2003.

Figure 5.1 Nicole Kidman as Grace, *The Others*, Dir. Alejandro Amenábar, Miramax, Canal+, Sogecine, The Kobal Collection, 2001.

Figure 5.2 Fionnula Flanagan as Mrs. Mills, *The Others*, Dir. Alejandro Amenábar, Miramax, Canal+, Sogecine, The Kobal Collection, 2001.

Figure 5.3 James Bentley as Nicholas and Alakina Mann as Anne, *The Others*, Dir. Alejandro Amenábar, Miramax, Canal+, Sogecine, The Kobal Collection, 2001.

Figure 6.1 David Duchovny as Mulder and Gillian Anderson as Scully, *The X-Files*, 20th Century Fox Television, The Kobal Collection, 1993–2002.

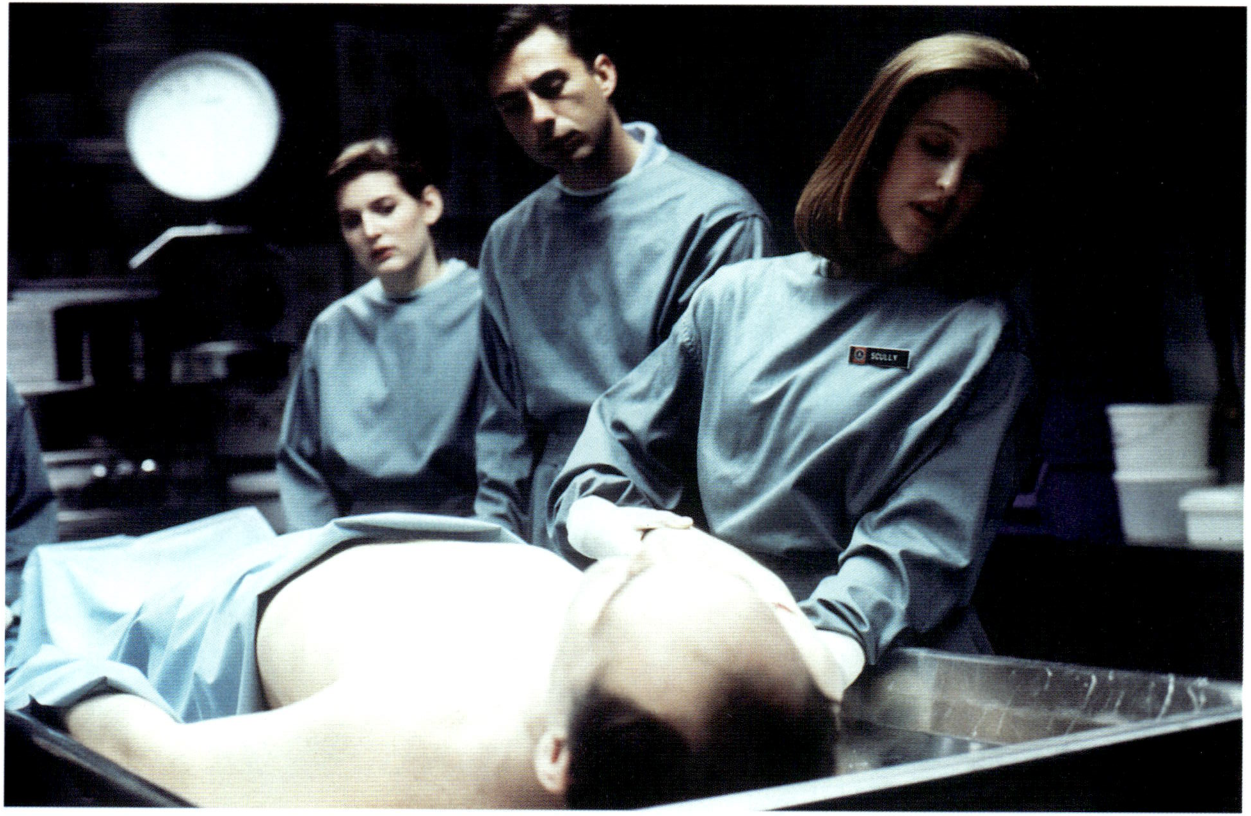

Figure 6.2 Gillian Anderson as Scully, *The X-Files*, 20th Century Fox Television, The Kobal Collection, 1993–2002.

Figure 7.1 Sheryl Lee as the wrapped-in-plastic Laura Palmer, *Twin Peaks*, Lynch/Frost Productions, Spelling, The Kobal Collection, 1990–1991.

Figure 7.2 Grace Zabriskie as Sarah Palmer, Sheryl Lee as Laura Palmer and Ray Wise as Leland Palmer, *Twin Peaks: Fire Walk With Me*, Dir. David Lynch, Lynch/Frost, CIBY 2000, The Kobal Collection, 1992.

Figure 8.1 James Gandolfini as Tony Soprano and Jamie Lynn Sigler as Meadow Soprano, *The Sopranos*, HBO, The Kobal Collection, Barry Wetcher, 1999–.

Figure 9.1 Ralph Fiennes as Spider, *Spider*, Dir. David Cronenberg, Sony Pictures, The Kobal Collection, Takashi Seida, 2002.

Figure 9.2 Miranda Richardson as Mrs. Cleg and Bradley Hall as boy Spider, *Spider*, Dir. David Cronenberg, Sony Pictures, The Kobal Collection, Takashi Seida, 2002.

Figure 9.3 Gabriel Byrne as Bill Cleg and Miranda Richardson as Yvonne, *Spider*, Dir. David Cronenberg, Sony Pictures, The Kobal Collection, Takashi Seida, 2002.

Figure 10.1 Mark Rylance as Jay and Kerry Fox as Claire, *Intimacy*, Dir. Patrice Chereau, Azor Films, France 2, Greenpoint, The Kobal Collection, Jack English, 2001.

Figure 11.1 Jennifer Saunders as Edina and Joanna Lumley as Patsy, Justin Canning, copyright BBC (Christmas Special) 2004.

Figure 11.2 French 16th century grotesques and animal decoration, Chambre des Arts, Francesco Primaticcio, (1504–70), The Kobal Collection.

Figure 11.3 Edina (Jennifer Saunders) using Saffy's baby 'Jane' as a fashion accessory as Patsy (Joanna Lumley) looks on, Tim Anderson, copyright BBC (5x7 'Exploitin), 2003.

product of this coniunctio, although not as overtly consecrated with holiness as his mum and dad, is nevertheless encoded with attributes of the saviour – the potential to realize the Self.

William may well be a metaphor for *the truth* that Mulder, Scully and their apostles seek, or *the absolute* that in classical Jungian terms unifies binaries, but more likely he represents the possibility of coexistence, exchange and plurality. In the final scene of the program, Scully and Mulder cuddling yin/yang-like in a Roswell motel room, acknowledge that they are looking for the same thing. Their only surety though is that they will experience 'the truth' differently from each other. As Kellner notes of the episode 'José Chung's from Outer Space', a parody on *The X-Files* itself:

> there is no unitary truth, but rather each individual had his or her own interpretation of the truth. Thus, in this vision, although the truth 'may be out there,' it is multiple, complex, difficult to access, and subject to a diversity of interpretations.
>
> (Kellner 2002: 143)

William, post-magnetite injection, may well be just a smartly dressed tot in a cot, stripped of his telepathic powers and destined to all-American boyhood under George Bush, but then again he may just as easily be the second coming. As with the question of his mortal or celestial origins, *X-Files* aficionados will be divided on the William-as-saviour hypothesis, but as Scully's farewell voice-over to her Kal-El tells us, 'the truest truths are what hold us together or keep us painfully, desperately apart.'

Chapter 7

Libidinal frenzy

Twin Peaks

> What else have the last years taught me if not that my father will take nothing less than all of me?
>
> Katherine Harrison, *The Kiss* (1998: 201)

Given *The X-Files*' homage to the myths of antiquity, it shouldn't come as any great surprise that the series' own mythology incorporates incestuous coupling as the ultimate trigger for transformation/rebirth. Scully and Mulder's Luna/Sol, sister/brother alchemy that spawned William the (maybe) divine, Mulder's spiritual reunion with his sister Samantha, and the various sacred 'fathers' throughout the series to whom Scully 'gives herself' (birth dad and 'Our Father' included), are all instances of how the incest archetype surfaces in popular culture through metaphor and allusion.

Jung argued that unconscious incestuous urges can in part be understood as the desire for transformation, and that these urges to merge with archetypal imagos of rebirth (puella, puer, mother, or father) have always been an integral dimension of the mythic. Counter to Freud, he theorized the libido as a life-force or creative energy that manifests in a variety of projections and behaviours that may or may not be sexual in nature. In analytical psychology libidinal regression to the incest archetype as a means of renewal is ordinarily satisfied through the metaphors of myth, ritual and the imagination. But as we know from current research, public discourse and media exposés, incest is not always held at the symbolic level. When the archetype is disowned, projected and acted-out, the soul can hemorrhage.

Chapters 7, 8 and 9 focus on the shadow aspects of the incest motif, still firmly embedded in screen mythology. This approach to incestuous imagery is conspicuously unexplored from the point of view of film and television, so I'm going to open up this area by looking at how the incest archetype is woven through Lynch and Mark Frost's series, *Twin Peaks*. This short-lived cult classic fixed the precedent for *The X-Files* and related prime-time dramas that immersed themselves in intertextual plays with popular culture, psychology, philosophy and religion.

The series is peppered with Lynch's signature themes of duality; eroticized/victimized female characters; ensemble cast; Badalamenti's score and orchestration; overlapping storylines; and unnerving subterranean presences. He directed only six of the thirty episodes (including the pilot); the rest were handed over to celebrities and guest directors, notably Diane Keaton (2×15) and Tim Hunter (1×4; 2×9; 2×21), director of the similarly pitched film *River's Edge* (1986). *Twin Peaks* was divided into the pilot and two oddly proportioned seasons, the first of seven episodes and the second of twenty-two. Although it's tempting to explore how this project made the postmodern television drama a 1990s prime-time must, from the present-day perspective, it's more fruitful to look at the theme least talked about in popular discourse – transformation via the libido's regression to the incest motif.

The pilot and first sixteen episodes revolved around the unsolved murder of high school senior Laura Palmer (Sheryl Lee). The personal story arcs of characters familiar with Laura and the mystery of her death overlap and merge to shape the narrative. Eventually Bob (Frank Silva) is revealed as the sadist who tortured Laura after sexually and psychologically raping her since puberty. But Bob, not quite of this world, is an indirect presence realized only through the dreams, visions and grisly flashbacks of select characters. In a recycled sweep of Lucifer, Mephistopheles, Satan, Pan and Mara, Lynch and Frost construct Bob as an 'evil entity' who dwells in, and operates through, Laura's father Leland (Ray Wise). When the force of Bob's nature explodes and a confession of Laura's murder ensues, the question of Leland's guilt and/or innocence becomes more morally complex. As a parable of libidinal chaos, various techniques in *Twin Peaks* set Bob up as a metaphor for the power of the repressed shadow/trickster desiring recognition. Lynch and Frost's densely packed play on imagery and all its attached maya (like *Mulholland Drive*) is the stuff of myth and its underlying archetypal structure.

I began this chapter with a line from Katherine Harrison's (1998) autobiographical account of her adult daughter–father sexual relationship. The unsentimental lyricism of her writing exposes the destructive nature of a parent's desire for his daughter as a way of sating an intense sense of lack. The emptiness and dread in the brief quote that introduces this chapter capture the ache implicit in *the frustration of archetypal intent* for father and daughter; a state where the energies of individuation have become blocked. 'The kiss is the point at which I begin slowly, inexorably, to fall asleep, to surrender volition, to become paralyzed. It's the drug my father administers in order that he might consume me. That I might desire to be consumed', writes Harrison (1998: 70) in what can clearly be read as a mirroring of the consumption of Laura Palmer.

Lynch's penchant for doubling and schisms

As intimated by the name of the series, *Twin Peaks* is concerned with duality and plurality. A fusion of respectability and indecency, Laura, the wannabe junkie, sex worker, overachiever and all around town darling, becomes the penultimate gazed-at-one. Her photographed image and corpse are visually cannibalized with an intensity verging on the necrophilic. More than a fetishized schoolgirl wrapped in plastic, she is an Ariadne of sorts who unfurls a thread for both audience and characters to grapple with as we pass through the labyrinth of the shadow.

Dialogue and visual clues make it clear that Laura led a double life, her popularly remembered innocence, moral integrity and social respectability were merely workable fronts for a darker energy fueled by sex, violence and drugs. Not so subtle signs of division repeatedly mark the Laura schism: one half of her heart-shaped locket is found at the murder site; Harold, the keeper of her secret diary, sends a hybrid orchid to her grave; Maddie, her cousin, is played by the same actress in a brunette wig (Lee); and each of the characters has their opposite realized in another character. Town psychiatrist and Laura's love-struck analyst, Dr Jacoby (Russ Tamblyn), eventually spells out what Lynch and Frost signposted from the first episode: 'It was her you see, a divided heart. Laura was in fact living a double life, two people' (1×7).

We become aware of Laura's strength of character through our gradual discovery of her acknowledgement and fraught acceptance of the underground playtime activities she was drawn into. As Leland tells us in his confession, while Bob was her most legitimate fear, she was willing to confront, rather than disavow him: 'they [evil spirits] wanted her, they wanted Laura, but she was strong, she fought 'em, she wouldn't let 'em in' (2×9). The difference between Laura and Leland's relationship with Bob, is that Leland is unaware of Bob's presence. Unable to access him, he's also unable to understand him as an unconscious shadow distortion.

Initially Bob was presented as a separate character played by Silva, but when exposed as part of Leland's psyche, Silva's image no longer carried the 'Bob' pathology. In the revealing 'Maddie murder' scene, the dancing, singing Winnebago trickster (Chapter 2) seeps through Leland's (Wise) obsessive behaviour. During the attack, trickster's terrifying shadow aspect is also signaled by a flash of Bob's previously established image (Silva) reflected in a wall mirror as Leland looks at himself slapping on lycra gloves in preparation for the slaughter. It's here that we're finally made aware that Bob is Leland. Both represent opposing psychological material:

> The [trickster] figure works, because secretly it participates in the observer's psyche and appears as its reflection, though it is not recognised as

> such. It is split off from his consciousness and consequently behaves like an autonomous personality.
>
> (Jung *CW* 9i, para. 484)

Twin Peaks is shaped through interwoven layers, each linked to the binary tensions that underlie trickster's lightweight or sinister mischief. On the face of it the series suggests that supernatural forces are beyond control or understanding, but Jung doesn't interpret the term 'evil spirits' to mean 'external beings' (Chapter 5). He sees them as a concept once used to make sense of psychological disorders: 'Possession, though old-fashioned, has by no means become obsolete; only the name has changed. Formerly they spoke of "evil spirits", now we call them "neuroses" or "unconscious complexes" ' (*CW* 18, para. 1374). Similarly Bob, or demonic forces, can therefore be interpreted as unconscious eruptions of unacceptable shadow impulses. FBI forensic expert Albert Rosenfield (Miguel Ferrer), called in for Laura's autopsy, points out that after Leland's confession, 'people saw Bob, they saw him in visions – Laura, Maddie, Sara Palmer'. He rounds off with the punch line, 'maybe that's all Bob is, the evil that men do, maybe it doesn't matter what we call it' (2×9).

Shadow patterning

Lynch and Frost take us to the place where the archetypal energy of incest becomes fused with the shadow. Public and media fascination with the abuse of power by child minders (priests, teachers, nannies or parents) and children who kill (like Robert Thompson, John Venables, Mary Bell, and Kipland Kinkel) is riddled with moral panic. Those transgressing the expectations of 'good' parenting or childhood 'innocence' are often imaged as 'aberrations'. Exposure to these more pathological aspects of human nature though, via myth and less sensationalist motivated media, can also encourage us to acknowledge that these behaviours aren't just acts of 'evil', but human possibilities. John Sanford (1987: 26) for instance notes that the archetypal shadow 'is the inferior part of our personality where we are incapable, irresponsible, psychopathic, and filled with infantile fantasies'.

The shadow, 'inferior personality' or alter-ego belongs to both the collective and personal unconscious and contains all that our social self and culture finds difficult to assimilate. Shadow manifestations vary according to personal and community ideals. No matter how disturbing this material appears, Jung argued for the need to consciously acknowledge and integrate the shadow, or risk its unpredictable, inevitably damaging effects: 'If you get rid of qualities you don't like by denying them, you become more and more unaware of what you are, you declare yourself more and more non-existent, and your devils will grow fatter and fatter' (Jung 1984: 53).

Twin Peaks movingly explores the urge to claim the shadow, via Leland and

Laura, who blindly juggle their amoral/moral – shadow/ego binaries in a space where the enemy is indestructible and within. Jung believed that to become conscious of the shadow as 'present and real' by understanding and accepting its multiplicity, takes 'considerable moral effort' (*CW* 9ii, para. 14). Of course it can also present as entirely positive or *golden*. If one's outward show (persona) is supported by an ego that embraces a sense of the nefarious, then the golden shadow would be formed from conflicting material necessarily withdrawn for the ego to sustain its 'darker' values.

Although Jung clearly acknowledges that 'evil' and 'good' are culturally and personally subjective labels, he maintained that their motivating tensions are embedded in our physical and psychic experience (*CW* 9i, para. 197). The perpetual oscillation of shadow energies within the personality are often tied to archetypal images that have the potential to draw our attention to the moral ambiguity and consequences of powerful impulses and desires (*CW* 9i, para. 310). When too confronting to acknowledge, these archetypal fusions (the incest or trickster motifs for example) can be outwardly projected and split off into multiple figures (Jaffé 1978: 110–111).

Bob as libido

'Fire walk with me' is written in blood on a scrap of paper found in the deserted train carriage where Laura was tortured and murdered (pilot). This phrase is echoed throughout the series and the post-series film that documents the build-up to Laura's death (*Twin Peaks: Fire Walk with Me*). 'Mike' (Bob's spirit world partner) repeats this line in chief FBI investigator (Special Agent) Dale Cooper's dream sequence (1×1) and again in later episodes (2×6; 2×9). Half of Laura's heart necklace is also found in the carriage, but placed on a mound of dirt encircled by twelve melted candles.

The candles are also seen alight in Cooper's (Kyle MacLachlan) dream sequence as a menacing key into the ritualistic murder. The implication of death is marked at the end of the scene when the candles are blown out by a gust of wind. Juan Eduardo Cirlot writes of Shiva's cosmic dance, performed in a ring of twelve candles, as 'the circular dance of nature in eternal process of creation and destruction' (Cirlot 1962: 274). The configuration not only alludes to *Twin Peaks*' many binary death/rebirth plays, but also the Self, if we understand the circle of candles to be mandala imagery. This clarifies Bob/Leland's impetus to ritualize his incestuous actions – transformation in the hope of individuation.

According to 'the Log Lady' (Catherine Coulson, 1×4), fire is 'a devil hiding like a coward in the smoke'. Throughout *Twin Peaks*, 'fire' becomes a sign of the chaotic libidinal forces binding the Leland–Bob–Laura triad. 'It is probably no accident that the two most important discoveries which distinguish man from all other living beings,' wrote Jung, 'namely speech and the use of fire, should have a common psychic background. Both are products of psychic energy, of libido or mana' (*CW* 5, para. 237). Fire is also associated with purification and the integration of opposites. As we saw in Chapter 3, the rubedo (red stage) is the final uniting rebirth process of the coniunctio. This climatic point in the 'alchemical marriage' also referred to unconscious material rising to consciousness, or in a broader context, the rise of consciousness itself (*CW* 14, para. 307). From this perspective, fire might also be interpreted as a sign of Bob's emergence from the unconscious.

While Freud's description of libido in *Three Essays on the Theory of Sexuality* (1905) clearly defines the concept in terms of instinctual sexual forces, Jung posits that while the libido can manifest itself sexually, it is not limited to sexuality: 'The sexual theory of psychic automatisms is an untenable prejudice. The very fact that it is impossible to derive the whole mass of psychic phenomena from a single instinct forbids a one-sided definition of "libido" ' (*CW* 5, para. 185). He best sums up this divergence from Freud by characterizing the libido as

> a desire or impulse which is unchecked by any kind of authority, moral or otherwise . . . From the genetic point of view it is bodily needs like hunger, thirst, sleep and sex, and emotional states or affects, which constitute the essence of libido.
>
> (*CW* 5, para. 194)

The fire that surrounds Bob and his associated shadow undercurrents can refer to the feral libidinal desire ensnaring and imploding upon Leland and Laura. Bob's primitive appetites and cruelty, explicit in the series, are most marked by his curdling howls of bloodlust that introduce us to a flashback sequence of Laura's murder where he repeatedly drives a knife into her stomach and chest (2×1). When he next murders cousin Maddie, we see him punching her in the head, brutally slamming her into a wall and kissing and biting her bloodstained face as his image shape-shifts from Leland (Wise) to Bob (Silva) (2×7).

In both murders, howling, indicative of the animal/human hybridity of trickster, is echoed over the action to signify Bob's pleasure. In shots where he's intercut into dream or spontaneous vision sequences, he maniacally smiles, laughs and bays to accentuate his pleasure of pain. Fellow spirit Mike tells Cooper of Bob's cruel playfulness, clearly paralleling the Winnebago's Wakdjunkaga and the ruthless Norse trickster Loki: 'He is Bob, eager for fun. He wears a smile, everybody run . . . he feeds on fear and the pleasures, they are his children' (2×6). When Bob speaks it is to brag about his exploits, reveal himself as an aspect of Leland (2×9), or to talk of killing: 'Cut you with my death bag. You may think I've gone insane, but I promise I will kill again' (1×1).

If Bob and the fire associated with him are projections of Leland's rampant libidinal energy manifesting as the greed, sex and violence that pathologically bind the emotional matrix of father and daughter, then what does this unbridled energy ultimately signify? What is the allegorical import of the *Twin Peaks* myth? As Jung argued, psychic energy/libido seeks transformation. As the surfacing archetype can direct psychic change by initiating discourse between the unconscious and consciousness, libidinal energy can direct archetypes toward the brokering of this transformation. After all, Jung was attracted to the concept of a *forward* looking psyche, and saw the concept of mythic incest not always as an Oedipal *looking back*, but a means of progression toward the Self via rebirth.

While Bob is often seen as pure libido, he can be clearly read (and is understood by the other characters) as 'the evil that men do'. He is the ultimate archetypal shadow or devil that in this instance acts as the catalyst for transformation on a number of levels within the series. More specifically, Bob-as-libido/shadow-devil surging through Leland can be understood as symptomatic of the desire to realize the Self. It seems like a long shot so far, but when incest is revealed as the act that sets the *Twin Peaks* myth in motion and propels it over seventeen episodes, this interpretation makes much more sense.

Images of incest

As discussed in previous chapters, the coniunctio, or divine marriage that produces the ultimate spiritual experience (knowledge of the Self), was imagined in various heterosexual formations within the nuclear family unit: son/mother, father/daughter, brother/sister. This myth, never intended to be taken literally, addresses our unconscious incestuous desires that Jung believed represented the urge to be reborn; a return to the maternal matrix/the chrysalis, in the hope of emerging with a more developed awareness. When coniunctio is taken out of its symbolic context and incest is literalized, we can see, according to Tacey (1990: 22), the degree to 'which the ego (or conscious personality) is held in thrall by it [the archetypal incest image]'. From the excessively brutal and sexual libidinal energy directed toward Laura, and by proxy her cousin Maddie, Leland is clearly held 'in thrall'. The hunger for incestuous union directly points to the urgency for Self.

When Juliet Mitchell (2000) argues that the life/sex and death drive (conflicting tensions according to Freud) are often combined or 'fused', as in cases of hysteria and incest where violence is sexualized, then the 'sexuality is unlikely to be about a relationship, it is more likely to be about a desperate need for something that is forever missing' (Mitchell 2000: 135–136). This idea echoes Jung's pioneering thoughts on symbolic and literal incest as a bid for metamorphosis. David Hughes (2001) makes a convincing sociological point when he says of *Twin Peaks* that 'God forbid that anyone should bring a respectable middle-class father's rape and murder of his own daughter into American homes, without some kind of supernatural possession to explain it away!' (Hughes 2001: 133). An archetypal reading of the overtly mythic layers of the series, though, helps us understand the father's 'supernatural possession' as more than a merely sugar-coated 'cop out'. It reads more as a clever device to connect the audience to the spiritual and psychological search for that intangible 'something that is forever missing.'

Although the procedural dramas of 2005 (*Crime Scene Investigation* and *Law and Order* spin offs) now blatantly bring the brutality of incest to prime time, I would argue that it's usually the spectacle, sensationalism and atrocity of the act that are most attended to. When engineered into the daytime soap, it's nearly always approached as a titillating and shock narrative device to jolt relationships between characters. Lynch and Frost must then be admired for their 'audacity' to see beyond the cliché and the moral panic.

Theorizing incestuous desire archetypally is not to argue, of course, that actualizing incest wishes, imagery or myth should be condoned. As Tacey (1990) notes of his experience in trying to approach the issue of incest from an archetypal perspective, the public resistance to this kind of thinking is intimidating, but understandable. Perhaps the core of this unwillingness to view the incest image/desire as an aspect of individuation lies in Freud's culturally entrenched psychoanalytic treatment of the Oedipal myth: the desire to supplant the father for the mother's affections, consequently repress the incestuous desire, and so enter the 'father-centered' realm of subjectivity. Going back to mother for Freud was *regressive*, for Jung *progressive*. In *Totem and Taboo* (1913), Freud justified his Oedipal theorizing by briefly tracing the incest taboo to indigenous cultures and consequently arguing that the various laws and rites in place to prohibit and inhibit any incestuous acting out, reflect/ed the deep psychological aversion to incest necessary for social development (Freud 1950: 28–29).

The incest taboo – transgression and redirection

Freud's interpretation of his patients' accounts of inter-family rape and seduction as purely imagined expressions of repressed incestuous wishes ran counter to his earlier 1896 findings in *The Aetiology of Hysteria* first read at the Society for Psychiatry and Neurology in Vienna. He validated incest claims as actual instances of child abuse and maintained that the repression of these disturbing memories caused and/or fed his patients' hysteria and neurosis. Jeffrey Masson's (1992) *The Assault on Truth* exposed what he saw as Freud's suspicious change of tack.

Masson (1992) argues that initially motivated by the isolation from his medical colleagues who rejected his 1896 theories, Freud explained away incidents of actual incestuous suffering as wishes and fantasies, paving the way for his theorization of the Oedipus complex and the consequent development of psychoanalysis. While his acknowledgement of childhood sexuality was progressive and central to Jung's work, Judith Herman and Lisa Hirschman

(1981: 10) in *Father–Daughter Incest* argue that in failing to accept the deeply traumatic female experience of incest by abandoning the seduction theory, Freud was consequently unable to grapple with female psychology, and in particular, female neurosis. It might reasonably be argued that 'the dark continent', his term for this blind spot, lies at the heart of the Freudian shadow.

Like Freud, Jung understood the significance of the incest taboo as a vital barrier against acting on incestuous impulses, but offered more guidance for dealing with the warping of this psychological safeguard. Murray Stein (1973), Tacey (1990) and Samuels (1993) agree that only by accepting the importance of incest on the mythic, religious and imaginal level, is it possible to understand its symbolic and spiritual meaning, and so redirect any pathologized desire to enact the motif. The effect of the incest taboo, according to Jung, 'is to stimulate the creative imagination, which gradually opens up the possible avenues for the self-realization of libido' (*CW* 5, para. 332). Stein argues that both the desire for incest and the incest taboo work together as a means of furthering psychological and spiritual growth:

> Repression of either the desire (as Freud, Malinowski and others suggest is essential for culture) or the prohibition is, in my opinion, obstructive to psychological growth. To understand this relationship, both the desire and the inhibition need to be viewed as aspects of one instinct.
>
> (Stein 1984: 32)

Confessing and accepting

Leland's confession scene in the final moments of episode 2×9 is a powerful mythic treatment of the craving to consume the child/daughter as a means of accessing a sense of Self. When suspected of his daughter's rape and murder, Leland is locked in a police cell and the force of Bob explodes in a confession where once again, as in the 'Maddie murder' scene, the darker libidinal energy is no longer entirely imaged through another actor (Silva), but finally identified as a split aspect of Leland (Wise) rising to consciousness:

> Oh Leland, Leland, Leland, you've been a good vehicle and I've enjoyed the ride, but now he's weak and full of holes . . . Leland's a babe in the woods, with a large hole where his conscience used to be and when I go children I will pull that rip-cord and you watch Leland remember, watch him, but not for long.

When the misdirected libido or psychic energy is 'ripped' from Leland via the mythic allegory of Bob's transmutation into another 'hosting' body, we see Leland accept his transgression, and in a movingly written coda, can understand him to be the victim of cyclic abuse:

Leland: Oh God Laura, I killed her, I killed my daughter. I didn't know. Forgive me. Oh God. I was just a boy. I saw him in my dream. He said he wanted me to play. He opened me and I invited him and he came inside me.
Cooper: He went inside?
Leland: When he was inside I didn't know and when he was gone I couldn't remember. He made me do things, terrible things.

From these brief words, it's possible to understand that robbed of his own childhood through sexual cruelty, Leland's craving to reclaim the child archetype, or that 'something that is forever missing', has been misguidedly filtered into a brutal chain of incestuous violence.

At this stage in the confession scene, a fire alarm has been activated in the police precinct and water streams from the sprinkler system in the ceiling onto the collapsed and depleted Leland, in what can only be read as an allusion to baptism, and, like the *Wizard of Oz*'s (1939) drenched Wicked Witch, an ousting of the shadow. As Leland lies on the cell floor, Cooper cradles his soaking body in the pre-death position, 'Lying Posture of a Lion', detailed in *The Tibetan Book of the Dead*. He ministers guidance taken from the following Book 1, Part 1 passage of the text:

> O nobly-born (so and so by name), the time hath now come for thee to seek the Path [in reality]. Thy breathing is about to cease. Thy *guru* hath set thee face to face before with the Clear Light; and now thou art about to experience it in its Reality in the *Bardo* state, wherein all things are like the void and cloudless sky, and the naked, spotless intellect is like unto a transparent vacuum without circumference or center. At this moment, know thyself; and abide in that state. I, too, at this time, am setting thee face to face.
> (Evans-Wentz 2000: 91)

In this self-conscious play on smoothing Leland's path to the afterlife, the final shots of this man who we've only ever known as a tormented father and abuser, are reminiscent of Laura's tranquility when we first see her 'wrapped in plastic' body freshly pulled from the river:

Leland: I see her. She's there
Cooper: Into the light, Leland
Leland: She's beautiful
Cooper: Into the light
Leland: Laura
Cooper: Don't be afraid
(Leland dies).

Cooper's evocation of Buddhist doctrine, functions as a catalyst for the redirection of the incest image, now appropriately returned to the symbolic state in order for Leland to negotiate the process of rebirth and transformation.

The transit of Bob

Although this section of the chapter looks at the series only up to the seventeenth episode when the Palmer case is solved, *Twin Peaks* continued for another twelve episodes before it was axed by the American Broadcast Company despite weekly U.S. audience estimates of between 9 and 10 million (Hughes 2001: 118). In terms of the shadow and trickster archetypes woven into the Bob-as-misdirected-libido, the final episode is a predictable conclusion to any archetypal reading of the series.

Lynch images Bob shape-shifting into owls during transition periods from one 'host' to another. The confession episode (2×9) enabled us to catch this metamorphosis. As the representatives of the FBI, army and police (the forces of good pitted against the forces of evil) gather in the woods after the confessions scene, Sheriff Truman (Michael Ontkean) tells Cooper that he finds it difficult to believe that Bob murdered through Leland. Cooper responds by asking if it's 'easier to believe a man would rape and murder his own daughter, any more comforting?' It's at this point that forensics ace Rosenfield links Bob to 'the evil that men do.' When Major Briggs asks, 'an evil that great in this beautiful world, finally does it matter what the cause?' Cooper, with the camera fixed upward to intimate an imposing aura of authority, tells his colleagues, 'Yes, because it's our job to stop it'. Briggs shrugs.

The imagery following this dialogue suggests a gust of wind passing at great speed through the forest debris. The implication here is that the spirit of Bob has left Leland's body and is 'in transition'. When the wind reaches the end of its tunnel-like journey, the image of an owl flying toward the camera is superimposed over the dark undergrowth to supposedly signal Bob's shape-shifting transformation. The last episode (2×22) reveals Cooper as the next character to be possessed, through a repetition of the mirror technique we saw in the 'Maddie murder' scene where Leland and Bob were shown to be one. With Luis Buñuel's *L'Age d'Or* (1930) in mind, Martyn Pedler and Saige Walton (2004: 117) argue that 'Lynch's swan song to the series parallels Buñuel's use of the mirror: the mirror isn't a reflective tool, it is an entry point to subconscious desire that visualizes an interior state of mind and Bob's possession of Cooper'. Bob's conquest isn't surprising considering how vulnerable Cooper makes himself by not acknowledging the importance of integrating interior shadow states. Analytical psychology, and it would seem Lynch and Frost, don't consider the avoidance of 'evil' and the fear it engenders, as any kind of option.

Twin Peaks graphically draws on the incest trauma of both abuser and victim.

Because of its intensely drawn-out emotional and mythic treatment of the issue, it is still a unique example of the libidinal excesses that inspired Ovid, Sophocles and Seneca's accounts of interfamilial sexuality. In the next chapter the father–daughter relationship in David Chase's series *The Sopranos* also plays on the theme of incest, but unlike *Twin Peaks*, the pattern is much more indirect. Mafia boss 'Tony Soprano's' daughter 'Meadow' is used quite differently from Laura. She functions as a soul-mate for Tony to venerate and a means of negotiating his crippling mother-complex. Both fathers' desires, though, expose an inability to shift a blocked libido that seeks movement.

In television, where the viscera of the central characters can be unwound over months and years, *Twin Peaks* and *The Sopranos* are easily able to identify the shadow and ego conflicts that make Leland and Tony such compelling deviants. As projections of the incest paradigm these mythic 'fathers' come to us as complex prisms of conflict that violently use the female others in their orbit (daughters, lovers, mothers) as ciphers for their frustrations. But Leland is unquestionably the darker energy. Unable to accept and hold incest in the symbolic realm, he perpetuates what might be called 'the evil' that frightened and inwardly crippled 'men do'. Nevertheless, as a fiction, he serves to demonstrate the abstract idea that regression to the incest archetype can be an expression of *forward* rather than *backward* development.

Chapter 8

Incest by goomah/ daughter proxy

The Sopranos

> Everyone knew that Livia kept Augustus in strict order and that, if not actually frightened of her, he was at any rate very careful not to offend her.
>
> Robert Graves, *I Claudius* (1979: 27)

Graves' take on the Roman Empire's Julio-Claudian dynasty, with all its incestuous intrigue and interfamilial butchery, was just begging to be revamped. David Chase creates a parallel universe to *I Claudius* with *The Sopranos* (1999–), HBO's prime-time drama of an American-Italian mafia diaspora. Although the Sopranos aren't as pedigreed as their Julian and Claudian role models, they're just as ruthless and corrupt. Now in its fifth season at the time of writing this chapter, the series is a fitting companion to *Twin Peaks* if we approach it from the angle of libidinal chaos and the incest archetype.

New Jersey's Don of the moment, Tony Soprano (James Gandolfini), resists facing up to the deep desire for renewal that lies at the heart of his random anxiety attacks, fits of uncontrolled anger and promiscuity. His struggle to negotiate work, play and the domestic, is imbued with the same mytho-tragic need for 'something that is forever missing' that motivated *Twin Peaks'* Leland. Like Caesar Augustus, Tony must also deal with 'Livia', who this time comes reincarnated not as a wife, but a formidable maternal presence. Both versions, though, are that rare breed of matriarch who would have their children killed for the greater good of 'the family'. Despite this, it's to her that Tony is bound and to her that he incestuously regresses. As Graves (1979: 24) tells us, 'Augustus ruled the world, but Livia ruled Augustus'.

Tony's relationship with women reflects the one problem he feels powerless to eliminate, or in mafioso speak, 'whack': the inability to transform the libido (life-force/creative energy) as a step toward individuation. 'Whenever this drive for wholeness appears', claimed Jung, 'it begins by disguising itself under the symbolism of incest, for, unless he seeks it in himself, a man's nearest feminine counterpart is to be found in his mother, sister, or daughter'

(*CW* 16, para. 471). This might seem like a sexually naive cliché, but it's appropriate for the way that Tony evolves over five seasons. Even the sometime 'Freud-by-numbers' approach of his regularly featured psychiatrist, Dr. Jennifer Melfi (Lorraine Bracco), is all about unraveling the import of Tony's relationship to his mother Livia (Nancy Marchand), wife Carmela (Edie Falco), daughter Meadow (Jamie-Lynn Discala) and the collection of 'goomahs' or mistresses who pass through his life. All appear more germane to his treatment than the carnage of his profession that he legitimizes to those not-in-the-know as 'waste management'.

Although it's easy to imagine that the various murders and tortures that Tony either commits or orchestrates are at the root of his anxiety, Chase has made the series much more vibrant by milking not only the incestuous intensity of the Roman Empire, but Sophoclean tragedy as well. Tony develops as a fusion of Oedipus/Augustus, and in the cannon of classic myth making, it's not so much the ramifications of battle, as the effects of family relationships that torment, haunt and expose his vulnerabilities. As his nephew and right-hand man, Christopher Moltisanti (Michael Imperioli), is told by the inner Soprano mafia circle after having nightmares about a man he'd just whacked, the more you kill, the less they chase you in your dreams ('The Legend of Tennessee Moltisanti' 1×8). In other words, the nature of Tony's work eventually takes on a kind of normality, while his emotional entanglements adopt an alien quality that he finds difficult to confront. These tensions become his most reliable source of chaos and stress.

Although Tony never commits incest directly, the incest-complex is a marked feature of the series. By not accepting his need for renewal, he is unable to symbolically move through the process of merging (or allowing for dialogue between) contradictory psychological positions to develop a deeper self-awareness. Unable to negotiate the coniunctio, Tony remains caught at the point of regression to the incest motif, so that instead of moving through to a sense of libidinal transformation, he only ever experiences the *desire* for rebirth.

This is of course only one limited aspect of Chase's intricate rendering of Tony Soprano, but it's pretty clear that Tony wants to sexually 'nail' what he can't grapple with internally – the mother/daughter other. In the pilot, the first and much discussed image of Tony is shot through the spread legs of a naked female statue in Dr. Melfi's waiting room (oddly enough we don't see this sculpture again). In a shrewd summation of the psychoanalytic dance begun here with his upward gaze at the vulva, Anna Dzenis (2004: 83–84) writes that 'the relationship between Tony and Melfi seems to repeat the relationship between Tony and the statue'. The uncomfortable gestation period he experiences in her circular, womb-like office continues to play itself out through each season. This is a man who isn't trying to cut the cord, as much as retrace it.

Code name 'Princess'

Meadow Soprano, a.k.a. 'Princess' by the ever-thwarted FBI surveillance team, along with her grandmother Livia, is Tony's ultimate Achilles' heel and the marker of his worth. Both women are intertwined shadow/mirrors of each other and the only figures able to direct, misdirect or stifle Tony's libidinal energy. Even early in the series, as Tony sits in his darkened kitchen, the belly of his domestic 'whale', stirred by the possibility of being jailed for murder, his dialogue with Meadow is illuminating: 'I tell people you're like your mother, but you're all me. Nothing gets by you and I know you think I'm a hypocrite . . .'. 'Sometimes,' she says in return, 'we're all hypocrites' ('Bust Out' 2×10). Donatelli and Alward (2002: 69) acknowledge Meadow's increasing complexity, sexuality and darkness as she matures through the series: 'Always close to her "grandma," she is skillfully manipulative and makes the system work for her; perhaps, she will toughen up even more to replace the departed Livia'.

Meadow is not as strongly featured in the early seasons as her mother or grandmother, but her presence is felt through the uses and misuses of Tony's goomahs. After Livia's death in 'Proshai Livushka' (3×2) she develops a darker persona that reveals a knowingness of, and simpatico to, her father's world. Not only does Meadow inherit Livia's cunning, but also her intellect, education and growing urbanity make her a potentially more formidable personality. She's as genetically and socially prepared for power as Tony's one-time business acquaintance, the beautiful Sicilian Mafia boss Annalisa (Sofia Milos), daughter of ailing Don Zi Vittorio ('Commendatori' 2×4).

Although Meadow is aware that Tony is involved in organized crime, his position and activities aren't made clear to her. The way she negotiates her affection for him, through her accumulating encounters with his mafia loyalties and her Ivy-league college life, is testament to the complex nature of their ties to each other. As Stein (1984) writes:

> In spite of the underlying soul-mate bond between father and daughter, the child is unable to experience her wholeness in relationship to him because of the incestuous triangle. Her relationship to him becomes increasingly fragmented and frustrating as she matures. The same pattern occurs with a male child in relationship to his mother.
>
> (Stein 1984: 30)

Unlike Livia, I would argue, Meadow is emotionally bound to her father, and like Carmela, creates blind spots to accommodate this connectedness. But throughout the series up until season five at least, while these blind spots gradually break down, her loyalty to Tony increases. 'You are the dad, the template for future lovers,' Dr. Melfi tells him in characteristic psychoanalytic-speak. 'She loves me,' he says, 'I know that, since she was a tiny baby' ('No Show' 4×2).

Tony periodically reiterates his love and concern for his daughter, but is also quick to disparage or 'whack' unsuitable boyfriends. When he orders the death of ex-boyfriend Jackie Aprile Jr. (Jason Cerbone), Meadow slips into a depression, not so much out of grief it seems, but because her father's world is becoming more transparent. In season five, when boyfriend Finn (Will Janowitz), having taken on part-time work at one of Tony's construction sites, confronts her with the venal and violent underbelly of this mafia front, her response allows us to see what was always suspected of her real loyalties. She shows no surprise at the assault Finn has witnessed nor any sympathy for the victim, rather she disparages his concern and supports the aggressive action by validating her 'other family's' codes of justice:

> You know you talk about these guys like it's an anthropology class, but the truth is they bring certain modes of conflict resolution from all the way back in the old country, from the poverty of the Mezzogiorno, where all higher authority was corrupt.'
>
> ('Unidentified Black Males' 5×9)

This is perhaps the most potent example of Meadow's complicity with her father's life and her mafia ancestry. Unlike Carmela whose desire and conscience remain compromised, Meadow is as smart and as potentially powerful as Livia. She knows exactly what she does, what she wants, and how to get it, but while Livia could only ever aspire to be a malevolent influence on her husband, brother-in-law 'Uncle Junior' and son, one suspects that Meadow would never be content in the background.

When asked directly by an adolescent psychiatrist if she was molested by her father ('No Show' 4×2), Meadow is bemused, and the question itself seems absurd given Tony's indulgent fathering. But throughout *The Sopranos* an incestuous link *is* thinly veiled. In the most blatant example of this, Tony contemplates an affair with his nephew's fiancée (niece of sorts) Adriana (Drea de Matteo), an act that, as Dr. Melfi reminds him, is akin to 'symbolic incest' ('Irregular around the Margins' 5×5). Although this incident is another symptom of his regression, Tony's goomahs or mistresses, higher up in the pecking order than his prostitutes, one-nighters, or dancers at the 'Bada Bing' strip club where the mafia 'crew' conduct their business, even more sharply reflect his relationship with Meadow, and as will be discussed later, Livia. While Tony tires of his 24-year-old Russian goomah, Irina Peltsin (Oksana Lada), her replacements begin to take on similar characteristics to Meadow. Not only do their swarthy looks, uniform long dark hair, defiance, and dedication to him act as signifiers for 'the daughter', but Tony also begins to fuse and eroticize female intellect and independence, qualities intrinsic to Meadow and Dr. Melfi.

Tony's involvement with Irina, girl-like and needy with no means of support or skill base, soon ends when Meadow leaves the family home and begins to develop her autonomy. It can be argued that Irina was no longer a proxy figure for Meadow. Tony's goomahs from season three on, the Mercedes Benz sales rep Gloria Trillo (Annabella Sciorra) and art saleswoman Valentina la Paz (Leslie Bega), reflect this quality of liberation, marked in Dr. Melfi (who he sexually fantasizes and dreams about), but more particularly Meadow. 'She can do whatever she wants', he proudly whispers to Carmela in bed, 'She's becoming a wonderful woman Carm, smart, beautiful, independent, [the] woman that you created. Isn't that what you dreamed about?' ('Eloise' 4×12). The image he describes is telling at this point in the series when Carmela, wanting to leave Tony, is dreaming of taking on this persona herself. But as we see in season five after a painful separation, they reunite, and the momentary independence that lured Tony back is once again reserved for Meadow, Dr. Melfi and the goomahs. The synthesis of daughter, lover and psychological catalyst (Dr. Melfi) brings us again to the incest image.

Apart from eroticizing the autonomy of these more 'sophisticated' women, Tony also plays out his incestuous desire through the various strippers-cum-hookers who work at the Bada Bing, always referred to as 'girls'. The age of these women varies, but many of the topless and heavily implanted/augmented dancers featured either working the raised dance floor poles or the customers seated at stage level below, appear to be only a few years older than Meadow, particularly in her later Columbia University years. Tony's offhand sexual banter and occasional grabs, kisses and cuddles with the Bada girls, coupled with our knowledge that they sexually service the Soprano mafia family on request, become a source of tension and discomfort during his more intimate interactions with Meadow. This is most noticeable at the family pool-side party ('Marco Polo' 5×8) where he kisses, grabs and cuddles her on his knee. Even though their 'horseplay' has no overt sexual intent, the Bada girls are an invisible presence.

When Meadow's boyfriend Jackie (pre being whacked) is caught in a compromising position with a Bada girl at the club ('To Save Us All from Satan's Power' 3×10), Tony brutally assaults him, offended at Jackie's betrayal of Meadow, but also perhaps affronted by the way that this infidelity connects the stripper to his daughter. Even earlier in the first season, this parallel is clearly established as Tony and his 'crew' find out that their daughters' soccer coach has been having sex with one of Meadow's friends ('Boca' 1×9). Instead of whacking the coach (the general consensus of the outraged crew), the episode ends with Tony watching a news report on the coach's arrest following an anonymous tip-off from a young female student, presumably a Baba girl set up by Tony to make the call. At this point we are made aware of the blurring boundaries between these two highly segregated and hierarchically positioned young female groups throughout the series. We are also alerted to the possible psychological interchangeability of the Bada girls and the daughters/princesses.

If the Bada girls are more or less Tony's sexual 'fast-food', while his goomahs sexually reflect his two main female role models, Dr. Melfi and Meadow, we need to ask why female beauty, intellect and independence has Tony in thrall. Simplistically one could argue that he desires these qualities in himself, caught as he is in the subterfuge of mafia politics as the paragon of obligation, loyalty and expectation: 'the sad clown' as he calls himself. I would venture to say that rather than the incest image being as obvious as this, it is fused, as Meadow is fused, with Tony's mother Livia, the shadow of beauty, intellect and independence. It seems as if he is trying to relocate *and* redeem his mother in an attempt to transform the libinal energy that remains stuck and frustrated. Looked at in this way, coniunctio with Meadow via goomah/stripper proxy, can be seen as an attempt to unclog his libido, stifled by the malignant Livia, and reconnect with the positive mother energy reflected in Meadow.

While the Bada girls and goomahs are substitutes for Meadow, Meadow is in turn a substitute for Livia. Perhaps the most telling episode that makes this connection is 'Isabella' (1×12). Dosed up on Prozac and lithium for severe depression, Tony fantasizes an encounter with an attractive Italian exchange student 'Isabella' (Maria Grazia Cucinotta), temporarily boarding next door. Not physically unlike Annalisa, the Sicilian Mafia boss, Tony is attracted to Isabella, but despite his desire there's no sexual contact; rather he dreams of her in an old Italian cottage, nursing a small baby she calls Anthony.

Dr. Melfi jumps on the dream as a mother/son image; a means of replacing Livia (who at this stage in the series is planning to have Tony killed) with an independent, educated and nurturing figure. Three women from his life entwine to form the imagined sexualized mother/daughter figure Isabella conjured here in Tony's fantasy and dream: Meadow (in the way he frames her as a young adult student), Annalise (because of her Italian background and exotic appearance) and Livia (in the mothering aspects of the dream). The incest image becomes clear. The desire to couple with the mother/daughter in order to be reborn/renewed supports one of the central themes of the series and is appropriately held at the imaginal level in this episode. The following quote from Jung helps make sense of the import of this fantasy:

> Moreover it must be pointed out that the basis of the 'incestuous' desire is not cohabitation, but, as every sun myth shows, the strange idea of becoming the child again, of returning to the parental shelter, and of entering into the mother in order to be reborn through her. But the way to this goal lies in incest, i.e., the necessity of finding some way into the mother's body. One of the simplest ways would be to impregnate the mother and beget oneself in identical form all over again. But here the incest prohibition intervenes; consequently the sun myths and rebirth myths devise every conceivable kind of mother-analogy for the purpose

> of canalizing the libido into new forms and effectively prevent it from regressing into actual incest.
>
> (*CW* 5, para. 332)

Non voglio fottere mia madre!

'I do not want to fuck my mother,' Tony says in a fit of exasperation at Dr. Melfi's continued probes into his mother-complex, 'You should have seen her in that house dress with that hairnet, the conversation would be over in two seconds' ('In Camelot' 5×7). As Mitchell (2000: 160) argues, from a Melfi perspective, 'Except for ego psychologists and Lacanians, for whom the position of father remains supreme, the relationship with the mother has been the dominant area for theorization right up to the present day'. Contrary to Freud, for whom the authority of the mother, literally and symbolically, remained subordinate to that of the father, Jung attributed a great deal of power to the mother archetype and imago, and argued that, ' "Entry into the mother" then means establishing a relationship between the ego and the unconscious' (*CW* 5, para. 459) – analytical psychology's primary aim.

In a similar vein to Kristeva's (1982) configuration of the abject (Chapter 6), as that which signifies the terrifying and yet much desired pull toward the symbiotic fusion with mother, Jung also acknowledges this powerful and primary longing for reunion as intrinsic to the human condition. He even referred to the desire for mother as 'the prime object of the unconscious' (*CW* 5, para. 465). Along with Johann Jakob Bachofen (1815–1887) before him, Jung favoured the instinctual and positive nature of seeking the symbolic mother image, 'the creative aspect of the unconscious' (*CW* 5, para. 182), in order to experience the transformation, transition or rebirth that he saw as central to the hero myth. While he wrote extensively on the positive and negative/devouring aspects of the archetypal mother (Chapter 5), he saw nothing intrinsically 'dangerous' in the desire for a symbolic return to the maternal matrix: 'The mother-imago, however, represents the unconscious, and it is as much a vital necessity for the unconscious to be joined to the conscious as it is for the latter not to lose contact with the unconscious' (*CW* 5, para. 457).

Because of Livia's impoverished mothering, narcissism and inability to form intimate connections, Tony becomes stultified by his cruel and shadowy mother imago. Although Livia, the malevolent Soprano matriarch who never wavers in her contempt or self-absorption, has much in common with Etienne Chatiliez's 'Danielle' (*Tatie Danielle*, 1990), she's more closely related to Graves' Livia. Livia Drusilla Julia Augusta, Empress of Rome (58 BC–AD 29) wife of Octavian, later Emperor Augustus, ruled with him as the mouth to his ear for fifty-two years. Her name, according to Graves, 'is connected with the Latin word which means Malignity' (1979: 32).

In DVD season two's interview with Peter Bogdanovich, Chase acknowledges his homage to Graves' Livia, even including a scene where Tony discusses with his 'Uncle Junior' the merits of Caesar Augustus' popularity, fairness and willingness to distribute his wealth with the people, as a means of teaching Junior (boss at this early stage in the series) the value of democratic leadership ('Pax Soprana' 1×6). The names Meadow and Carmela also have resonance in Graves' work, as versions of Claudius' first love, the young Medullina Camilla, murdered on their wedding day (Graves 1979: 90).

Like Livia Augusta, Livia Soprano is just about the only one who has the ear of Uncle Junior, even to the point of ordering Tony's death and teaching his nephew Christopher 'a lesson' (code for mock assassination warning). As Joseph Walker (2002) writes, Livia does all her scheming without ever vocalizing 'a command, or even such a suggestion; her agency is expressed through silence, analogy, innuendo' (Walker 2002: 118). Throughout the first season she plotted to have Tony killed because of her bitterness at being put in a nursing home and her disappointment at his meetings with Dr. Melfi. In a flashback sequence of Tony's childhood she yells at him, 'I could stick this fork in your eye'. The scene is rounded off in Medea-eque histrionics, when learning of her husband's aspirations to buy into a supper club, she screams, 'I'd rather smother them [the children] than take them to the theatre' ('Down Neck' 1×7). This is the kind of high melodrama that Meadow reproduces in her fight with boyfriend Finn, as she convinces him not to do a 'runner' after he's been terrified by Vito, a mob heavy at Tony's construction site who is coming onto him. Brushing aside Finn's anxiety and Vito's sexual menace, she throws herself into fits of self-pity until exasperated and intimidated he says, 'Why don't we just get married?' ('Unidentified Black Males' 5×9)

For Tony, 'going back to mother' is an abject and raw enterprise, fraught with the fear of being devoured and sucked into the abyss of Livia's blackness. So potent is his need for coniunctio, and so unable is he to totally hold this at the symbolic level, that he takes the archetype beyond internal imagery and enacts mother/son coitus through sexual relationships with mother proxies. It is then not so surprising, that in a bid to usurp Livia's power over him, Tony throws himself into his father's Alpha-male obsessed mafia subculture, a hotbed of sexual hypocrisy and machismo.

Despite this overcompensation for Livia's castrating presence, enough to trigger his panic attacks and fainting fits, Tony's emulation of his father's lifestyle, accelerates through the series. The underlying subtext of *The Sopranos*, then, might accord with Bachofen's (1967) summation of the power of the maternal that he details in his thesis on 'mother-right':

> The mother's connection with the child is based on a material relationship, it is accessible to sense perception and remains always a natural truth. But the father as begetter presents an entirely different aspect. Standing in no visible relation to the child, he can never, even in the marital relation, cast off a certain fictive character. Belonging to the

> offspring only through the mediation of the mother, he always appears as the remoter potency.
>
> (Bachofen 1967: 109)

Tony's father ran his own mafia crew, romanced his goomahs, and bullied his way through New Jersey, but by the time he died Livia had turned him into, as Tony tells Dr. Melfi, 'a squeaking little gerbil' ('The Sopranos' 1×1). Throughout the series his henpecked father remains a romantic and sentimental fiction, 'the remoter potency' and perhaps a prophetic warning for Tony. Livia, though, is always a devouring and immortal psychological reality, incarnated over and over again in his relationships, particularly with his goomah Gloria Trillo.

In 'Amour Fou' (3×12), Tony's heated fling with Gloria, the tempestuous Mercedes Benz saleswoman, is played out like an incestuous mother–daughter–lover triangle. While embodying the qualities Tony fosters in Meadow (autonomy, savvy, intelligence and urbanity), Gloria also, and more potently, incarnates Livia's nihilism and egocentrism. The hysterical arguments between Tony and Gloria, sparked by her masochistic need to draw him into conflict and live out a self-constructed victim persona, reflect Tony's dealings with Livia. Dr. Melfi picks up on the connection. She intimates that Tony is fatally attracted to Gloria because of her likeness to Livia. The incest by proxy coniunctio doesn't work though. He ends his connection with her and she eventually commits suicide. Tony is unable to shift both the psychic energy that Liva always manages to curb, and the shadowy mother imago that remains linked to her. Jung wrote:

> The paradox lies in the fact that, like the mother who gives life and then takes it away again as the 'terrible' or 'devouring' mother, the father apparently lives a life of unbridled instinct and yet is the living embodiment of the law that thwarts instinct . . . the paternal law is directed against incest with all the violence and fury of uninhibited instinct.
>
> (*CW* 5, para. 396)

As the paragon of patriarchal sensibility, Tony cannot cede to the positive mother image. Although Carmela presents a more genuine role model of mothering, she's no match for the formidable Livia, who has become so bound up in Tony's mother imago, that her physical and psychological presence is fused.

This fear of symbolically 'going back to mother' is palpable given all we know of Livia: 'To be "entwined" or embraced is the same as to be "devoured," which . . . means entering into the mother's womb' (*CW* 5, para. 425). This takes us back to the first image we have of Tony, shot between female legs in the waiting room. His driven incest-by-proxy relationships, attempts to shift the libido and move through the process of coniunctio transformation, are, in

Dr Melfi's womb-like office, gradually and painfully directed back to the symbolic level where they belong (as in the Isabella fantasy/dream). 'What happens in here is like taking a shit', Tony tells Dr. Melfi. 'OK,' she says, 'although I'd prefer to think of it more like childbirth' ('Unidentified Black Males' 5×9).

To capture the heart of Tony's penchant for the incestuous over five seasons we would need to spend more time unpicking Chase's complex text. I've only scratched the surface here. Tony's emotional and psychological immobility becomes even more obvious if we apply Jung's rationale on incest further by microscopically detailing the way in which Meadow, Dr. Melfi, the Bada girls and the goomahs function as clues to help Tony work through the labyrinth of his mother-complex.

It has to be said that apart from the more peripheral Bada strippers, these characters are given strongly developed presences beyond Tony's serrated path through the series. Nevertheless, the mythic sense of renewal, rebirth and regeneration is largely wrapped up (often allegorically) in forms of sexual expression, and these characters are *all* either directly or indirectly sexualized in relation to him. Finding a way to energize the libido causes Tony a great deal of distress. Because he tries to access this 'life-force' through the mother/daughter/wife/one-nighter/mistress combo, these women become attached to his suffering. In light of the shit/rebirth analogy, they are his laxatives – the key to effective waste management.

The next chapter continues with the incest theme begun in Chapter 7, but in an umbilical whiplash back to the primal mother, Cronenberg's *Spider* challenges us by inverting the power play. Instead of a parent's misdirected libido generating the tension of the narrative, a child's stifled psychic energy becomes the pivotal perversion. The boy, Spider, struggles with Oedipal tensions as much as Tony, but his desire and revulsion toward the mother/other, takes the Madonna/whore cliché beyond anything Chase allows Tony to dream up. While Tony may scream that he does 'not want to fuck' his mother, there's no doubt that Spider does.

Chapter 9

Motherly and slatternly creatures

Spider

> You frighten me, Mother, but I like being afraid, since the more afraid I am, the more I love you.
>
> George Bataille, 'My Mother' (2000: 119)

As much as Tony Soprano talks of his mother as 'dead' after he learns she put a hit out on him, David Cronenberg's *Spider* (2002) takes this rejection of mother as monstrous/desired other to its matricidal ends. Much like *Twin Peaks*' sexual brutality and *The Sopranos*' daughter/mother proxy dalliances, *Spider*'s Dennis Cleg (a.k.a. Spider) is also held in thrall by the underlying incest archetype. This chapter dissects the incest imago as even more primal/maternal, by looking at the unbearable tensions created in the coupling of Spider's emerging sexuality and the uneasy desire he feels for his mother. As he reinvents childhood images, we are able to see this desire for and revulsion of mother–son union. Like Tony, Spider as a boy (Bradley Hall) constructs mother as a devouring force, but unlike Tony, it's the overwhelming terror of sexuality that lies at the heart of his complex. While Tony's inability to understand his incest/mother exposes his puer (eternal boy) aspect, Cronenberg's Spider is a much more explicit example of this retardation.

Leaving a psychiatric institution to board in a men's halfway house, the middle-aged adult Spider (Ralph Fiennes) traces the landmarks of his childhood. Although we see the way that he remembers interacting with his parents in these spaces, we can never be sure if these images are flashes of his past or complete fabrications. Through this labyrinth of plays on memory, imagination and psychosis, Spider painfully begins to acknowledge his most deeply repressed secret; that as a child he intentionally devised an elaborate scheme to murder his mother. Various takes on childhood sexuality are interwoven to create a world that exposes the energy-consuming process of suppressing the unacceptable.

The psychologically claustrophobic *Spider* pivots on the pioneering psychoanalytic view that shadow material is repressed until the ego is able to cope with its rise to consciousness. Nevertheless, it's important to keep in context the mythic nature of Cronenberg and writer Patrick McGrath's text, for as McNally (2003: 275) insists, the idea 'that the mind protects itself by repressing or dissociating memories of trauma, rendering them inaccessible to awareness, is a piece of psychiatric folklore devoid of convincing empirical support'. Even Cronenberg confesses that after reading Richard Webster's (1995) *Why Freud was Wrong*, he doesn't take the idea of repression seriously either (Hoberman 2003: 52).

Despite the freedom that Cronenberg wanted for Spider's interior complexity, he also acknowledges the 'many Freudian resonances in the movie' particularly the Oedipus complex (*Weaving the Web*, 2002). In this chapter, though, I'm more interested in moving past the Freudian model to the Jungian incest archetype as a way of negotiating another, perhaps less overt, reading of the film. Louise Kaplan's (1991) take on perversity in *Female Perversions: The Temptations of Emma Bovary* holds some relevance to Spider's fear of, and inability to, navigate his mother and incest complexes, when she argues that:

> A man who is driven to a perverse fantasy is terrified of open, ambiguous spaces that remind him of his wish to be swallowed up in the womb, and he is frightened also of soft, friendly things that invite him to cling and remind him of his shameful feminine wishes.
>
> (Kaplan 1991: 74)

True to Kaplan's generalization, the adult Spider *is* terrified of the engulfing 'ambiguous' spaces of his neighbourhood that threaten to take him back to the desired and feared matrix of rebirth. As a child we never see him embrace or cling to his mother and yet his need to be the sole object of her affections becomes almost pathological. The only physical contact between them is his affectionate brushing of her hair. Cold, distant, and safe in the cocoon of his imagination, Spider, as a child and adult, is wary of the *affect* physical tenderness, trust or intimacy might produce in him.

Rorschach, 'Dog and Beggar', gasworks

The opening credit sequence of *Spider*, underscored by a maternal Elizabethan melody, is made up of a series of water-marked/stained/rotted wallpaper patches mimicking Hermann Rorschach's inkblot test. The abstract images fused with deliberate allusions to decrepitude, psychological disturbance, female sexuality, the womb and birth, combined with the angelic/spiritual dimensions of the score, introduce us to the key themes of the film. Having been released from the 'asylum' (as the psychiatric hospital is archaically referred to), the adult Spider begins his life in a dilapidated halfway house for released patients run by Mrs. Wilkinson (Lynn Redgrave).

Although the film is set in the present day, the sparsely furnished boarding house gives the impression of an earlier period, as though nothing has been done to maintain or update the building since the 1950s. The wear and decay of the intervening years reflects Spider's inner and outer state of displaced and arrested time. Fiennes shapes Spider as an almost pre-Oedipal figure, who writes in illegible self-styled script, has no articulate speech, bathes in the fetal position, and is haunted by images from his childhood. The hints that Cronenberg offers in relation to the puzzle of Spider's intricate web spinning, like Lynch and Nolan's films (Chapters 3 and 4), can be deciphered only in hindsight. The multiple shirts Spider wears and newspapers he wraps around his body suggest the many overlapping layers of real, distorted and fabricated memories that shield his fragile soul. As fellow boarder Terrance (John Neville) says, 'Clothes maketh the man. The less there is of a man the more the need for the clothes'.

The most haunting clue to the jigsaw of Spider's past is the recurring image of the looming gasworks that he sees from his bedroom window, outside the boarding house, and along the canal where he wanders. Again Terrance offers a narrative voice to his silence and internal distress: 'Gasworks got you have they? I'm not surprised, nasty stuff gas.' The design of Spider's small room, bare except for a single iron bed, chest of drawers and bedside table, lends the small, hissing gas heater a more imposing presence as a conduit for the invisible monster that takes on gigantic proportions in Spider's psyche: 'I smell gas', he says as he sniffs the heater, strips to his underwear, and wraps newspaper around his waist with string as a sort of protective device, or as Cronenberg says in his DVD commentary, to stop the gas escaping from his body.

What we learn at the end of the film is that as a child Spider murdered his mother by attaching an elaborate string pulley from his bedroom to a lever of the gas stove in his family kitchen, so that he could gas his mother while she dozed after a night at the pub with his father. This is the climatic memory that Spider is trying to unearth by revisiting landmarks of his childhood: the family house, the Dog and Beggar pub, and his father's garden plot. He illegibly records distorted impressions and memories from these sites in a secret diary that he guards as if its discovery would be his undoing. The scenes of his childhood are coded as flashbacks to the past and/or embellished memories (we are never sure) by the adult Spider (Fiennes) who always appears in the background of the action, looking on as if both observing and orchestrating these memory grabs.

Ikto-mi and maya

In our first encounter with boy Spider via one of these many 'observed' scenes, the child sits in the kitchen with his mother (Miranda Richardson) weaving a 'cat's cradle' from a length of string he manipulates between his hands and spread fingers. As the film progresses and each childhood scenario unfolds toward its climactic revelation, imagined by the adult Spider who either stands or sits scribbling the reconstructed/fantasy event in his diary to preserve it as a kind of reality, we become aware of the child's 'weaving' skills. His ability to fuse fact and fiction by projecting anxieties onto his parents culminates in a web of fabricated reality that ultimately ensnares him in a chaotic network of sexual signs.

The evocation of trickster throughout the film has strong resonances with Leonard's trickster function in *Memento* (Chapter 4). For like Leonard, although trickster can be utilized for one's own purposes, the archetype itself as a function that trips us up to incite change, remains unconscious and uncontained by the ego. While boy Spider may think he can manipulate his trickster aspect, the way the motif unsettles and traps him in later life shows us just how vulnerable the ego is to unconscious energies. Cronenberg's insistence that Spider is a fictional, intuitive and creative invention doesn't negate the character as a contemporary mythic trickster figure. As Radin (1972) notes in his analysis of North American trickster cycles:

> The Winnebago word for trickster is *Wakdjunkaga*, which means *the tricky one*. The corresponding term for him in Poca is *ishtinike*, in the kindred Osage, *itsike* and in Dakota-Sioux, *ikto-mi*. The meaning of the Ponca and Osage words is unknown, that of the Dakota is *spider*.
>
> (Radin 1972: 132)

We have to ask what Spider is trying to 'trip up' in himself. The most obvious focus of the film is the way in which heterosexual desire becomes located and locked into the mother figure. It seems as though sexual arousal to boy Spider is an entirely foreign and threatening experience that the trickster function works consciously keep at bay *and* bring to awareness, so that he can loosen his libido from this point of fixation. Jung wrote that spiders can sometimes function in dreams as symbols of an unfamiliar reality which might translate as psychological material incapable of breaking through to consciousness (*CW* 10, para. 671). With this idea in mind, *Spider* can be interpreted as a mythic or dream narrative of the alienated world of arrested sexual development, where the incest archetype remains forever attached to the mother imago because it is unable to shift into the next stage of coniunctio (the discourse of opposites often illustrated through sexual metaphors).

As in the dream imagery of *Mulholland Drive*, the concept of maya, or as Jung called it the 'projection making factor' (*CW* 9ii, para. 20), also pervades the themes and structure of *Spider*, particularly in its relationship to conflicts with, illusions of, and allusions to, 'the feminine'. In Vedic and post-Vedic frameworks, maya was intrinsic to creation and transformation, as the power to transform and an energy that could activate shape-shifting (Pintchman 1994: 89). Its ability to create new forms alludes to notions of mother. As mentioned in Chapter 8, Jung accorded enormous weight to the archetypal mother in both her positive and 'terrible' aspects, arguing that she could draw 'him [the son] into life with her Maya – and not only into life's reasonable and useful aspects, but into its frightful paradoxes and ambivalences where good and evil, success and ruin, hope and despair, counterbalance one another' (*CW* 9ii, para. 24) This 'drawing in' is of course determined by the child's projection of, and relationship to the motif, making Spider's various maya-like projections of mother a transparent key into his shadow pathologies.

The nickname 'Spider' given to him by his mother because of his fascination with spiders and webs, seems to initially suggest clichéd ideas of arachnids as phobic symbols of distress tied into the idea of mothers/women as potential castrators/devourers. Films like *Black Widow* (1987) and *Along Came a Spider* (2001) for example, play on the feminine shadow as a seductive, treacherous, calculating, overwhelming and toxic. While Cronenberg too plays on these primal hooks, his spider symbolism has a broader scope. The boy and adult Spider's fascination with webs, as metaphors for his multilayered realties and arrested psychological state, is also coupled with vulnerability and death as we see from his favourite childhood story:

Mrs. Cleg: . . . if you knew where to look you could find the spider's web bags.
Boy Spider: What happened to her after she laid her eggs?
Mrs. Cleg: You like this bit don't you? She just crawled away without looking back once.
Boy Spider: And then she died?
Mrs. Cleg: Her work was done. She had no more silk left, it was all dried up and empty.

This exchange pre-empts the death of the spider mother/Mrs. Cleg and underpins the death/rebirth motif as the mother who can take and give life and whose life is metaphorically taken over when she gives birth.

But this cuts both ways, for Spider is also creator, destroyer and destroyed. He's a child who kills and is psychologically condemned by the act; doomed like Ovid's Arachne, to forever spin inside the sticky framework of his own cunning. Spider's downfall begins when his sexual libido/psychic energy becomes fixed to the mother figure or more specifically the fusion of mother and shadow. Mrs. Cleg who bears this projection loses all identity and agency in line with Jung's theory of libidinal regression: 'The libido that will not flow into life at the right time regresses to the mythical world of archetypes, where it activates images which, since the remotest times, have expressed the non-human life of the gods' (*CW* 5, para. 466). Cronenberg and McGrath have highlighted this warping of the mother as projected sexualized other by casting Miranda Richardson as both Mrs. Cleg, and an excessively sexualized specter of boy Spider's imagination, Yvonne Morganson, a character who Cronenberg in his DVD commentary repeatedly refers to as 'the slut'.

Yvonne the slut

This projection began to take shape in Spider's imagination after a flashback encounter with three prostitutes at the Dog and Beggar pub where he was sent to fetch his father, Bill (Gabriel Byrne). Yvonne (Alison Egan), the most dominant of the group, a loud platinum blonde with figure-hugging clothes and 'easy access' unbuttoned blouse, begins to tease him, as he stands transfixed, shocked and turned on by her overt sexuality. In a ribald attempt to both embarrass and excite him, she exposes her breast, laughing at his humiliation as he runs from the trio to his father. From this point on, the blonde woman is reinvented as a split-off version of the mother, with Miranda Richardson, still playing Mrs. Cleg, now transformed into the brassy, monstrous Yvonne. In her paper 'The Teacher's Breast', Jane Gallop sees 'a' breast as an idealized symbol of maternal nurture, opposed to 'breasts' which she reasons are more sexually suggestive (Gallop 1994: 11). This sheds some light on Spider's synthesis of the whore and mother's breast as sexual *and* maternal.

This blurring of boundaries is reinforced by a later flashback scene where Bill, out for a night at the pub with his wife (Richardson), suggestively eyes Yvonne (now also Richardson) in the lounge area. Yvonne, a cartoon 'scrubber', with her pointed bra, faux leopard skin coat, jagged black teeth, lecherous cackle and white-bleached hair, is original sin incarnate. She is a presence embodying the stereotypical signs of impurity, sleaze, corruption and dirt, which for Mary Douglas (1996) signals disorder. In her thesis, the idea of 'dirt as matter out of place' indicates a rupture in the systems of structure that we build around ourselves, so that, 'our pollution behaviour is the reaction which condemns any object or idea likely to confuse or contradict cherished classifications' (Douglas 1996: 37). The emergence of Yvonne as a split-off 'dirty' projection of the sexualized devouring mother (matter out of place) also coincides with boy Spider's burgeoning awareness of his mother's sexuality and the sexual feelings she arouses in him.

Having 'lured' Bill, a plumber, to come and 'fixed her pipes for her' (a line rich in innuendo that a child in the 1950s and 1960s might have picked up), Yvonne, stroking her cat (pussy/genitals) seduces him as they stand bantering in front of her decrepit toilet pretending to examine 'the pipes'. The setting is of course a blatant signifier for Yvonne as a form of refuse, waste, abjection. They later meet in the pub and drunkenly walk along the canal. After Yvonne masturbates Bill, she moves toward the water bank and sullenly shakes out her cum-wetted hand. At this point, Bill is shot with his back to camera, but as he turns to face us, we see the adult Spider. It is as though he has been experiencing Bill's pleasure in Yvonne, replacing the father to have the mother in an overtly Oedipal play.

This desire that Yvonne-as-sexualized-mother imago evokes in the adult Spider is once again made clear in a present-day scene where, taking a short break from his outdoor gardening, he pulls out of his small tin case an old 1960s soft porn double shot of a topless woman. He covers each figure with his hands and as he slides his fingers down from the images in an erotic shudder, Yvonne's face is grafted to the model's body.

As the film develops, Spider's memories become more transparent as fantasies. After Mrs. Cleg/mother catches Bill and Yvonne having sex in Bill's garden plot shed, he kills her with a spade and buries her in his vegetable patch. From here on Yvonne takes the place of Mrs. Cleg, moving into the family home and adopting her wardrobe. The mother imago has now become totally sexualized and devouring. 'It's true he murdered your mother,' Yvonne tells boy Spider, 'try to think of me as your mother now'. This total absorption of mother by Yvonne triggers boy Spider's rigging of string to the gas stove and the consequent murder of his mother.

As this memory emerges through Spider's exploration of his past and the fantasies of his childhood, we see the Yvonne figure infiltrating his present life in the boarding house. Unable to kill off a specter/projection, she takes over the role of Mrs. Wilkinson, with Richardson at first adopting Redgrave's portrayal and then gradually introducing Yvonne into the characterization, until, as with Mrs. Cleg, Yvonne has totally consumed Mrs. Wilkinson. Once again Spider tries to kill her off by holding a hammer and chisel to the sleeping Mrs. Wilkinson/Yvonne's head, but as the memory of matricide begins to surface, Mrs. Wilkinson, now Redgrave once again, turns to confront him. 'What have you done?' she says.

It's not too much of a leap, given all the Freudian tip-offs along the way, to assume that boy Spider has a fairly heavily entrenched Oedipal complex. That is, desire for the mother cannot be actualized because of the incest taboo, and is therefore split off as the sexual carnivore Yvonne, a vagina dentate (toothed vagina) with the twinkle of castration in her eye. Following the classic Freudian approach, in Cronenberg's fairly Freudian-faithful myth, is highly appropriate, but a more archetypal reading is able to offer a further twist to our understanding of the incest dilemma.

Blocked regression of the libido

Early on in the boarding house scenes Terrence mumbles about his African travel experiences: 'Now there's a dark continent for you', he says. This cheeky inclusion of the Freudian catch cry for the *supposed* mystery of female sexuality helps us to pinpoint Spider's agony. Although Jung's work on women/the feminine was caught in sexist clichés of the early twentieth century, he was entirely comfortable with the regenerating power of the mother archetype as a necessary channel for the development of Self-awareness. Having established Richardson as Mrs. Cleg/mother before her transmutation, we can understand the projection of Yvonne as an inflation of the sexually devouring 'terrible mother' archetype to which Spider has attached his libido.

Jung champions Freud's rare use of myth to validate the authenticity of the incest image as an innate psychological reality, but bitingly adds that the Oedipal drama is 'by no means the only one' (*CW* 3, para. 564), and should not, because of its male-oriented approach to the incest-complex, be held in higher esteem than other vast mythic incest allegories. Rather than fight the natural desire to regress to the maternal matrix, or succumb to the power of the mother imago or archetype, Jung argued that it should be encouraged, with the incest taboo in place, not to negate the desire or power of the maternal, but to prevent incestuous acting out. He argues that myth, religion and the unconscious all echo with metaphors for this desired return to the womb that allows for a regression to the incest image and a transformation of the libido (*CW* 5, para. 313). He even reasons that the relationship of sponsus (Christ) to sponsa (Church) is analogous to a sacred marriage of the alchemists' coniunctio templates Sol and Luna, whereby the son re-enters the womb in order to be reborn (*CW* 14, para. 106).

It's then not such a stretch to argue, in purely mythical terms, that Spider desires rebirth. The most potent image of this need for return and transformation is a single shot of his angular adult body, curled (fetal position) in the reddish water/embryonic fluid of his bath, a stock vessel of coniunctio that alchemists called the 'womb' (*CW* 14, para. 75). Because the archetypal mother is such a powerful, and necessary, presence in Jung's work as a symbol for the unconscious and the oscillation between return to, and separation from, this source of nourishment, he claimed it must also have a considerable role in childhood development and trauma. He even went so far as to argue that 'mother' is *always* related to the core of infantile or childhood neurosis (*CW* 9i, para. 161).

Whether in the twenty-first century we can still swallow this or not, it makes sense within the mythic parameters of *Spider*, where the child's instinct for regression to the incest archetype is disturbed, curtailed and forever constellated in an incest/mother complex:

> for whoever sunders himself from the mother longs to get back to the mother. This longing can easily turn into a consuming passion which threatens all that has been won. The mother then appears on the one hand as the supreme goal, and on the other as the most frightful danger – the 'Terrible Mother'.
>
> (*CW* 5, para. 352)

Thwarted matricide

The splitting of the mother imago into Mrs. Cleg, the nurturer devoted to her child, and Yvonne the sexual predator, becomes more distinct after Bill has buried Mrs. Cleg in the vegetable plot. In early scenes when the adult Spider revisits this site, he lays down on the shriveled plants, clasping the earth, as boy Spider did after the imaginary interment, in a mythic cliché of his need for the 'great (earth/matter) mother' and all her nurturing, regenerating qualities. It is as though boy Spider has relegated the Mrs. Cleg aspect of his mother to a romantic mythology as the more dominant sexual energy of mother/Yvonne begins to consume him in a metaphor for the devouring process of rebirth.

In negating the full regression though he remains arrested, caught, terrified by this specter of change. He imagines that the only way out is to kill Yvonne, but as we saw in *Twin Peaks* when Cooper talked of stopping evil, one cannot kill off an archetype. The more it is relegated to shadow material, the more it seeks to become conscious. One might argue that in resisting the incest regression, and the craving for rebirth it entails by killing his mother and the attempted killings of the ubiquitous devouring mother archetype (Yvonne), Spider is resisting his own death. That is, he resists ending one stage of his life so that another can begin.

In his director's commentary, Cronenberg talks about the ambiguity of the climactic murder of Spider's mother at the end of the film. Because the text is totally constructed around Spider's fantasies and fragmented memories, we are never quite sure if we can believe such a subjective ending. The film has surprising resonances with the way David Chase incorporates Tony Soprano's fantasies about his mother long after her death, whether reliving her legacy through his goomahs, dreaming about her, or trying to redeem her through his daughter. Both texts give vent to Jung's impassioned insistence that the mother image is the most powerful libidinal pull of the psyche.

If the creative energy of the unconscious comes to us through a labyrinth of layered images, with archetypal projections shifting and infiltrating our conscious and unconscious realities, then Cronenberg's *Spider* has to rank as one of the most shrewdly rendered contemporary myths of the incest-complex. If the disturbed little Spider had not constructed Yvonne's exposed breast as beast, but had been able to reacknowledge the excitement of that inviting expanse of skin as the first bodily appendage to be craved, perhaps *la petite mort* that he so feared and desired, would not have been forever postponed.

Dennis (Spider) Cleg, like Tony Soprano and Leland Palmer, is caught in the knot of his complex sexuality. Because he can't navigate the incest image, his frustrated libido remains transfixed at the point where transformation should have occurred. When denied and neglected psychological material, like the incest, mother, and coniunctio archetypes, constellate as carnivorous specters of the imagination, it is easy to read the result (to refer back to *Twin Peaks*) as 'the evil that men do'. All three characters kill in order not to be killed. Instead of working their way through the regression that takes them to the place where change is possible, they react violently against this perceived threat of ego annihilation.

The next chapter also approaches this idea of arrested development from a more emotionally intense and less surreal perspective than the almost monstrous worlds of Leland, Tony and Spider. Although *Intimacy* is a fairly torturous 115 minutes, there's a sense of 'evolution' about the central character 'Jay'. While the pathological excesses presented to us in *Twin Peaks, The Sopranos* and *Spider* are able to offer a breathing space (simply because they are *so* fantastic), the more pedestrian emotional ride of *Intimacy* has a claustrophobic feel about it. This might be why the film is so uncomfortable to watch. There is no respite. But in comparison to the last three texts, we have the benefit of movement *into*, rather than a cyclic retreat *from*, uncomfortable 'points of transition'. I'm going to argue that this is possible via the archetype of anima, which in this instance can be understood as the introspective dynamic able to cultivate, monitor and direct the libidinal energy of eros.

Part IV

Excesses of the sad and the sassy

Chapter 10

The fear of exposure and connection

Intimacy

> There are few creatures more despised than middle-aged men with strong desires, and desire renews itself each day, returning like a recurring illness, crying out, more life, more!
>
> Hanif Kureishi, 'Nightlight' (1997: 144)

Since the mid 1990s, there's been a steady stream of films, in what might be called 'the wounded male' genre, that deal with folding back, entering into and recovering a sidetracked libido. While examples like *American Beauty* (1999), *Magnolia* (1999), *The Man Who Wasn't There* (2001), *Solaris* (2002), *About Schmidt* (2002) and *In my Father's Den* (2004) look at either men's rejection of, or inability to handle, qualities often culturally fixed to that wooly term 'the feminine', Patrice Chéreau's *Intimacy* (2001) doesn't buy into any preconceived ideas of sex/gender disavowal appropriateness. The film adds another dimension to its emotionally floundering centerpiece, the relationship of 'Jay' and 'Claire', by working under the surface of the renunciation–reintegration equation. The problem isn't that these characters don't engage in the eroticism and force of the eros love/sex paradigm, or that they totally disavow these overwhelming energies, Jay and Claire's real frustration is their desire *and* resistance to lock onto and move within these experiences. They replicate the tricksterish, teflon play of *eros* by freefalling *through*, rather than *into*, the other. Their lust becomes an animating pulse that forces them into an intensely intimate relationship with the 'bonding agent' I'll be referring to as *anima*.

Intimacy opens with the camera scrutinizing tangled male limbs snuggled in a fetal position. The frame is so tightly dominated by skin and fabric that the sleeping body remains fragmented until the camera eases its intensity, finally and briefly settling on the face of this adult puer. There is something too intimate about the relationship of the spectator's eye to the details of Jay's body. As Tania Modleski (1982: 100) writes about flesh-hugging close-ups of film and television, a gaze that before celluloid was privileged to lovers and parents, this how we are 'trained' to read the tacit feelings of others on screen. Stuart Staples' moody vocals collude with the camera to create an ambience of stillness and underlying conflict. The spectator is invited to search the surface of this man who curls like a child with his arm between his legs, in these, the only moments of the film when he is not caught in chaotic inner and outer movement.

Jay (Mark Rylance) is suddenly jolted out of his sleep by Claire's (Kerry Fox) arrival; an in-your-face metaphor for what's about to unfold. As he rushes to the entrance, we see her blurred form behind a cracked glass window in the door. Their minimal conversation and barely exchanged glances, signifying either a reluctance to admit attraction or a lack of interest in the subjectivity of the other, gives way to awkward clutching at clothes and skin. The raw, frenetic sex and the snatched gratification these moments of primal impulse offer both lovers show us how, as Linda Williams (2001: 21) writes of this scene, 'the two bodies work so hard to stay connected'. It's through this attempt to reach to, and into, the other, unadulterated by words or the artifice of sexual technique, that Jay and Claire's desperation for connection is spilt onto the screen. As Chéreau says of the sex between the lovers, what you're really exposed to are 'two actors conveying a psychological situation' (Porton 2001: 18).

Chéreau and Anne-Louise Trividic collapsed Hanif Kureishi's novella *Intimacy* and short story 'Nightlight' to form the basis of their screenplay. Kureishi's fictional characters often flounder in the empty spaces of their craving for, and dread of, emotional attachment, where the promise of fulfillment and the farce of being kept in limbo work as binary forces. Their crying out 'for more' is indicative of living in less. In Chéreau and Trividic's adaptation of Kureishi's work, the need to guide eros via anima, is expressed through the oscillation from passion to feigned apathy, that Jay, a 40-something ex-musician turned barman, feels for Claire, a struggling, married actress in her thirties. His need for animation/reinvention, coaxed along by her intense and direct sexuality, develops into a deep attachment. While she is a much more perceptive and resolute character caught in her own story of loss, the greater part of this analysis concentrates on Jay's course toward the desired intimacy of the title. In this case, intimacy as an anchored sense of relatedness *and* a privileged/exclusive exchange. Jay's swings to and from realizing this experience with Claire force him to acknowledge the futility of merely wanting 'more life' while remaining a safe distance from it, as opposed to integrating the 'gearing' energy of anima, 'the *archetype of life itself*' (Jung, *CW* 9i, para. 66).

Wednesday man

From the sexual images of intense bodily commitment to the contrasting wider shots of Jay's room, a chaotic fusion of clothes, cigarette butts, grimy dishes and flaking wall paint, we get a pervading sense of his inner and outer damp, dishevelment, and longing for more. 'I just spill things and there's no one to see', he says to Claire, ushering her to the grimy kitchen for a pre-coital coffee. *Intimacy*'s fly-on-the-wall feel is simulated by set design, location shooting, minimal lighting, downbeat wardrobe/make-up design, and lack of extraneous dialogue. While this is indicative of British cinema's infatuation with realism it also alludes to Danish director Lars von Trier's 'Dogma 95' filmmaking manifesto but without any pretentious replication of Trier's austere rules. Still, like the raw intensity of a Dogma text, Chéreau concentrates on characterization and the interpersonal to place the spectator in an uneasy and demanding proximity to the psychological drama.

As Jay and Claire fuck, the props and set surrounding the foregrounded bodies echo Jay's unraveling. There's no ambiguity about this defensive slide into apathy, transience and slow decay. Only in his brief, naked encounters is there a sense of authenticity that allows us to see the gradual emergence of anima as it works to pin down the ephemeral, competing and frustrating energies of the eros love/sex compound festering inside this bitter and pretty unlikable character.

Jay's indifference to any form of intimate contact is sharply contrasted with the sexual episodes that cumulatively work to expose his need for connection. His Wednesday 2–4 p.m. meetings are informal agreements to engage in sex without engaging in the other. It's an impossible situation to begin with. Claire's forthright entry to his house intrigues him. He never refuses her as she enters and leaves barely speaking. At first each lover appears to be using the other body to release some deeply held hunger, but as the narrative unfolds Claire and Jay become aware of their need not just for *another*, but for *each other*. What is shown is not merely the impulse to escape the self through orgasm, but an expression of the desire for intimacy through a consuming eroticism. It is in this anima generating lust that the eros energies at play are eventually made conscious.

Their *amour fou* is explicit without falling into the pornographic clichés or orchestrated art-house sensuality of films like *Damage* (1992) or *Last Tango in Paris* (1972). The graphic fumbling in *Intimacy*, unlike the stock conventions of porn, can hardly be misread as a stimulating voyeuristic sex-fantasy. The following quote from Williams (2001) alerts us to Chéreau's unique metaphors:

> Its hunger, urgency, and desire are unprecedented in any known repertoire of cinematic representation. Neither the kind of reverential penis worship that so commonly occurs in pornography and which is predictably organized around demonstrating the penis's outward extension from the body in phallic display, nor organized to elicit the overtly visible climax of a 'money shot,' it is a gesture that makes us see the fleshy vulnerability of the organ at the same time as its pulsing hardness.
>
> (Williams 2001: 21–22)

Williams is spot on in her decoding of the flaccid and erect penis as symbolic of the character's extreme vulnerability and determination as he works to 'stay connected'. The camera's gaze from the waste littering Jay's room where each encounter takes place, to the details of his flushed, excited body, suggests a shift of the deadening aggression of the outer, to a sense of inner animation.

As the primary story of Jay and Claire's affair unfolds, the background to his emotional impasse, via verbal disclosures and flashbacks, provides a revealing subplot of abandonment that Chéreau takes from Kureishi's thinly veiled confessional *Intimacy*. Frequent attempts to justify his actions via the misplaced illusion of needing to be 'free' help Jay avoid confronting the discomfort of his condition. The snappy and tightly edited shots where we see him operating within his spaces of home and work, accentuate the ephemeral nature of his social self. We get the impression that like mercury, he doesn't 'stick' to anything except the trendy inner city bar where he's worked for six years. And that's only because, as he says, he's 'stuck in a rut like a fucking arse-hole'. The transient and detached nature of the clientele and casual staff reflect the impersonal contact he feels most comfortable with. When this indifference is mirrored though, Jay reacts defensively: 'I'm surrounded by arse-holes', he says of the bar staff, 'who are doing this job only while they're waiting for something else to turn up'.

The intensity of his anxiety here provokes surfacing memories from the time he deserted his wife and two small children. This life prior to Claire is opened up to us through a number of flashbacks. Jay as middle-aged puer wants to be unburdened, blameless. As Mitchell writes of men prone to hysterical turns (the same kind of emotional flailing that Chéreau and Rylance have sutured into their version of Jay), there's an inherently 'desperate need never to feel guilty. This non-guilt reaches the point where he is not responsible for anything' (Mitchell 2000: 148). It's from this self-absorbed pivot point that Jay takes from, and abandons, those in his orbit. Despite his trail of harm, he reserves all sympathy for himself as perpetual wounded victim, never wounder. Such an extreme denial of compassion coupled with his wariness of attachment (except perhaps to his bar job), suggests the inevitability of an equally extreme response to this evasive behaviour in the form of anima. It is not that anima automatically steps in as a compass for eros rather it is Jay's unconscious need to mobilize his anima that gives it the go-ahead.

Eros and Phanes

Jung expressed the psychological function or eros as that which effects 'psychic relatedness' (*CW* 10, para. 225), 'feeling' (*CW* 14, para. 664) and love (*CW* 7, para. 78). In *Civilization and its Discontents* (1930), Freud most notably tied eros to the sexual and erotic energy of the libido and theorized the conflicting instincts of thanatos (death) and eros (life) to be central to the death drive that he rationalized as the key to human evolution (Gay 1995: 755–756). As mentioned in Chapter 7, Jung, on the other hand, understood libido as psychic energy, desire and appetite, not essentially sexual in nature (*CW* 7, para. 33; *CW* 5, para. 195). He demoted eros from the governing position Freud gave it within his libido schema, and fixed it in a combined oppositional, compensatory and balancing relationship with logos (discrimination, rationality, objectivity), aligning each archetype respectively to the outmoded notion of feminine and masculine consciousness (*CW* 10, para. 255; *CW* 14, para. 224).

Although this categorization of gendered conscious states is problematic (to say the least), there is nevertheless, as Rowland argues, a sense that Jung's essentialist ideas can be reread if we consider that the gender binaries he set up were really a means of negotiating his 'lifelong dialogue with an inner "opposite" other' (Rowland 2005: 49). Within the suspect sexism of his writing though, we can still see Jung's progressive desire for a balance or dialogue between eros and logos in a culture lacking and aching for relatedness (*CW* 10, para. 275).

While eros filters through *Intimacy* as both sexual energy intrinsic to the life-force *and* as a quality that operates unconsciously beyond the rational, I want to take eros out of these psychoanalytic binaries for the moment and think of the archetype as plural, evolving *and* regulated. To do this I'm going back to myth. Although there are no romantic clichés or shallow archetypal projections in *Intimacy*, the text can be read as a twisted borrowing of Apuleius' *The Marriage of Cupid and Psyche* (Adlington's 1639 translation) and the Orphic creation myth of Phanes. In side-stepping the 'star-crossed lovers' factor, exploring the inner workings of the central eros/phanes energy in both myths, and trying to understand one of the ways in which these archetypes network with each other, *Intimacy*, like all of the screen texts looked at so far in *Mis/takes*, can be read as a reworked version of archetypal configurations.

In Apuleius' *The Golden Ass*, Eros/Cupid was the winged trickster-cherub son of Aphrodite/Venus, eternal lover of Psyche (after many tribulations), and a very naughty boy:

> rash enough and hardy, who by his evil manners, contemning all publique justice and law, armed with fire and arrowes, running up and downe in the nights from house to house, and corrupting the lawful marriages of every person, doth nothing but that which is evil.
>
> (Apuleius 1946: 91)

Although more updated versions of the classical *Eros and Psyche* myth redeem him as an almost heroic figure personifying romantic love and connection with Psyche as the personification of both conscious/unconscious processes and soul (psyche is Greek for soul), he is nevertheless still a trickster god, highly sexed, infantile, shape-shifting, and as an agitator, prone to the amoral wiles of his species (see Chapter 2). Not only does he come and go from Psyche's bed at will, vanishing during the day and expecting her to obey his rules of virtual household imprisonment, but also he nicks off when Psyche dares to reveal his identity. Alone and unprotected, she's exposed to the wrath of Aphrodite (the mother of all mother-in-laws). Despite his/its penchant for love sickness, Eros (the god) and eros (the psychological energy/ archetype) are nevertheless, at base, contained little globules of non-stick mercury with toxic potential.

In the Orphic Hymns, Eros had an earlier incarnation as 'Phanes' or 'The Shining One', imagined as a bisexual primal being, born fully winged from the cosmic egg. He was the embodiment of equality, harmony and creation, symbolizing emerging light/consciousness from primordial darkness (personified as the goddesss Nyx) (Kerenyi 1985: 55). Orpheus associated Phanes (also called Protogonus) with Dionysos/Pan (Campbell 1974: 299) and in his sixth ancient hymn elevated him to an 'Ineffable, occult, all-shining flow'r . . . All-spreading splendour, pure and holy light' (Taylor 1824: 18–20). The imagery throughout this poem is evocative of the hermaphroditic Mecurius, child of Aphrodite and Hermes, and the product of the divine alchemical marriage (coniunctio).

Although Kerenyi (1985: 55) tells us that in Aristophanes' *The Birds* (*c.*414 BC), Phanes is referred to as Eros, Jung thought him to be the 'father' of Eros and in another version, Kama the Indian love god, 'who is likewise a cosmogonic principle' (*CW* 5, para. 198). According to Neville (1989: 260), the Greeks fused Phanes with Psyche's Eros to produce a hybrid 'god of union and communion, relationship, newness and process, romance and delusion, procreative power'. I would argue that in applying eros to *Intimacy*, both these myths can still be mobilized. It's possible to retain the phanes-esque quality of the energy where its mercury aspect takes the form of an amalgamating agent, without dismissing or automatically blurring it with eros, who will always bring us back to the archetype's more infantile Cupid-trickster nucleus.

Phanes therefore can be read as the *potential* within eros. Although, as Samuels (1989: 188) points out, eros has no fixed meaning and operates as a floating 'winged' signifier that manifests as multiple yet interlocking signifieds, we can at least draw from the two reasonably concrete mythic strands discussed above that filter through *Intimacy*. After all, myth, as Jung has it, is the best tool we have for representing the psyche in all its protean potentiality.

While Jay's extreme rejection of any form of physical or emotional commitment, dominates the narrative, the final sequence, where he exposes the depth of his feeling for Claire and his need to move *within* not *around* the experience of relationship/connection, allows us to understand just how potent the transformative eros-to-phanes energy can be. It's not that Jay doesn't love, but as we're told by his friend Victor (Alistair Galbraith) he 'probably doesn't know how to love'. If it wasn't for the six sex scenes throughout the film, Jay's hysterical rants and behaviours, enhanced by the frenetic 1980s music score and well-paced editing, might be easily dismissed as unconvincing defenses against the emptiness of his transitory state. Instead, his manic ploys to deflect attachment and accountability seem symptomatic of unconscious conflicting wishes for 'more life'/relationship *and* detachment. It's a situation that he finds increasingly difficult to sustain as his connection to Claire strengthens with each fuck.

The second time they meet the sex is more sensual. There seems to be a joint climax. The ivory-pink bodies are tightly shot in striking contrast to the spartan and lifeless room they move in. During the third sequence, Jay carefully untangles himself from Claire's sleeping body and watches. As he sits in the chair above her we see him drink in the erotic curve of her hips, breasts, belly and limbs. The stillness is brief, but it's enough to let us know that the 'psychological situation' is shifting. Anima as the gearing agent for eros motivates a change in Jay's perspective, whereby Claire's status is elevated from object to subject. She abruptly wakes, and as if to take back any projections Jay's gaze might have stirred, dismissively dresses and leaves. He begins to follow her in a move that takes both of them from the dark interiors of his London terrace, to the lightness of the late afternoon. He darts through a marketplace, half-heartedly trying to trace her between anonymous faces before losing her to the crowd.

There's an easy mercurial play in this shadowing of Claire, but now eros is beginning to be seen in relation to the gradual rise of anima. The metaphor of inner to outer locations, muted light to daylight, and intensity to play, signals another fleeting hint of transformative psychological movement inspired by the need not only to affix agency to this woman who arouses him, but also to prolong the aroused state. This developing phanes aspect (light, awareness) emerges via the psychopomp energy of anima (*CW* 12, para. 74) as it disciplines, curbs and directs the flight-prone eros toward consciousness.

Anima

Although eros and anima are separate ideas, they were previously understood as fibers of the same archetypal paradigm (*CW* 9ii, para. 34). Hillman (1985: 21) reads them as interconnected: 'where anima withdraws toward meditative isolation – the retreat of the soul – eros seeks unions'. However, in my differing view, it is the more alive, free, non-judgmental anima that has the capacity to mentor eros so that it can maintain and reflect upon the unions it seeks. And while anima, in Hillman's reformulation of classical Jungian theory, is seen as the target of eros, the aim of cupid's arrows, or 'that which love works upon', he stresses that it is 'an archetypal structure of consciousness. As such it provides a specifically structured mode of being in the world, a way of perceiving, feeling that gives events the significance not of love but of soul' (Hillman 1985: 21–23).

Jung argued that the numinous concept of 'soul', and in its Latin root 'psyche', 'is too general and too vague' to be applied to anima (*CW* 9ii. para. 25). Soul, then, might be read not as a principle interchangeable with, but as another byproduct of, the anima, which rather than being the *target* of eros activity, guides that activity to conscious, giving it a 'structured mode of being in the world'. Soul (as fuzzy as this term seems) can therefore be understood to emerge from the *grounding of love*, in making creative connections between body and psyche – a way of being with/in the other. Maybe anima has always presented a threat for characters like Jay who resist depth by straddling the margins.

Jung's anima concept was gendered feminine and read in conjunction with its spirit/masculine other *animus* to expand the emotional repertoire of the sexes and personal relationships (*CW* 9i, para. 134). He argued that this coupling of opposites or *syzygy*, fixed in Daoist Yin/Yang and Egyptian Ba/Ka formations, was also projected in divine form through the heterosexual partnership of mythic deities (*CW* 9i, para. 120). The etymology of anima and animus is central to Jung's rationale for both structures as the following citation shows:

> The Latin words *animus*, 'spirit', and *anima*, 'soul', are the same as the Greek *anemos*, 'wind'. The other Greek word for 'wind', *pneuma*, also means 'spirit'. In Gothic we find the same word in usanan, 'to breathe out', and in Latin it is *anhelare*, 'to pant'. In Old High German, *spiritus sanctus* was rendered by *atum*, 'breath'. In Arabic, 'wind' is *rih*, and *ruh* is 'soul, spirit'. The Greek word psyche has similar connections; it is related to *psychein*, 'to breathe', *psychos*, 'cool', *psychros*, 'cold, chill', and *physa*, 'bellows'. These connections show clearly how in Latin, Greek and Arabic the names given to the soul are related to the notion of moving air, the 'cold breath of the spirits'.
>
> (*CW* 8, para. 664)

He embedded the archetypal motifs of eros and logos in anima and animus respectively, sexing and gendering these patterns at the same time, so that anima was assumed to be unconsciously projected in *a* female form and animus in a *collection* of male forms (*CW* 9ii, para. 34; *CW* 7; para. 338). The acknowledgement and integration of anima in men and animus in women were the central thrusts of the contra-sexual schema. But Jung's work on the supposed 'female masculine aspect', in all its assumed multiplicity, is now seen as an inadequately developed adjunct to the much pored/pawed over concept of anima that he endowed with a sense of religious and sexual awe (Emma Jung 1957; Binswanger 1963; Harding 1965; Wehr 1987; Douglas 1990).

Jung even went so far as to describe anima as 'something that lives of itself, that makes us live; it is a life behind consciousness that cannot be completely integrated with it, but from which, on the contrary, consciousness arises' (*CW* 9i, para. 57). In short, as mentioned earlier, 'the *archetype of life itself*'. It's important to remember, though, in a period where the rigid sex/gender inequities of 'the law of the father' guided Freudian psychoanalysis and Western, particularly Swiss culture where women didn't achieve full suffrage until 1971, the anima concept was progressive. It signified the personal and collective necessity of integrating the often disregarded and socially disempowered *other* associated with women and the concept of the feminine.

While the equilibrium of anima/animus within both men and women feeds into contemporary feminist and New Age discourses, Jung argued quite assertively that men have no animus and, in one of his most reviled assertions, 'Woman has no anima, no soul' (*CW* 17, para. 338). Hillman (1985: 55) modified this problematic claim by arguing that 'the anima, as archetype, is too wide to be contained by the notion of contrasexuality. Anima, released from this containing definition, bears upon the psyche of women too'. Hillman argued that 'all that is female is not necessarily anima' (1985: 27), but throughout Jung's writing and Hillman's (1985) review, the motif is inevitably equated with femaleness, and consistently referred to as 'her' or 'she'.

Samuels is not unsympathetic to the idea of peeling away sex and gender in preference of talking 'simply in terms of "focused consciousness", or "fantasy", or whatever qualities we wish to examine' (Samuels 1985: 212). This seductively postmodern/postfeminist cleansing though is also packaged within his more direct revision of anima and animus, as motifs of otherness, that because of their unconscious nature, can be projected *symbolically* in (and as) the opposite sex. To Samuels these energies, more 'contrapsychological' than 'contrasexual' (1989: 104; 1993: 143), offer the possibility for personal and cultural gender expansion.

Having applied the coniunctio motif to *Mulholland Drive* (Chapter 3) and *The X-Files* (Chapter 6), and symbolic regression to the incest archetype in *Twin Peaks, The Sopranos* and *Spider* (Chapters 7, 8 and 9), it's possible to appreciate the psychologically transformative nature of identifying (making conscious), and therefore having the option to integrate, disparate and/or conflicting aspects of the psyche *with* or *without* recourse to sex or gender associations/projections. If one links the *value* of love, sexual *intensification* or *lust*, the *forging* of emotional connection/relationship, and the *guidance* of eros to consciousness, as 'feminine' or 'female', then anima is likely be imaged in that anatomy. If not, it will be projected in an analogous image depending on the associations brought to the concept.

In this analysis of *Intimacy*, the characters aren't read as anima projections. I am exploring the archetype through the intricate behaviour patterns of Jay and Claire, for as Jung writes, the ultimately irrepresentable archetype is not always represented in images, but in ideas and patterns (*CW* 8, para. 417). I've done this not just to free the concept from dated genderisms, but because this kind of clichéd application would reduce the bite and breadth of the text. My position is a reaction to the original anima recipe and a response to post-Jungian revisions of the concept that redress problematic female/feminine ascriptions and/or notions of polarity with animus (Hillman 1985; Wehr 1987; Samuels 1989; Douglas 1990; Ulanov and Ulanov 1994; Young-Eisendrath 1997; Rowland 2002, 2005).

John Lennon and red shoes

Anima presents itself most acutely in *Intimacy* through images of loss. In three flashback sequences, a physically transformed Jay and his cozy middle-class family home contrast markedly to the minimalist/miserable interiors of his present house and hurriedly thrown together appearance where the marks of distress are self-consciously 'written' on his body. 'One day I just walked out', he says to the new barman Ian (Philippe Calvario). The scenes of Jay's past expose the trauma that sparked the emergence of the manic persona we are now asked to identify with. Chéreau couples the deadening coldness between Jay and his wife Susan (Susannah Harker) with the painfully fragile love of his sons. In two flashback episodes in particular, Chéreau allows us to enter into Jay with some compassion.

In the first, the house is empty. He hurriedly packs his bag to leave and looks around his office as if taking in the last traces of what is now his former life. Impulsively he takes an autographed photograph of John Lennon from the wall, who we might imagine here as an Orphic figure from the underworld that clues us into Jay's sense of grief, attempted retrieval and the inability to get back that which he cannot salvage. He places Lennon on the floor against the skirting board adjacent to a small red pair of baby shoes. These objects together, as well as being Orphic images of loss, are also the most tangible signifiers, not of anima, but anima's ability to stimulate phanes throughout the film. Each object is wrapped in the sense of play, creativity, imagination, inspiration, sharing, harmony, 'light' and attachment that the centering of eros is able to bring. But Jay is so unwilling to channel his love and deepen his relationships, that all this potential embodied in Lennon and the red shoes, is unavailable to him.

In the next episode, directly following the above scene, he substitutes his inability to sexually contact Susan, with frenetic masturbation. He stimulates himself in the bathroom by taking deep breaths of her underwear, already turning her into a memory or a chimera without agency. The inhaling of some irretrievably lost 'essence' of his wife, a Eurydice figure perhaps sliding from Orpheus' grasp into Hades, also alludes to Jung's original attachment of breath, wind and 'moving air' to anima. This impulsive sexual breath suggests an unconscious acknowledgement of the need for anima as an anchoring force, and his inability to find it through Susan.

During this fraught period where Jay is confronted with the futility of his situation, this anima energy becomes anathema to the flight, detachment and the independence of eros that he ironically believes will give him the chance to breathe. His younger son, who has wet the bed, knocks on the bathroom door, forcing him to hurriedly wipe the cum from his body. This mirroring of leakage leads into a playful scene, a beautifully crafted image of anima, where we are confronted with Jay's fragility and tenderness as he openly reciprocates the affection of his little boy. The libido as life-force is embodied in this union. There's a sense that this easy exchange is the very thing Jay is seeking to recapture. There is no resistance to the centering of eros, and love in all its conscious and unconscious force is showing itself in a last-ditch attempt to stave off the trickster impulse.

These sequences of his loosening grip, expose the magnitude of the emotions he has tried to bury as they are reignited by Claire. In the following present-day scene, a sharply intrusive contrast to the stillness of parental tenderness Chéreau has created, Claire and Jay are pushed naked against each other. This intensity reads as a desperate bid to spark some of the eros/anima rhythms lost to him. It is therefore possible to argue that lust is more intrinsic to anima than eros, in its directedness and inexplicable capacity to attach one person to another so that, to varying degrees, flight is impossible.

In this episode, the fourth time we see them together, the sex is even more emotionally loaded. It's here where actress Kerry Fox fellates Rylance that has caused some controversy. She sucks his penis, coaxing a response with her mouth and later her hand. After Jay comes, he moves his face between her legs reciprocating the gesture. Claire, though, brushes his head to one side, suggesting that her pleasure, her play, her lips, were given to him as an act of affection not in expectation of being gratified in return. 'It's all right', she says gently, smiling at him.

Unlike the excess of controversial French/English dramas like *Romance* (1999), *Baise-moi* (2000) and *9 Songs* (2005), where actual oral and genital sex takes place, this scene of attempted mutual pleasuring isn't about sensationalizing fellatio, as much as signaling the move between Jay and Claire from the desire for self-gratification, to the desire to gratify the other. The psychological *affect* of play and touch in this scene, an intimacy that has escalated from the previous encounter where Jay gazes at her sleeping, is sharply juxtaposed to the sexual avarice of earlier encounters. It demonstrates the willingness of Jay and Claire to extend their sense of animation even further through a more intense connection *to*, rather than *through*, the other. In an irresistibly cheeky play on the act of oral-genital 'going down', one might read Jay and Claire's eros energy as being directed away from flight, to an 'interiority' indicative of 'a movement of deepening downward' that Hillman (1985: 23) associates with anima.

In thrall to our desires

Jay again surreptitiously follows Claire. This time to a small theatre at the back of a pub where the only access to the performance space is through a door marked 'Theatre and Toilets': one signpost among many for the way creativity, harmony (phanes) is defensively rendered abject by the central characters. He secretly watches Claire play Laura in a season of *The Glass Menagerie*. Although the role is obviously inappropriate for a woman of her age, Claire's skill at evoking Laura's anxiety when the 'gentleman caller' arrives, rather than reflecting her own possible hidden anxieties, is an acute mimesis of Jay's hysterical fear of intimacy. During these and following scenes at the theatre/pub, Jay ingratiates himself into the life of Claire's husband Andy (Timothy Spall), cruelly baiting him and daring him with each suggestive barb to find out about his affair.

Jay later tells Andy that the decision to leave his family was his greatest act of bravery, 'because after all Andy, it's so very easy to stay isn't it?' Jay's calculated and acidic one-sided conversations in these scenes, accentuate his defensiveness and resistance to signs of attachment. While Andy's blind, 'husbandly' devotion is merely a way of avoiding his deadening marriage, Jay's 'lone ranger'/'Don Juan wannabe' artifice is just as much of a ruse to dodge his situation. To maintain the pretence of otherness, he must reduce, and rise above Andy by constructing himself as heroic, daring and beyond the clichés of 'cop-out' suburban life. Despite Claire's attack on Andy, where she calls him, 'the least alive person I know', Andy seems to have the capacity to anchor eros. This stage of relationship play that, while emergent, is for Jay, only in its infancy. 'That you should be so close to someone tears me apart,' he later admits to Claire, 'you're being close tears me apart.'

In a cruder form of self-approbation, Victor, Jay's low-life mate in desertion and squalor, tells barman Ian, 'Jay and me we've both done our share of drifting, but at each bend in the road we always did what we wanted to do. And that makes one fuck of a difference. In thrall to our desires, that's us.' Chris Blazina (1997: 65), in a study on male misidentification with 'the feminine', aptly writes that, 'To ride off into the sunset alone is the surface façade of the masculine ideal'. Blazina's twist on the cinematic cliché of romanticized independence allows us to read this final act of pseudo-heroic machismo, as little more than an acceptable way of representing abandonment.

Running away from cut-off fragments of the self does indeed leave one in thrall to one's desires, where craving for the next adventure/conquest becomes a seductive ploy to defer uncomfortable realities. It's a form of avoidance that can be likened to Don Juanism: 'With his endless women Don Juan never loses anything; but he never has anything either, which is why the hysteric goes on wanting' (Mitchell 2000: 262). Jay's edgy sense of being in constant want, constant tricksterish transition, contrasts with Claire's determination to unswervingly pursue her wants for marriage, sex and an acting career, regardless of, and despite, the consequences. And yet both, in different ways, have to learn to claim what they pursue through the resilient anima energy both are resisting.

The attachment Jay develops, despite himself, is acted out in his frantic clearing of household debris in preparation for Claire's Wednesday visit. This rush of domesticity is at odds with his petulant denial of feeling in the previous scene, where he disingenuously moans to Ian, 'Can you believe how desperate that woman must be? Wednesdays two till, I don't know four, wanting that and only that.' When he realizes she isn't coming he lies on the yellow bedspread where they usually have sex, and cocoons himself in a tight fetal position as though rewrapping himself in the womb (or *hystera* in Greek).

The following and fifth sexual encounter is punishing. Jay's sense of rejection at Claire's failure to meet him triggers a vicious defensiveness. The sex works possibly as an assault for this perceived insult, and/or her ability to reduce him because of his growing attachment. He pumps her body leaving his top, shoes and trousers on. The makeshift furniture and yellow chenille bedspread beneath their bodies become blurred props as they're swept into the tension of yet another wave of their 'psychological situation'. Traces of the bedspread's cheap raised stripe design can be clearly seen in pressure marks on Kerry Fox's back, where the fabric has been pressed into her skin through the weight of Rylance's body. This imprint of Jay's inner and outer debris and anger, now stamped into Claire, signals the end of her alliance with him. After he comes, she rolls over, gets up and quickly leaves. There is the sense here that Jay is finally aware of his need for Claire. Something has stuck that he is unable to run away from.

Theatre and toilets

Jay wants to prolong his attack. He returns to the theatre, continues to indirectly torment her husband, and confronts her backstage in the first scene between them of direct verbal communication. The unconscious, sensory play of eros now finds expression through words, as Claire and Jay defend themselves against each other. The way that anima has worked on eros to pin Jay to Claire, painfully stirring an experience of loss and possibility, is pummeled in this space that to Claire is a refuge, and to Jay, a 'half arse little theatre that stinks like piss.' His demeaning of Claire, her work, her ability to create opportunities for herself, and her effect on him, is a way of discarding the fragile need for connection she has evoked. The sense of life and animation previously offered to him, mutates into the possibility of death. For Jay, eros and anima become abject: the discarded matter that once nourished; everything that for Kristeva (1982: 9) is 'opposed to I'. Freud's eros (life) and thanatos (death) that fuels libido, is thumped out in this quaternity-like space already marked as one enters it, by the 'warning' sign, 'Theatre [life/animation]' and Toilets [death/abject]'.

Mitchell (2000: 146) adds *hate* to the life–death libido mix mentioned earlier: 'One hates when one's survival is threatened . . . anything that echoes that predicament evokes hate'. She twists Freud's claim that hysterics love where they hate, by arguing that 'hysterics sexualize hatred' (2000: 146). This love/hate reworking as it applies to hysteria is reflected in the way that Jay manages, or rather mismanages, this theatre-based, theatrical, tiff with Claire. 'Hate is a reaction of the need for survival,' argues Mitchell (2000: 145), 'the urge to humiliate the other when one is in danger of being annihilated oneself'. Indeed Jay sexualizes his hate, as his callous and punishing last fuck with Claire showed. Even their early non-committed meetings might be alternatively read as a means of focusing his disdain toward that which might be his undoing. 'Jay's a big, big Tennessee Williams fan,' Andy quips off-handedly, in perhaps the most acerbic line in the film, 'all the women in it, they always seem so hysterical don't they?'

This fight-scene, where Jay indirectly articulates his need to anchor eros, is contained within the enclosed four-pronged-cornered theatre space, that like the hermetically sealed boxes in *Mulholland Drive* (Chapter 3), can be read as a metaphor for the Self (the 'higher' state of multiple, merging and unfettered options, or 'the bigger picture'). Finally we see him making conscious his desire to understand and admit to his connection with Claire. If one wanted to introduce the animus concept at all into this reading, it could be argued that having focused eros and consequently directed this transformed energy to consciousness, anima is now pushing Jay even further toward action and examination, a function that might be taken up by animus in order to fully develop the phanes dynamic. Eros/thanatos, eros/phanes, and anima/animus, enclosed and dialoging within the Self-like prism of Claire's theatre, is a fitting climax to the closure and renewal theme of the epilogue.

The day I died

As the relationship moves beyond redemption, Claire confides in her acting student Betty (Marianne Faithfull). She masks her personal distress by saying that someone has died before confessing to her failed affair. 'Well if no-one's died that must mean it's you,' says Betty, 'when I died there was no-one there, I had to go through the whole thing on my own.' Betty's ambiguous play with grief and death as markers of change takes us back to the mortificatio, rebirthing and transformation of the coniunctio, where, as we saw in previous chapters, regressing to a metaphorical death allows for a transformation of awareness.

In the final sequence Jay and Claire meet for the last time. Claire tells him that she is going to stay with her husband. Jay's dialogue, particularly the repeated pleas for her to stay, are so uncharacteristic of the detachment associated with him, that it's clear a more concrete release has taken place: 'I didn't know it would be like this, I didn't know I would become so closely tied to you . . . Stay with me. If you've come back, stay. Come back. Stay. Now. Stay now.' Jay's tears suggest that all pretence to avoid the chaos of misdirected feelings of attachment has dissipated. His vulnerability is exposed so completely that this focusing of love by anima and the implosion of a warped ideal of autonomy was the unavoidable outcome of his disavowal. Rather than falling *through* each other, Jay and Claire have found themselves *in* the other, and while this sits outside the romantic *Eros and Psyche* happy-ever-after-together ending, there is the sense that both characters are able to move within, and more fully explore the libidinal energy of eros.

The film ends where it begins, with Claire and Jay pressed against each other's bodies in a struggle for connectedness. This wordless exchange is the way that both characters have understood themselves and each other. If language inducts us into culture, rigour, focused consciousness, then wordless symbiotic union can take us back to a less armoured reality, where knowing through feeling, connection, touch, exploration and risk, is far from annihilation, but an opportunity to dwell and die *a little death* in the realm of the other before stepping, phanes-like, into a more illuminated sense of awareness. We might now more comfortably return to Jung when he tells us that 'anima no longer crosses our path as a goddess, but, it may be, as an intimately personal misadventure, or perhaps our best venture' (*CW* 9i, para. 62).

The sexual 'abandon' of *Intimacy* is far from the liberation Jay and Claire are after, although it is a way to the other. The next chapter takes a 180-degree turn on expressions of excess, by looking at how the cathartic pleasure of physical and emotional abandon is woven into television comedy via the archetypal grotesque. Because trickster is an intrinsic aspect of this paradigm, there's no sense of the need for fixity or the 'gearing' element of anima to negotiate relationships. In my framing of the concept, the grotesque functions as an unrestrictive energy that arises through a need for release from containment and convention. In this context, excess is not about an inability to anchor oneself, but a means of freeing oneself from being anchored.

While this chapter has focused on the story of a male character who can be seen to encapsulate an entire film genre built on the unspoken and often unacknowledged grief of middle-aged men, the next chapter looks at another face of middle adulthood – the unruly woman. In channeling the grotesque, the characters of *Absolutely Fabulous* peel back the 'rules' that have kept (or have attempted to keep) women silent. In leaving Jay, now able to express intimacy, it's time to move on to the more disruptive and self-centered intimacy of the Patsy/Edina unit. Although these women have an enviable commitment to each other, moving in sync through the superhighway of celebrity, their attitude to the world around them is ultimately 'teflon'. There is nothing thwarted, lost or indecisive about the grotesque. It allows us work through ideologies that are failing us and rethink the viability of outmoded ways of seeing.

Chapter 11

Grotesques, Bakhtin and rupture

Absolutely Fabulous

I name the child Eurydice Colette Clytemnestra Dido Bathsheba Rabelais Patricia Cocteau Stone. Now, take it away . . . Bring me another lover.

Jennifer Saunders, *Absolutely Fabulous 2* (1994: 147)

After the intensity of the last chapter it's a relief to talk of excess and non-fixity (sexual or otherwise) as liberating rather than symptomatic of emotional inertia. While *Intimacy*'s Jay and Claire, with their tangled Wednesday trysts, may find it difficult to embody anything authentically Dionysian, Vicky Pollard, *Little Britain*'s chav princess mentioned briefly in Chapter 2, would be right at home with the grotesqueries of this chapter. Although she's had a fair amount of cult exposure in the United Kingdom, Vicky and her breed of second wave trickster-cum-grotesques have yet to eclipse the global longevity of their televisual forerunners Patsy Stone and Edina Monsoon, the loud, middle-aged and ribald exhibitionists from the BBC sitcom *Absolutely Fabulous*, a.k.a. *AbFab* (1992–).

When the series began, its appeal lay in the cathartic novelty of Patsy (Joanna Lumley) and Edina's (Jennifer Saunders) frantic search for self-gratification, violation of social codes, and ability to provide a respite from the clichés of 'womanliness' that pervade the very medium through which *AbFab* became so popular. They remain unbound by a sense of duty, personal anxiety or fear of retribution. Like the recycled myths that run through *Mis/takes*, Patsy and Edina's craving for 'dis-play' echoes the older stories of female unruliness that intermittently punctuated carnival, literature and comedy.

It is not surprising that images of subversive women have reerupted amid a climate of social and political discomfort that has forced the twentieth and twenty-first centuries to acknowledge the mutability of various power systems. What we have been (and are still) experiencing is an oozing, seeping, bleeding, abjection of much that was assumed sacrosanct. Uncertainty and rupture seem to be the only surety. Both are symbolized through the grotesque image. The re-emergence of the pattern/image/story that I have called the grotesque is indicative of a shifting awareness. It offers a genderless 'space of play' that provides an alternative to the ultimately damaging ideologies that contain and suppress. We might think of this energy in terms of an oscillation to and from a much-desired otherness.

The grotesqueries explored here aren't clearly documented by Jung, but his descriptions of the excesses of impacting archetypal motifs, particularly trickster and Dionysian ecstatic experience, feed into what is known of the grotesque. Bakhtin's thesis of carnival practices, *Rabelais and his World* (1965), and Rabelais' epics *Gargantua* (1532) and *Pantagruel* (1534) are more closely aligned to my understanding of this particular unconscious eruption. While not championing analytical psychology, these texts nevertheless allow for archetypal thinking.

The first half of the chapter traces the idea of the grotesque and the way it reverberates through *AbFab*, while the second half looks at the connections between fertility and the carnivalesque. Although the grotesque is fused with the death/rebirth motif, it's often characterized as a non-nurturing figure that breeds and abandons at will. I'm going to demonstrate this idea by focusing on the archetype's capacity to rupture the maternal/motherhood nexus; a breech of the 'sacred' that has become one of *AbFab*'s signature themes. In a tricksterish play with seemingly inviolate rules, the grotesque leads us to question the worthiness of the rule and the benefits or drawbacks of upholding it.

Now a five season sitcom written by Jennifer Saunders, *AbFab* was initially developed from the *French and Saunders* comedy skit, 'Modern Mother and Daughter' (French and Saunders 1991). The initial popularity of the show led to the marketing of clothing and accessories; Patsy and Edina look-a-like parties and competitions; posters and greeting cards; a rap-style single and video clip featuring Patsy, Edina and the British duo *The Pet Shop Boys* (1994); an *AbFab Mag* inserted in *Marie Claire*'s 1994 Christmas edition; and a comprehensive BBC website (bbc.co.uk/comedy/abfab). Set around the fashion industry and satirizing the shifting trends of popular culture, the situation around which the half-hour series pivots is the acrimonious triangle of Patsy, Edina and Edina's daughter Saffy (Julia Sawalha). In topsy-turvy carnival mode, mother–daughter roles are reversed. Saffy functions as the parental figure desperately trying (and failing) to subordinate the excesses of her mother, a public relations businesswoman, and Edina's best friend Patsy, an executive fashion magazine editor turned stylist to the stars. The mother and daughter bond is maintained by Edina's need for a live-in companion, Saffy's need to find something maternal in her mother, and their mutual need to disempower each other. Patsy's role is to ensure that any maternal feelings Edina might inadvertently act upon are promptly curbed.

As well as core and satellite characters, the series is strewn with cameos by pop culture luminaries featuring as inflated versions of themselves to more effectively strengthen the program's take on celebrity as asinine and ephemeral. Although *AbFab* initially boasted an impressive following from critics and audiences, it may not have been as well received if it hadn't been for the play with female unruliness popularized in the 1980s and 1990s by American comedian 'Roseanne'. Her link to Patsy, Edina and the disruptiveness they signify was heightened by her 1995 purchase of the adaptation rights to the series. Before introducing Saunders and Lumley at the 1996 American Comedy Awards, she joked about her futile attempts to pitch the idea to American networks, who, in allowing only a certain degree of female autonomy and belligerence, never picked up the project. Ten years later, few American television comedies equal the parodic and unsettling tone of *AbFab*, except perhaps Trey Parker and Matt Stone's *South Park* (1997–). It also has to be noted that the hedonistic Nina Van Horn (Wendie Malick) of *Just Shoot Me* (1997–2003) was an inspiring (yet more tame) Patsyesque prototype.

In the 1990s I gave a paper on female images of the grotesque at a university seminar accompanied by a number of short *AbFab* clips before reruns and media grabs of the best gags had sucked the early episodes of their punch. In the scene where Patsy and Edina crawl around a bathroom floor passing a joint to each other while pontificating on their lost youth and the imaginary rotting corpses of surgically made-over icons ('Birthday' 1×6), the laughter from the women in the group led to a pretty obvious bleeding of mascara. 'But I don't think any of this is funny', a male voice piped up after we'd all calmed down a bit. A few men 'mmmed' in agreement. 'They're just a couple of drunks,' he went on, feeling more affirmed by the support, 'I don't get the joke'. In order to get the joke, in line with Umberto Eco's theory on comedy and cathartic pleasure, the rule being broken has to be innately understood and, according to Eco (1987: 275), 'inviolable'.

Patsy and Edina undermine socially constructed notions of the 'feminine', lampoon the non-fixity of the postmodern condition, and viciously challenge the customs governing the ways that women are expected to appear and behave. Understanding female indulgence and excess to be no more than a 'sad' loss of dignity, doesn't take into account women's desire for spectacle and transgression. These often 'behind-closed-door' urges most probably constitute the archetypal pattern of the grotesque reflected in Patsy, Edina and the fabric of *AbFab*. It's not surprising that female grotesque imagery should arise *through* the media as a compensatory factor for a mode of expression that has been largely repressed *by* the media. The more female indiscretion, vulgarity, gender-bending, overt sexuality, autonomy, excess and self-indulgence are denied, the more likely they are to demand recognition.

Rather than surfacing as a destructive energy, the grotesque manifests as a positive source of empowerment that transgresses and redresses. As a motif that wraps around the rebirth paradigm, it can also signify the need for change and the inevitability of death as a precursor to renewal. While the 'monstrous' of the horror genre intimates a fear of transformation and destruction (and here we can look back to Chapters 7, 8 and 9), the grotesque projects the developmental possibilities of this shift. Two of the most prominent and widely recognized theorists of the grotesque, Bakhtin and Wolfgang Kayser, differ markedly on interpretation, but neither identifies the concept as archetypal. Kayser (1981: 185–189) insists that it refers to things individual and abject, 'the estranged world', 'a play with the absurd' and 'an attempt to invoke and subdue the demonic aspects of the world', whereas Bakhtin (1984: 19) reads it as an entirely constructive phenomena linked to carnival practices and the collective, growing, transforming and abundant body of the people. Although these opposing views are pivotal to what is known of the grotesque, Bakhtin's interpretation of carnival and grotesque imagery is a more useful framework for seeing into *AbFab*.

From grottos to cathedrals

The term 'grotesque' was used to describe bizarre and excessive images of male and female forms interwoven with plants and animals common to the decorative wall paintings of fourteenth- to sixteenth-century Italian grottos. Kayser maintained that the noun and adjective grotesque was derived solely from the Italian *grotta*, but the word's etymology can be traced to the Greek *Kryte* (a vault) and *krytein* (to hide) (Thompson 1982: v) implying that the grotesque, as Geoffrey Harpham (1982: 27) notes, 'gathers into itself suggestions of the underground, of burial, and of secrecy'. The *grottesche* art movement of the late Middle Ages and Renaissance was adopted from frescos embellishing Nero's Domus Aurea (Golden Palace) excavated from ancient Roman ruins in AD 1480 (Harpham 1982: 23), but according to Harpham Roman grotesque art (that dated back to 100 BC), was copied from more ancient Asian cultures which in turn were influenced by prehistoric cave paintings (Harpham 1982: xi).

The grotesque style had a wide-ranging influence. It was used to decorate public and religious structures as well as household items, posters, art works and private homes. Many artists were commissioned to adorn architecture in this way: Signorelli's painting of the Cathedral at Orvieto (1499–1504), Pinituricchio's decoration of the cathedral's library ceiling in Sienna (1502), and Raphael's ornamental work on the pillars of the papal loggias (1515) gave the form a sense of legitimacy (Kayser 1981: 20–21). Because of its seeming lack of closure, dependency on plants/animals and association with unconscious dream images, the appealing and threatening grotesque disturbed notions of harmony and restraint. It represented opposition to civilized Europe and came to be closely associated with women, who for the most part were defined as 'other' through the discourse of men and their institutions. As Russo (1994: 12) reminds us: 'the expression "female grotesque" threatens to become a tautology since the female is always defined against the male norm'.

The prolific nature of grotesque imagery in ritualistic practices and various forms of entertainment, from the prehistoric Venuses of the Palaeolithic, Gravettian-Perigordian and Magdalenian eras (*c.*25,000–10,000 BC) through to ancient mythology and contemporary screen texts, suggest that there is some 'purpose' behind the image. It can be argued that the grotesque in its various cultural projections serves as a conduit through which to 'communicate' (as Bakhtin might phrase it) an underlying 'message'. The prolific display of female versions of the grotesque in contemporary television comedy also suggests the need for exposure to *female transgression*, as a form of compensation for the sanctified ideal of *female restraint*.

Harpham (1982: 45) alludes to the ubiquity of the grotesque when he argues that rather than 'being confined to a particular time, place, and aesthetic mode, this message, in endlessly diluting forms, can be found anywhere'. In tracing these images to prehistory, he begins to think of them as having no documented origin: 'From the moment of its appearance in Western culture, grottesche represented an invocation of "some other phase of being" of a mythological culture that was permanently lost' (1982: 51). The grotesque then takes on the dimensions of a psychic force; a point further supported by Harpham's acknowledgement of the way it straddles consciousness and the unconscious: 'Whether considered as a pattern of energy or as a psychological phenomenon, it is anything but clear' (1982: xv). In taking his assumptions further, the 'phenomenon' can easily be interpreted as an archetypal motif rather than a purely socio-political art form as Miles, Russo, Bakhtin and Kayser have argued.

This notion of archetypal merging/morphing/interplay, mentioned earlier, is worth bearing in mind again here. When viewed from this perspective the grotesque, while remaining a distinct archetypal pattern, can be interpreted as a fusion of various other archetypal motifs (trickster and the ecstatic in particular). To talk about the essence of the grotesque as transgressive, boundless, volatile, intrinsic to nature, or carnivalesque, is a little misleading because these qualities apply to a number of culturally recurring images. What distinguishes the grotesque is the *combination* of impacting archetypal features and *how* those elements are embraced and expressed.

Sexing the grotesque

It doesn't take a great leap of the imagination to link *kryte*, *grotto* and consequently grotesque to notions of the womb (a dark, hidden, mysterious, contracting receptacle); an organ that from the time of Plato's *Timaeus* (*c.*360 BC), through to the Middle Ages and Renaissance, was commonly believed to exceed its own boundaries and wander through the body provoking bursts of hysteria and sexual insatiability (Davis 1975: 124). Descriptions of the uterus as a shifting, unruly anatomical 'problem' that in conception and birth linked the internal to the external in a rush of abject waste, secured a connection between female corporality and the unbound, bestial and transgressive nature of the grotesque (Waddell 1999: 208). Both were seen to defy rationality and containment: 'Low, hidden, earthy, dark, material, immanent, visceral. As bodily metaphor, the grotesque cave tends to look like (and in the most gross metaphorical sense be identified with) the cavernous anatomical female body' (Russo 1994: 1).

Grosz (1994: 5) reads the relationship between mind and matter (since Plato), as gendered into a mind/man–woman/body configuration. Woman as matter was bereft of the high ideals of ancient Greek and later Christian philosophy. Miles (1991: 153) asserts that the grotesque, created and popularized by men for male pleasure and female humiliation, was specifically designed to debase the sexual female body, reducing it to an object of ridicule. In contrast, Bakhtin (1984) insisted that carnival empowered the grotesque woman, enabling men to extend their consciousness to nature and in so doing overcome their fear of it. He theorized that the lavish attention thrust on the spectacle of female unruliness connected humanity with its origins and that the carnival tradition, in offering a cathartic respite from the repressive hold of the church, was far from hostile to women.

This idealization is admirable if naive, for it's highly unlikely that the female body was seen solely as a symbol of birth, death and renewal (Bakhtin 1984: 240). Defining and debasing women through an intense obsession with the body is of course unhelpful, but using the body as a transgressive spectacle for overt and covert political means, is entirely viable, as Kathleen Rowe writes:

> Because public discourse is predicated largely on visibility, men have long understood the need to secure their power not only by looking but by being seen, or rather, by fashioning – as subject, as author, as artist – a spectacle of themselves.
>
> (Rowe 1995: 11)

Miles' (1991) sense of 'ridicule' though could be applied to the way that Patsy and Edina have evolved, particularly in seasons four and five. Although no less transgressive than previously drawn, they triumph less over those around them, and Patsy's sexuality (in particular) is unsupported and belittled by ancillary characters, unlike previous seasons where she enjoyed many willing conquests. Despite their waning sexual 'drawing' power, both characters never give up or are humbled by rejection. What we are led to is an oscillation between pity and praise.

This ambivalence or blurring of boundaries is exactly the kind of trickster ammunition the grotesque thrives on. Fresh from a 'Marilyn Manson' concert and fully decked out in Goth garb, Patsy and Edina in no way see their pursuit of the 'now and happening' as 'tragic'. The humour of the scene, though, rests on their failure to recognize the conventions of age-appropriate behaviour as it applies to them, while having no difficulty in fobbing off the aging 'Rolling Stones' as 'a bit sad' ('Fish Farm' 4×2). Their wannabe masquerade can easily be seen as 'unfortunate', but in their enthusiasm, blind acceptance of each other's anarchic wants, and inability to ultimately render *any* activity inappropriate, they can also be recouped as empowering comic presences. I would argue that the impacting trickster function here, more than in earlier seasons, compels us to come to our own conclusions about the progressive/regressive nature of grotesque defiance. For as we saw in Chapter 2, trickster doesn't take a stand but shifts between positions so that we can begin to develop a greater sense of awareness from the endless contradictions it puts forward.

Men as grotesque

As Russo (1994) and Miles (1991) point out, men are able to adopt grotesque characteristics only if their bodies are connected to the feminine. According to Miles, such bodily associations exist when the male form is seen to be penetrable, obese, deformed or in some way robbed of its original shape and 'integrity' (1991: 151). She theorizes that grotesque imagery is always constructed as female in one way or another and that any analysis of the genre must recognize the political gravity of this 'demeaning' form of representation (Miles 1991: 168). Although Rabelais' central and marginal characters are dominantly male (Gargantua and Pantagruel in particular), Bakhtin (1984) interprets their actions and bodily discharges as symbolic of reproduction.

To highlight this concept of all pervading femaleness within grotesque images, Bakhtin drew on Rabelais' obsession with the seepage of bodily wastes, particularly urination: 'In the "Extraordinary Chronicle" Gargantua urinates for three months, seven days, thirteen hours and forty-seven minutes, thus giving birth to the river Rhone and to seven hundred ships' (Bakhtin 1984: 150). This spirit of creation is repeated when in 'Rabelais (Second Book) all the warm medicinal springs of France and Italy were generated by the hot urine of the sick Pantagruel' (Bakhtin 1984: 150). The male body when endowed with grotesque proportions (as we saw in Chapter 2) is thus likened to images of pregnancy and procreation.

Aside from Bakhtin's gendering of the grotesque, women adopting grotesqueness (physical and emotional) is important because of the insubordination attached to this behaviour. While male figures have been 'allowed' to parade their various grotesqueries and excesses in public, women (generally speaking) have not. The pioneering work of 1970s British comedy team Monty Python's films and television sketch comedy series *Monty Python's Flying Circus* (1969–1974) along with *The League of Gentlemen* (1999–2002) and *Little Britain* can be productively read in relation to Bakhtin, but it's not the intention of this chapter to analyze specific male images of the grotesque (although these programs include countless drag acts like *Little Britain*'s Vicky Pollard). I don't believe that they have had as much impact on contemporary television in recent years as have female projections of the archetype, nor do I see them to be as clear an expression of transgression and subversion as female grotesqueness.

As an archetype, the grotesque is neither male nor female, and yet it appears rooted in more female than male images. This might be based on the historically so-called transgressive/other nature of the female body *and* the need for women to embrace the unruly nature of the archetype. Roseanne comments on this lack of 'excess equality' in one of her stand-up comic routines documented in the 1992 television exposé *Feeding the Monster*:

> Men drunk in public, everybody's just OK about that aren't they? There's no big deal, they're like 'Oh look there's Frank again, he's really fucked up, he's drunk again, he's shit-faced, look at that [laughter] he's got his penis on the pool table . . . nice shot though [laughter] . . . that Frank what a card'. That's OK, but women drunk in public, everybody just freaks out you know . . . cause there you are at this party, you're having a great time, you're over in the corner dancing with your dress pulled up over your head having a great time – and everybody's saying 'sad, isn't it?'

Narcotic appropriateness

In ancient Greece, to partake of wine, much like the Christian myth, was to ingest the spirit of Dionysos god of the vine (Evans 1988: 58). Patsy and Edina are constantly searching for ways to absorb Dionysos as they collude and uncritically support each other's pursuit of pleasure. This character 'given' suggests an entwining of grotesque and ecstatic archetypal energies. Unlike the subject of Roseanne's joke who is ridiculed for excess, Patsy and Edina live to experiment with as many euphoric experiences as they can.

The vicarious audience satisfaction that might be felt here comes from the pair's refusal to be intimidated by ridicule for overindulgence. They achieve various degrees of pleasure by submerging themselves in the sensuality of music, alcohol, sex, and drugs. Patsy exists on a diet of cocaine, marijuana, cigarettes, Stolichnaya vodka, and the chemical designer drug appropriately named 'ecstasy' supplied by Edina's dealer 'Don Alfonso de Colombo' ('Poor' 2×5). Edina, not as hard drug dependent, seeks euphoric release in food, fads and Bollinger champagne. A significant portion of each episode revolves around Patsy and Edina's addictive behaviour, often highlighted by flashbacks to their stoned and drunken youth. It's this inability to develop a sense of civic/Apollonian 'responsibility' that becomes the source of Patsy and Edina's transgression.

In their quest for altered states, both actively pursue the ultimate narcotic experience. But as the episode 'Hospital' (2×1) indicates, they're unable to distinguish legal from illegal drug taking, sedation from elation, or medication from intoxication. This kind of confusion resonates deeply in Western culture. The anarchy Patsy and Edina create, in their attempts to source out the next ecstatic moment through sanctioned medical drug use, permits us to see beyond their addictive chaos to the trickster function at play. They remind us that ordinarily pleasure (as merchandised and accessible as it has become) is still contained, controlled, and publicly modified. Ironically in this ownership and regulation of ecstasy, Dionysos has the potential to become repressed, relegated to shadow material and therefore liable to resurface in more pathologically abstract forms.

Drug and alcohol addiction can be understood as the by-products of a culture, while selling pleasure overtly and covertly, is nevertheless unable to nurture or candidly celebrate ecstatic experience as a process of psychological well-being. While Patsy and Edina can be claimed as victims of our culture (addicts to sex, drugs and the beauty myth), their pure enjoyment of life, spectacle, pleasure and dis-play, remind us of the grotesque's deep-rooted connection to the unpathologized realm of Dionysos.

The abundant body of the people

In his analysis of Rabelais' *Gargantua* and *Pantagruel*, Bakhtin (1984) analyzed medieval and Renaissance carnival as a site of disorderly play where the pervading official religious and social ideologies of the sixteenth century gave way to abandonment and pleasure. During these periods of celebration the cathartic explosion of marketplace revelry replaced the asexual, 'closed' rigidity of the church that dominated civic life. Rich in humour, profanity, spectacle, transgression, sexuality, birth and death, carnival, was itself a matrix of fertility best symbolized through images of the grotesque body which Bakhtin saw as 'a body in the act of becoming . . . never finished, never completed' (1984: 317).

Both Rabelais and Bakhtin's interest in subversion, born out of the social revolutions of their time, are reflected in the desire to breech imposed political ideologies. In his prologue to *Rabelais and his World*, Michael Holquist writes that their idealization of the masses, carnival, vulgarity, and political satire allowed them to extricate themselves from the official: 'In treating the specific ways Rabelais sought holes in the walls between what was held to be punishable and what unpunishable in the 1530's, Bakhtin seeks gaps in those borders in the 1930's' (Holquist in Bakhtin 1984: xvii). While he acknowledges that Bakhtin's idea of the homogenous mass is romantic and excessive, he supports this determination to celebrate the 'unofficial' during the imposed official socialism of Bakhtin's time (1984: xviii).

In seeking to rupture the official/high and unofficial/low aspects of culture by claiming carnival as a site of play where all levels of society freely participated, Bakhtin's analysis of the carnivalesque can also be seen as an attempt to embody the postmodern ideal. This is problematic though because of his insistence that the masses were goal oriented: a view that allowed him to theorize carnival play as the collective desire to embrace regeneration, fertility, death, and cathartic release. This vision is incompatible with postmodernism as it's understood today, for as Jim Collins (1989: 5) argues, while 'class cohesiveness may be disappearing, no great leveling process is at work in which all classes slowly fade into one'. In Collins' view there is no master system, no grand plan, no 'uniform call' as Bakhtin would have it, but a situation where the subject 'is being hailed by multiple, competing messages all issued simultaneously' (Collins 1989: 142).

The seemingly endless choices and Baudrillardian simulacra of postmodernism is another key theme of *AbFab*. It is as if in some bizarrely nostalgic way, Patsy and Edina, by trashing celebrity, multiplicity, individuality, fleetingness and endless competition (a culture to which they are inextricably bound), are admitting to a desire for some kind of unity. This desire of course can't be realized because they are never allowed to be anything other than creatures of the clashing trends of consumerism. After all, Edina was catapulted into the national eye of the public relations glitterati with the catchphrase, 'I don't want more choice I just want nicer things' ('Jealous' 3×4).

It's important to remember that Bakhtin didn't envisage the carnival spirit or the collective drive toward catharsis from the official, as transferable to the twentieth century. He posited that the philosophical elements of carnival have been debased over time and replaced by crude sexuality. Along with other nihilistic readings of the postmodern condition, he saw the individual of his day as cut off from the masses and isolated within a world of infinite choices (Bakhtin 1984: 109). It can be argued, though, that the postmodern view of mass culture as a splintering of overlapping, conflicting, disjointed theories, messages, art works and so on, can embrace the carnivalesque if we read past Bakhtin's more precious views of Rabelaisian folk culture in the fourteenth to sixteenth centuries.

We might think back to Jung's concept of the Self where conscious and unconscious energies meet and inform each other, now theorized (as mentioned in Chapter 1), not as a process of 'unity' as much as a meaningful interaction between these contrary energies or a site of free flowing plurality. Carnival can indeed be metaphorically idealized as a site of such processes where archetypal structures (in trickster mode) freely break through to consciousness in order to play with, test, and stretch the margins of the ego. In claiming *AbFab* as a space of reimagined carnival and grotesque carousing, we can see just how relevant Bakhtin's theories of carnival might be, after all, *Rabelais and his World* reads like an ancestral history of Patsy and Edina who as components of the excessive world of televisual spectacle, personify key aspects of excess, abundance, fertility, pleasure and transgression. Even the adoption of 'Rabelais' as one of Patsy's many middle names suggests the conscious influence of his brand of satire ('Birth' 2×6). In positioning *AbFab* as carnivalesque, it has to be remembered that Bakhtin's romantic theorization of the homogeneity of carnival masses, and his failure to adequately address issues of gender, *is* to be generous, problematic.

Carnival

Bakhtin (1984: 5) divided the humour of sixteenth-century carnivals into 'Ritual spectacles', 'comic verbal compositions' and 'various genres of Billingsgate' or verbal blasphemy. During these pagan revelries religious dogma gave way to its shadow, the antithesis of officialdom where a 'second life, a second world of folk culture is thus constructed; it is to a certain extent a parody of the extra carnival life, a "world inside out" ' (Bakhtin 1984: 11). Davis (1975) writes of the social inversion of carnival play where women were able to assume the freedoms of power, control, and perversity, ordinarily denied them, and where both men and women adopted the behaviours and physical appearance of the opposite sex:

> In hierarchical and conflictful societies that loved to reflect on the world-turned-upside-down, the topos of the woman-on-top was one of the most enjoyed. Indeed, sexual inversion – that is switches in sex-roles was a widespread from of cultural play in literature, in art, and in festivity.
>
> (Davis 1975: 129)

European carnivals like *Fastnacht*, *Mardi Gras*, *Careme-prenant*, *Feast of Fools*, *Feast of the Ass* and *Easter Feast* were theoretically accessible to all social classes and focused on the more instinctual aspects of human behaviour: eating, drinking, copulating, laughing, defecating, farting, belching, birthing, and play. This double aspect of the world, embracing the entire community and blurring hierarchical social structures, allowed a respite for the general public and the clergy. As mentioned earlier, Eco (1984) argues that one must experience what is being transgressed in order to both understand the nature of the transgression and to transgress:

> The Coena Cypriani quoted by Bakhtin, a burlesque representation based upon the subversion of topical situations of the Scriptures, was seriously enjoyed as a comic transgression only by people who took the same Scriptures seriously during the rest of the year.
>
> (Eco 1984: 6)

While tragedy states an essential 'rule', breaks it, then reinforces it, in comedy, writes Eco (1984: 4), 'the broken frame must be presupposed but never spelled out'. He sees satiric violation of the rule as the prime source of humour and pleasure:

> Carnival, in order to be enjoyed, requires that rules and rituals be

> parodied, and that these rules and rituals already be recognised and respected. One must know to what degree certain behaviours are forbidden, and must feel the majesty of the forbidden norm, to appreciate their transgression. Without a valid law to break carnival is impossible.
>
> (Eco 1984: 6)

Eco is also careful to remind us, though, that the infringement of the rule can also serve to intensify the rule's potency. If we apply Eco's theory, the humour propelling *AbFab* presupposes that the audience understands certain social codes and how they are subverted (Waddell 1999: 216). Because the program comments on the socially dominant paradigm to which the viewer might return after each episode, watching the series is like taking part (albeit from a considerable distance) in a mini-carnival. But we have to be careful here, for while Bakhtin insisted that carnival made no distinction between performer and spectator, the relationship between television and the viewer is highly hierarchical. Whether *AbFab*'s audience (or its creators) see the infringement of social codes as a mechanism for strengthening *or* questioning those codes is, like the supposed transgressions of carnival, anyone's guess.

Davis (1975: 143) convincingly argues that the play of carnival has the potential to 'spill over'. Like the secreting, transgressive nature of the female grotesque, the behaviour allowed in carnival could be carried beyond its boundaries and in so doing provoke reflection on the nature of subordination. The unruly woman, though, could also be an unruly victim. While lusty, violent, courageous, energetic, able to organize riots and festive play, this figure was (and still is), like her fellow revelers, not immune to the violence of carnival.

Although Davis (1975: 131) argues that 'comic and festive inversion could undermine as well as reinforce that assent through its connections with everyday circumstances outside the privileged time of carnival', she prefaces this by noting that 'a world-turned-upside-down can only be righted, not changed' (1975: 131). Stallybrass and White (1986: 201), in their analysis of the political import of carnival, argue that the bourgeois desire to cyclically rediscover the other through carnival play is merely a way of confirming their middle-classness, so that class/political/religious identity is not lost, but potently re-established. According to Davis (1975), though, the female 'spectacle' in carnival *could* influence other women, inspiring reflection on their situation rather than merely confirming their social position.

In drawing on the examples of Rabelais' Gargamelle, Chaucer's Wife of Bath and the wife in *Les Quinze Joies de Mariage* (Rychner 1963), she claims that these female grotesques were 'full of life and energy, and they win much of the time' (Davis 1975: 135). Davis' 'woman-on-top' was able, often through comedy and carnival, to comment on the dubious nature of social conventions. Still active in popular culture, the woman-on-top ethos is evident in Patsy and Edina's scathing attacks on the fashion and media industry's notion of womanliness: 'There must be a moment about a week after death when all those women finally achieve the figure they desire,' Edina says to Patsy of the cosmetic surgery obsessed, 'when all the flesh has rotted from their bones, the bumps will still be there. Little coffins filled with bones and bumps' (1×6). In a topsy-turvy tricksterish somersault, the next episode 'Hospital' focuses on Patsy's vanity (2×1). She's so carried away with *Hello* magazine's offer to do a feature on her as a beautiful, youthful, stylish mistress of the politically influential, that after a failed attempt to temporarily smooth her wrinkles with sticking plaster, she decides to have a facelift for the photo shoot. 'I can't wait,' she says from her hospital bed, 'The day after tomorrow my life begins again. Goodbye aging obscurity and *Hello* magazine'. Both the embrace and disdain of social expectations placed on women to remain youthful and attractive allow us to laugh at the ludicrous nature of the rule and the kind of culture that ensures it remains in place.

Eco (1984) helps unpack this comic convention of endless contradiction by making a distinction between comedy and humour. The former is character driven while the latter operates (as was earlier mentioned) through the character's inability to obey the rule:

> the performance of humour acts as a form of social criticism. Humour is always, if not metalinguistic, metasemiotic: through verbal language or some other sign system it casts in doubt other cultural codes. If there is a possibility of transgression, it lies in humour rather than in comic.
>
> (Eco 1984: 8)

AbFab incorporates both aspects of the comic and humorous in its slapstick-overblown characters that emulate their idols at the same time as they deride them. Patsy and Edina's desperate attempts to be fashion icons are continually thwarted by the fashion industry. The series provides 'the contradiction between the character and the frame the character cannot comply with' (Eco 1984: 8) by juxtaposing their enslavement to the hyperreal media world with their contemptuous positions on fame. We only have to listen to Patsy's drug-induced advice to Edina on the nature of celebrity:

> That's not what you want to be, a celebrity . . . you don't want to be one of those skinny bitches who sticks on two patches of elastoplast and some dental floss [presumably as a G String] and calls it an outfit. You don't want to wrap your fanny out at a prem[iere] or slither your tits out in the back of a taxi . . . they're just trash, they're just mag[azine] fillers. They're just recycled vomit.
>
> ('Small Opening' 4×5)

As she goes on to ponder the downside of Edina's flirtation with a nude celebrity magazine shoot, Edina rounds off the conversation with an exasperated, 'I just want to be famous!'

. . . getting back to fertility

Having discussed the idea of the grotesque, its origins, and its configuration in carnival practices, I'd like to spend the second half of this chapter concentrating on the grotesque's relationship with fertility. *Mis/takes* has talked a great deal about the mother archetype and the way that its devouring and regenerative qualities have been linked to the death/rebirth process. Motherhood and its associations with seepage (lactation, afterbirth, sweat, urine, blood, mucus, expulsion of embryonic fluid, and ripping of flesh) is an abject enterprise. The clear, clean and defined bodily boundaries that signify the symbolic order are most violently disturbed by the juices and fluids of the procreating woman. Like the grotesque's excessive intermarriage of rambling forest flora with beast and/or human, the permeable body of 'mother' is beyond containment. The link between mother, as the site where inner and outer fuse, and the grotesque, is reinforced not only by the concept of the abject (which compels the subject to periodically acknowledge her/his desire to return to the maternal matrix), but also by the grotesque's historical (crude) association with the womb and reproduction mentioned earlier.

Because the grotesque sharply divides the maternal (that I'll define as nurturing, mothering, and care-taking aspects of childcare) and motherhood (the biological act of giving birth), it is asking us, in trickster mode, to address the culturally accepted link between the act of giving birth and the capacity to nurture. The rupturing of this ideological 'given' is one of the key themes throughout the five seasons of *AbFab*. It's also one of the central precepts that binds the series and its central characters to the notions of the grotesque.

In keeping with the topsy-turvy nature of carnival, there is never any suggestion that the central mother characters of *AbFab* are bonded with their daughters. In the very first episode 'Fashion', the lack of Patsy and Edina's maternal receptivity sets the tone for the rest of the series. While the schism between Edina and Saffy is clearly established in the opening dialogue, Patsy's loathing of anything that might interrupt her lifestyle is more covert. As she offhandedly re-pregnancy tests herself by urinating in an empty wine bottle between shopping, lunch and a quick call to her doctor, it becomes clear that she doesn't see herself as mother material.

AbFab is a product of the shifting status of televisual mothers from other to subject. This movement suggests that understanding nurture, as an instinctual by-product of birthing, is an inconclusive assumption. In response to Adrienne Rich's (1979: 12) foreword to *On Lies, Secrets, and Silence: Selected Prose, 1966–1978*, where she attacks television as a passive and shallow medium, Patricia Mellencamp (1992: 259) argues that 'several things are wrong with her dismissal as a strategy for the 1990's – including the fantasy of escaping television representation, which from the beginning has addressed women as subjects (albeit zany wives and crazy mothers) and rearranged everyday life'. Over two and a half decades after Rich's comments, female characters on television (mothers in particular) are far from submissive domestics.

Fictional television 'mums' have become speaking (often loud, unruly and vulgar) subjects who contribute to the redefining of mother as anything *but* selfless, passive, and bound to the maternal: a fact that Mellencamp believed, back in the early 1990s, that feminists were 'leery of noticing, let alone celebrating' (1992: 258). Even though a great deal has changed since then, the motherhood–maternal equation is a given for the majority of television 'mums' (we just have to return to *The X-Files*' Scully and her über offspring in Chapter 6). Even *Sex in the City* (1998–2004) had a fairly in-your-face mothering element, redeemed only by Carrie's (Sarah Jessica Parker) maternal ambivalence and Samantha's (Kim Cattrall) refusal to breed.

AbFab though shows us a variety of mothers, unwilling and unable, to embrace the concept of maternal nurture. This rupture of the assumed motherhood–maternal relationship is repeatedly illustrated in the series via Patsy's hurried pregnancy termination; Edina's mother who displays few caring impulses for Edina (those that are shown occur only in flashback sequences when Edina is an adolescent); the neglect of Patsy's mother, a self-centered bohemian who sees her daughter as sexual competition; Edina's refusal to compromise her independence for Saffy; and every other female character's reactions to Saffy's pregnancy in season five. Although each episode is scattered with comments on the crippling bind of motherhood, in a satirical stab at the sacred nature of mothering and the ambivalent relation between mother and daughter, Saunders finishes the second series with the episode 'Birth' (2×6) and shapes the fifth series around Saffy's pregnancy. Both are scathing comments on the social expectations of mothers to adopt a maternal approach to parenting despite any desire for autonomy.

Although Nancy Chodorow's *The Reproduction of Mothering* (1978) takes a psychoanalytic approach to the sociology of mothering and gender in its treatment of the division between motherhood and the maternal, her work has resonance in archetypal interpretations of the grotesque. She refutes the, then, popular theoretical position that nurturing behaviour is as biologically instinctive as giving birth (Chodorow 1978: 14). She also examines, and to a large degree discounts, the view of feminist and social psychologists who argue that maternal nurture is solely mimesis, so that a child's role-play with gender and notions of mother is encouraged by the stereotypes of literature, the media, advertising and parental behaviour. However, despite arguments that the maternal is either biological or socially constructed, she comes to the conclusion that maternal feelings are psychologically based and rooted in one's idea of self:

> Whether or not men in particular or society at large – through media, income distribution, welfare policies, and schools – enforce women's mothering, and expect or require a woman to care for her child, they cannot require or force her to provide adequate parenting unless she, *to some degree* and *on some unconscious or conscious level*, has the capacity and sense of self as maternal to do so.
>
> (Chodorow 1978: 33)

Chodorow posits that while both sexes have the capacity to mother and display maternal behaviour, girls are more prepared to cope with these types of behaviours than boys because of their differing psychological identifications with the mother. Claiming that mothering is in essence genderless, she sees maternal behaviour (and the dismissal of maternal behaviour) as socially learnt and psychologically instilled.

In an archetypal reading, we can argue that the maternal aspects of the mother motif, like other genderless and multifaceted a priori forms, varies in dominance from culture to culture, ideology to ideology, and individual to individual. Though a significant piece of work, I think we've moved on from Chodorow's fixed psychoanalytic perspective where the relationship to mother of 'boys' and 'girls' (as units) are decoded through a 'one theory fits all' methodology.

Bakhtin's grotesque mother motif

Mother's fertile body represented the carnival participant's conscious acknowledgement of the potency of mother as the embodiment of the life/death cycle that Bakhtin (1984) attributed to the exaggerated dimensions of all that was bodily in the rituals and farces of carnival, including exaggerated bodily protrusions like humps, noses and bellies. The gluttonous communal feasting of medieval carnival contrasted markedly to the relative gentility of private dining. He interprets this public activity where bodies were exposed to a point of inner and outer exchange, as another way of celebrating fertility. Edina's public indulgence in fads, food, drugs and alcohol also suggests a desire to be part of 'everything'. Despite her ambivalent attitude toward some of her 'chemical' indulgences and food binges, this kind of gluttony can, in carnivalesque mode, symbolize fertility and abundance. In trickster mode, though, she is of course mocking overabundance, so that gluttony, rather than indicative of fertility, comes to represent the nihilism of 'too much choice'.

Much of the humour that pervaded medieval carnival, and continues to be the backbone of contemporary comedy, relies on sexual innuendo and bodily expulsions. Bakhtin explains this dependence on the 'base', by positing that all connected with the 'lower stratum' (sex, birth, farting, belching, vomiting, defecation, urination) is both beyond authority and symbolic of fertility. He explains that the earth and the lower stratum of the human body are procreative areas: 'Grotesque knows no other level: it is the fruitful earth and the womb' (Bakhtin 1984: 21) and as such are central to the laughter of carnival.

The dialogue between Patsy's sister Jackie (Kate O'Mara), Edina's gay ex-husband Justin (Christopher Malcolm) and his partner Oliver (Gary Beadle) illustrates a carnivalesque fusion of the low and the base with fertility. Both women discuss their mother as a promiscuous bohemian who cavorted around Paris, giving birth, as Jackie says, 'like a great sprinkler scattering bastard babies to the four corners of the earth' ('Happy New Year' 3×2). *Little Britain*'s Vicky Pollard who first became pregnant at 14, also reproduces in a similar ad hoc fashion. On a return trip to her old school after a stint in a young offenders' institution, Vicky, with pram, gives her standard incomprehensible gossip to the class. As she prepares to leave, having forgotten her baby, the teacher, Mr. Collier, gives her a reminder, 'Huh? Oh it's alright,' she says, 'you can keep it. I've got loads more at home anyway' (Lucas and Williams 2004: 232).

Rabelais' images of mother

Through Rabelais' *Gargantua and Pantagruel*, Bakhtin (1984: 352) argues that the 'world is shown as a pregnant and regenerating death'. Gargamelle (meaning gullet), mother of Gargantua and wife of Grandgousier, is one of Rabelais' central *female* grotesques. Her excessive eating and drinking, her labour in giving birth to Gargantua and her extended and protruding internal organs, fuse her with the external and internal world/decay and renewal. More specifically, in terms of the archetypal mother, Bakhtin declares that 'We see looming beyond Gargamelle's womb the devoured and devouring womb of the earth and the ever-regenerating body of the people' (1984: 226).

Also known as the daughter of the king of the butterflies, Gargamelle lusted almost as much as she devoured, even rivalling Patsy and Edina's love of indulgence and spectacle. Rabelais (1990: 14) exaggerated in freakish proportion every aspect of Gargamelle's motherhood from conception to birth: 'And they whacked away at making the beast with two backs, happily whipping their lard together, so successfully that she conceived a handsome boy and carried him for eleven months'. During the last months of her excessively long pregnancy, while still revelling in carnival dance and play, Gargamelle 'ate sixteen barrels, two casks, and six pots besides. Oh, the lovely load of shit that must have swollen up inside her!' (Rabelais 1990: 16). The result of her excess is described in graphic detail: 'It was her asshole, which was falling off, because the right intestine (which people call the ass gut) had gone slack, from too much guzzling of tripe' (1990: 21).

Ribald as this portrayal may be, Rabelais saves his most bizarre descriptions of mother for the birth sequences. In these passages the world is turned topsy-turvy so that bodily interior spaces meet the external in an inner/outer exchange (Rabelais 1990: 21). Such explicit descriptions of the body exceeding its own boundaries during pregnancy and childbirth are also woven into Saunders' dialogue over five seasons, as Patsy, in trying to remind Edina of her sacrifice, says, 'You've been a fantastic mother. You've let them ruin your figure. You've stretched your stomach beyond recognition. You've got tits to your knees. And for what?' (1×1). In the satirical and exaggerated style of Rabelaisian 'lower strata' humour, *AbFab* fixes mother within the grotesque mould by drawing our attention to the bodily excesses of pregnancy, childbirth and the forever transformed flesh of the post-natal woman.

The sacrificial mother

Edina and Patsy never compromise themselves for motherhood because, for them, the concepts of mother and death are frequently fused. Patsy likens motherhood to a dark, crippling, smothering monster waiting to pounce and ensnare. She reminds Saffy, in a heated exchange, that when she found out Edina was pregnant, she begged her to abort with a knitting needle (2×6). On the birth of Saffy's baby 'Jane', she relives this sense of disgust by attempting to steal the infant for Saffy's stepfather and mother, now Hollywood baby brokers, but she's so inept at anything to do with birth and babies that she swaddles the placenta instead, presumably because she can't distinguish (to her way of thinking) this form of abjection from the (baby) other ('Birthin' 5×6). The thought that pleasure may have to be sacrificed because of Edina or Saffy's pregnancy is offensive to Patsy and, as we're constantly reminded, Edina.

In Rabelais' farces and traditional mythology, mothers (grotesque or not) *do* sacrifice themselves for their newly born child. This act symbolizes the life cycle of death and rebirth. This sacrifice is sometimes expressed through the literal dying body of the mother, the psychological death of her adolescent self, or the death of her autonomy in the world. Bigmouth or Babedec, Gargantua's wife and mother of their son Pantagruel, is an example of renewal through mother. Her death resulted from trying to give birth to an enormous baby much bigger than her body could tolerate. Descriptions of Bigmouth's labor were also linked to excessive amounts of food and bizarre images of human and animal forms. Like Gargamelle, she is typical of the grotesque mother:

> For when his mother was in labor, and all the midwives were waiting to receive him, the first thing that came out of her womb was sixty-eight mule drivers, each one leading a mule loaded with salt by its halter, after which came nine one-humped camels loaded with hams and smoked beef tongue, and then seven two-humped camels loaded with pickled eels, followed by twenty-five carts all loaded with onions, garlic, leeks, and spring onions. The midwives were frightened out of their wits.
>
> (Rabelais 1990: 141)

This mythological rule of motherly sacrifice that Rabelais capitalizes on so grossly doesn't influence Patsy and Edina's behaviour. They may give life (or have the potential to) but they don't die, physically, psychologically, or in anyway symbolically, in the process. Instead, they continue to celebrate their bodies, ecstasy, freedom and the unruliness of their consumer-driven lives. *AbFab* suggests that the enjoyment the spectator is allowed to feel through this break with tradition rests on the desire to be released from the assumption that excess, spectacle and self-absorption must be repressed after giving birth. This catapults us back to the idea that humour is generated from attempting to violate the presumably inviolable.

Rupturing the motherhood/maternal nexus

Televisual grotesque mothers like Vicky Pollard, Roseanne, Edina, Kim (*Kath and Kim*), Evelyn Harper (*Two and a Half Men* 2003–) and even Nina van Horne (who 'discovers' a daughter) don't lose their transgressive edge or sacrifice their individuality, sense of spectacle, or space in the world to embrace the maternal. Despite popular constructs that would have us believe in a nexus between motherhood and the maternal, these two behaviours are not necessarily synonymous. By reconstructing the mother–daughter relationship, from the socially acceptable convention that insists on mother's nurturance and support of her daughter, to one where these factors are negligible, *AbFab* suggests that mother has a choice *and not* a predisposition to nurture. During the episode 'Birth', in topsy-turvy mode, Saffy's becomes the parental dupe to Edina's adolescent rebel. She represents the closed sleek bourgeois ideal of civility and order, as opposed to Patsy/Edina who personify the loose, unbound lower strata of carnival.

This 'world inside-out', in all its abjection and rejection of authority, is inscribed as 'normal' within the series. Saffy's behaviour may be parental but she is not a maternal figure, nor does she embody the physical dimensions of mother (seeping, transgressive, fertile, large) until the fifth season, when her pregnancy becomes the butt of *AbFab*'s 'joke' of motherhood. Previous to this season, there was little evidence to suggest that she came anywhere near the seepage of copulation, pregnancy or birth. Bakhtin's definition of the classical ideal could well be applied to Saffy, who over the duration of four seasons came to represent 'the classic images of the finished, completed man, cleansed, as it were, of all the scoriae of birth and development' (Bakhtin 1984: 25).

Except for one almost aberrant incident in the episode 'Morocco' (2×3) where she allowed a servant boy to cover her with yogurt before he licked it off, Saffy was (until season five) portrayed as an intrusion in the grotesque reality of *AbFab* through her disengagement from any form of sexuality, sensuality or spectacle, the dull clothing that camouflaged her body shape (shirts often buttoned to the neck, baggy jumpers and jeans), and her sarcastic criticism of Patsy and Edina's sexuality. Her virginity is so scathingly attacked throughout the series, that even when she became pregnant, Edina needed some clarification as to how this manoeuvre was possible ('Book Clubbin' 5×2).

Although Saffy and Edina epitomize the central mother–daughter relationship in *AbFab*, other relationships operate similarly. In 'Birth', where the central and peripheral mother/daughters of the series (Saffy and Edina, Patsy and her mother, Edina and her mother) are clustered together in one episode, negating the maternal as a dominant theme. The episode exposes the fallacy that 'mother' as biological parent is necessarily a figure of nourishment and self-sacrifice. But again in trickster mode, it's difficult to tell whether the motherhood/maternal rule is broken or reinforced through the character's caustic attacks on each other.

During the episode various accounts of Patsy, Edina and Saffy's birth, and the attitudes of their mothers toward this event, are explored in flashback sequences. After Edina's mother (June Whitfield) has accidentally (although this is not certain) locked Edina, Patsy and Saffy in Edina's sitting room, Patsy and Edina in a mix of parody, exaggeration and fantasy begin to relate the details of their birth. The sequence of Edina's delivery satirizes the 'antiseptic' 1950s approach to childbirth. Here Edina's mother happily acquiesces to the sterile handling of her baby and its abrupt departure. There's no evidence to suggest any instinctive maternal behaviour. Distaste for the physical messiness of childbirth (and by association the grotesque itself) is also emphasized by the hygienic, non-tactile nature of the characters (Nurse and Mother) toward the infant Edina, born 'untouched by human hands'.

In contrast, Patsy's mother personifies the hedonism of post-war France. In the second sequence Patsy introduces her birth by announcing: 'my mother didn't give birth, she had something removed'. Sitting heavily pregnant in a French bohemian garret and surrounded by a painter, dancer, singer and writer, all expressing the birth experience through their various art forms, Patsy's mother (Eleanor Bron) appears Gargamelle-like in her carnivalesque excesses. As she talks of her bodily sensations, smokes, drinks brandy during her quickening contractions, and lays sprawled on a heap of cushions, she is the center of attention in the mise-en-scène. The episode not only is another instance of mother displaying no maternal feelings for her newborn child, but also in Patsy's mother's graphic descriptions of her seeping, pregnant body and immediate desire upon giving birth to have sex (the outcome of which may produce another child), it is an interesting illustration of the mother-like aspects of the grotesque in all its regenerating excess.

In comparison to Patsy's birth experience, Edina describes her labour in 'Jane Seymour fantasy' overtones. This concocted flashback, embroidered to pacify Saffy's torment over being an unwanted child, exaggerates romantic images of childbirth. Conventions established over the last two series that made clear Edina's almost total inability to nurture anything or anyone allow the spectator to 'be-in-on-the-joke' that her excessive display of maternal love toward the as-yet unborn Saffy (shown in the fantasy) is an obvious fabrication. The element of sacrifice is also parodied in this sequence and again our awareness of Edina's love of spectacle and her penchant for drugs is used to generate the humour and farce of the episode. But even this last flashback in 'Birth' cannot compare to the 'amaternal' act of selling Saffy into slavery while holidaying in Morocco (2×3) or Patsy's failed baby broker incident.

The grotesque world, into which we as audience are thrust in each episode of *AbFab*, turns the extra-carnival world of our everyday experience upside down. Not only are the grotesque and her perception of life inscribed as normal, orthodoxy and social artifice (in the form of Saffy) become abnormal. Mother as a maternal nurturing figure (the kind of figure that Saffy is constantly hoping Edina will become) is naturally counter to the nature of the grotesque who, while an image of regeneration and abundance, is far from maternal.

Although the physical nature of childbirth is ultimately transgressive in its testing and breaking of bodily boundaries, the maternal side of childcare (even childcare itself) does not figure largely, if at all in the archetypal pattern that characterizes the grotesque. Whether literally represented in the form of mother, or more symbolically in the rounded bumps, humps and bellies of male revelers, the female body remains a prominent and immutable reference point in relation to both the greater themes of carnival and personified images of the grotesque.

AbFab is only one among many voices of the grotesque that presents us with a sense of liberation from socially imposed codes and conventions that control and contain. Although symbolically gendered, the motif is neither male nor female, it's simply other to the dominant paradigm. Using the body to transgress, whether through spectacle, gender play, sexuality, or ecstatic indulgence, is another way of reminding us that we are regulated by taboos governing how the body is to be used and displayed. The grotesque, intertwined with the mother, trickster and Dionysian motifs, asks us to think through the body, to desire the body, and to accept the chaos, ecstasy, and unruliness of the body.

In its lack of closure and manifold projections, this energy has proved to be as abstruse and eclectic as television itself. It surfaces in contemporary culture so that another way of viewing and understanding can be acknowledged. While this analysis has put forward the proposal that the grotesque is archetypal in essence, and that its resurfacing suggests a collective desire to think outside unworkable ideologies of power and containment, I acknowledge the open-ended nature of this idea. The irony of conclusions is that they are rarely conclusive. There is always another approach that can be taken to measure, understand or simply view a popular phenomenon.

Much of the humour in *AbFab* comes from the infectious wit and sarcasm of Patsy and Edina's scathing commentary on the culture with which they are so familiar and yet clearly separate from. So while words, integral to the culture with which I am familiar, cannot adequately express the full dimensions of the grotesque, or indeed any archetypal structure, they are a way of contacting it, a way of reaching into that subterranean grotto and playing in the possibilities of otherness.

Conclusion

The application of Jungian and post-Jungian ideas to popular television and film offers a rich insight into the psychologically complex nature of identity. Jung is an equal opportunity philosopher. He tells us that 'the other' is us. Cinema and television, like the symbols and archetypes of analytical psychology, can be seen to function for our pleasure and progress beyond the confines of race, gender, religion and politics. I believe that my X generation has a fair understanding of this kind of universality (yes, a gross generalization I know). Gen. Y and especially gen. Z have grown up in a borderless culture thanks to media advances (for those lucky enough to have access).

There is some optimism in the way that audiences are being brought more intimately together because of the sheer reach of film, television and the net. These often cyber communities provide a sense of collective pleasure and fascination in and beyond particular screen texts. The way they splinter into ever more specialized interest groups indicates a yearning for the type of collectivity that encourages a plurality of discourses. Despite the shadowy climate of political unrest in 2006, much of it generated through racial and religious prejudice, I sense that we are becoming less tied to the business of othering. My work as a media academic, the research interests of my colleagues and what I've learnt from my students have strengthened this feeling. And although this might seem a crass assumption to some, it seems to me that 'the screen', in all its diversity, has been one of the key portholes through which we have been able to locate each other/the other and found 'them' to be us. It is an atemporal space where the mythic past is continually reflected back to us. There is repetition, but always reinvention, progress, futurity. In many ways screen cultures echo Jung's version of the psyche.

As much as Jung's detractors will maintain their prejudice toward the mythic and esoteric abstractions of his thinking, they have to admit that he was an optimist. His evaluation of the 'unknowable' unconscious as something that works *for* us and not *against* us is worthy of further consideration. If the biological matter of the body rushes to expel infection, scab us over and smooth our gashes, why shouldn't the psyche operate through the same healing impulse? Is it Pollyannaish to believe that the unconscious functions in sync with the body to help us survive? In *Mis/takes* I have looked at instances of television and film where archetypal patterning can be seen to work furiously as a means of rescuing troubled souls. These mythic plays or allegories on how unconscious processes might kick in to re-energize, are stories without end: endlessly reshaped signs of our collective ability to mend ourselves – if we listen.

Yet, it's important to remember that no philosophy or intellectual model is an absolute. I have a favourite scene from the television series *Northern Exposure* (1990–1995), where the central character 'Joel' (Rob Morrow) fantasizes a conversation with Freud (Lou Hetler):

> *Joel:* There's been almost a century of psychoanalytic practice. Untold millions spent in dark offices cluttered with expensive oriental rugs and Hindu art on Park Avenue, this huge quasi scientific, monolithic edifice based on your principles, and now people are beginning to question those very ideas, postulating in fact that the whole sexual orientation of Freudian psychoanalysis is in fact misguided and wrong. How would you respond to such criticism?
>
> *Freud:* It's just a theory.
>
> ('Jules et Joel' 3×5)

With similar vitriol levelled at him, we might imagine Jung answering in the same way.

Bibliography

Adams, M. V. (2004) *The Fantasy Principle: Psychoanalysis of the Imagination*, London and New York: Routledge.

Aden, R. C. (1999) *Popular Stories and Promised Lands: Fan Cultures and Symbolic Pilgrimages*, Tuscaloosa, AL: University of Alabama Press.

Alschuler, L. R. (1997) 'Jung and Politics', in P. Young-Eisendrath and T. Dawson (eds) *The Cambridge Companion to Jung*, Cambridge and New York: Cambridge University Press.

Apuleius (1639/1949) *The Golden Ass of Lucius Apuleius*, trans. W. Adlington, London: Richard Lesley.

Aristophanes (c. 392 BC/1967) *The Congresswomen (The Ecclesiazusae)*, trans. D. Parker, Ann Arbor, MI: University of Michigan Press.

Aristophanes (411 BC/1987) *Lysistrata / The Acharnians / The Clouds*, trans. A. Sommerstein, Camberwell, Vic.: Penguin.

Aristotle (1967) *Aristotle on the Art of Poetry*, trans. I. Bywater, London and New York: Oxford University Press.

Bachofen, J. J. (1967) *Myth, Religion and Mother-right*, trans. R. Manheim, Princeton, NJ: Princeton University Press.

Bakhtin, M. (1965/1984) *Rabelais and his World*, trans. H. Iswolsky, Bloomington, IN: Indiana University Press.

Barr, R. (1989) *My Life as a Woman*, New York: Harper & Row.

Barthes, R. (1972) *Mythologies*, trans. A. Lavers, New York: Hill and Wang.

Bataille, G. (1956/2000) 'My Mother', in *My Mother, Madame Edwards, The Dead Man*, trans. A. Wainhouse, London: Marion Boyars.

Baudrillard, J. (1983) *Simulations*, New York: Semiotext[e].

Binswanger, H. (1963) 'Positive Aspects of the Animus', *Spring*, pp. 82–101.

Blazina, C. (1997) 'The Fear of the Feminine in the Western Psyche and the Masculine Task of Disidentification: Their Effect on the Development of Masculine Gender Role Conflict', *Journal of Men's Studies*, 6(1): 55–77.

Boccaccio, G. (1473/1973) *Libri Johanis Boccacii de certaldo de mulieribus claris*, Ulm: Johann Zainer.

Bonnet, J. (1999) *Stealing Fire from the Gods: A Dynamic New Story Model for Writers and Filmmakers*, Studio City, CA: Michael Wiese Productions.

Bronfen, E. (1992) *Over her Dead Body: Death, Femininity and the Aesthetic*, London and New York: Routledge.

Campbell, J. (1959) *The Masks of God: Primitive Mythology*, New York: Viking Press.
Campbell, J. (1974) *The Mythic Image*, Princeton, NJ: Princeton University Press.
Charet, F. X. (1993) *Spiritualism and the Foundations of C. G. Jung's Psychology*, Albany, NY: State University of New York Press.
Chodorow, N. (1978) *The Reproduction of Mothering: Psychoanalysis and the Sociology of Gender*, Berkeley, CA: University of California Press.
Churchill, C. (1984) *Top Girls*, London and New York: Methuen.
Cirlot, J. E. (1962) *A Dictionary of Symbols*, London and New York: Routledge.
Collins, J. (1989) *Uncommon Cultures: Popular Culture and Post-Modernism*, London and New York: Routledge.
Coupe, L. (1997) *Myth*, London and New York: Routledge.
Creed, B. (1993) *The Monstrous-Feminine: Film, Feminism, Psychoanalysis*, London: Routledge.
Davis, N. Z. (1975) *Society and Culture in Early Modern France*, Stanford, CA: Stanford University Press.
Dean, J. (1997) 'The Familiarity of Strangeness: Aliens, Citizens, and Abduction'. Available http://muse.jhu.edu/journals/theory_&_event/v001/1.2dean.html (accessed 2 July 1999).
Delasara, J. (2000) *PopLit, PopCult and The X-Files: A Critical Exploration*, Jefferson, NC: McFarland.
Denton, A. (2003) *Enough Rope with Andrew Denton*, New South Wales: ABC TV. Available http://www.abc.net.au/enoughrope/stories/s932331.htm (accessed 13 July 2004).
Denzler, B. (2001) *Lure of the Edge: Scientific Passions, Religious Beliefs, and the Pursuit of UFOs*, Berkeley, CA: University of California Press.
Derrida, J. (1967/2001) *Writing and Difference*, London and New York: Routledge.
Dijkstra, B. (1986) *Idols of Perversity: Fantasies of Feminine Evil in Fin-de-Siecle Culture*, London and New York: Oxford University Press.
Donatelli, C. and Alward, S. (2002) ' "I Dread You"?: Married to the Mob in *The Godfather, Goodfellas*, and *The Sopranos*', in D. Lavery (ed.) *This Thing of Ours: Investigating The Sopranos*, New York: Columbia University Press.
Douglas, C. (1990) *The Woman in the Mirror: Analytical Psychology and the Feminine*, Boston, MA: Sigo Press.
Douglas, M. (1966/1996) *Purity and Danger: An Analysis of the Concepts of Pollution and Taboo*, London: Routledge.
Dzenis, A. (2004) '*The Sopranos*: 21st Century Television', in A. Rattigan and T. Waddell (eds) *Lounge Critic: The Couch Theorist's Companion*, Melbourne: Australian Centre for the Moving Image in association with La Trobe University.
Eco, U. (1984) 'Frames of Comic "Freedom" ', in T. Sebeok (ed.) *Carnival! Umberto Eco, V. V. Ivanov, Monica Rector*, New York: Mouton.
Eco, U. (1987) *Travels in Hyperreality*, London: Picador.
Edinger, E. F. (1994) *The Mystery of the Coniunctio: Alchemical Image of Individuation*, trans. J. D. Blackmer, Toronto: Inner City Books.
Ellis, B. E. (1991) *American Psycho*, New York: Vintage.
Engels, D. (1999) *Classical Cats: The Rise and Fall of the Sacred Cat*, London and New York: Routledge.
Enright, A. (1995) 'Diary', *London Review of Books*, 21 September, p. 25

Epstein, J. and Straub, K. (eds) (1991) *Body Guards: The Cultural Politics of Gender Ambiguity*, New York: Routledge.

Euripides (431 BC/2002) *Medea*, D. J. Mastronarde (ed.), New York: Cambridge University Press.

Euripides (428 BC/1995) *Hippolytus*, trans. M. R. Halleran, Warminster: Aris & Phillips.

Euripides (405 BC/1960) *Bacchae*, E. R. Dodds (ed.), Oxford: Clarendon Press.

Evans, A. (1988) *The God of Ecstasy: Sex Roles and the Madness of Dionysos*, New York: St Martin's Press.

Evans-Wentz, W. Y. (trans.) (1927/2000) *The Tibetan Book of the Dead*, London and New York: Oxford University Press.

Fiske, J. and Hartley, J. (1978) *Reading Television* (New Accents Series), London: Methuen.

Fredericksen, D. (2001) 'Jung/sign/symbol/film', in C. Hauke and I. Alister (eds) *Jung and Film: Post-Jungian Takes on the Moving Image*, London and New York: Routledge.

French, C. C. (2001) 'Alien Abduction', in R. Roberts and D. Groome (eds) *Parapsychology: The Science of Unusual Experience*, London: Arnold.

French, D. and Saunders, J. (1991) *A Feast of French and Saunders*, London: William Heinemann.

Freud, S. (1900/1953) *The Interpretation of Dreams (first part)*, *Complete Psychological Works* Vol. 4, trans. J. Strachey in collaboration with A. Freud, assisted by A. Strachey and A. Tyson, London: Hogarth Press.

Freud, S. (1900–1901/1953) *The Interpretation of Dreams (second part) and On Dreams*, *Complete Psychological Works* Vol. 5, trans. J. Strachey in collaboration with A. Freud, assisted by A. Strachey and A. Tyson, London: Hogarth Press.

Freud, S. (1901/1960) *The Psychopathology of Everyday Life*, *Complete Psychological Works* Vol. 6, trans. J. Strachey in collaboration with A. Freud, assisted by A. Strachey and A. Tyson, London: Hogarth Press.

Freud, S. (1905/1953) *A Case of Hysteria, Three Essays on Sexuality and Other Works*, *Complete Psychological Works* Vol. 7, trans. J. Strachey in collaboration with A. Freud, assisted by A. Strachey and A. Tyson, London: Hogarth Press.

Freud, S. (1913/1950) 'Totem and Taboo', in *Totem and Taboo and Other Works*, *Complete Psychological Works* Vol. 13, trans. J. Strachey in collaboration with A. Freud, assisted by A. Strachey and A. Tyson, London: Hogarth Press.

Freud, S. (1914/1957) 'On Narcissism – an Introduction', in *On the History of the Psycho-Analytic Movement, Papers on Metapsychology and Other Works*, *Complete Psychological Works* Vol. 14, trans. J. Strachey in collaboration with A. Freud, assisted by A. Strachey and A. Tyson, London: Hogarth Press.

Freud, S. (1919/1955) 'The Uncanny', in *Infantile Neurosis and Other Works*, *Complete Psychological Works* Vol. 17, trans. by J. Strachey in collaboration with A. Freud, assisted by A. Strachey and A. Tyson, London: Hogarth Press.

Freud, S. (1920/1955) 'Beyond the Pleasure Principle', in *Beyond the Pleasure Principle, Group Psychology and Other Works*, *Complete Psychological Works* Vol. 18, trans. by J. Strachey in collaboration with A. Freud, assisted by A. Strachey and A. Tyson, London: Hogarth Press.

Freud, S. (1923/1961) 'The Ego and the Id', in *The Ego and the Id and Other Works*, *Complete Psychological Works* Vol. 19, trans. by James Strachey, in collaboration with A. Freud, assisted by A. Strachey and A. Tyson, London: Hogarth Press.

Freud, S. (1930/1961) 'Civilization and its Discontents', in *The Future of an Illusion, Civilization and its Discontents and Other Works, Complete Psychological Works* Vol. 21, trans. by James Strachey, in collaboration with A. Freud, assisted by A. Strachey and A. Tyson, London: Hogarth Press.

Gallop, J. (1994) *Jane Gallop Seminar Papers*, J. J. Matthews (ed.), Canberra: Humanities Research Centre Publications, Australian National University.

Garber, M. (1992) *Vested Interests: Cross-dressing and Cultural Anxiety*, New York: Penguin.

Gay, P. (1995) *The Freud Reader*, London: Vintage.

Goldman, L. R. (1998) 'A Trickster for All Seasons: The Huli Iba Tiri', in L. R. Goldman and C. Ballard (eds) *Fluid Ontologies: Myth, Ritual and Philosophy in the Highlands of Papua New Guinea*, Westport, CT: Bergin & Garvey.

Graves, R. (1934/1979) *I Claudius*, London: Penguin.

Grosz, E. (1989) *Sexual Subversions: Three French Feminists*, North Sydney, NSW: Allen & Unwin.

Grosz, E. (1994) *Volatile Bodies: Toward a Corporeal Feminism*, North Sydney, NSW: Allen & Unwin.

Hall, N. and Dawson, W. R. (1989) *Broodmales*, Dallas, TX: Spring.

Harding, E. (1965) *The 'I' and the 'not-I'*, Princeton, NJ: Princeton University Press.

Harpham, G. (1982) *On the Grotesque: Strategies of Contradiction in Art and Literature*, Princeton, NJ: Princeton University Press.

Harris, R. (1994) *Punch Lines: Twenty Years of Australian Comedy*, New South Wales: ABC Books.

Harrison, K. (1998) *The Kiss*, London: Fourth Estate.

Hauke, C. (2000) *Jung and the Postmodern: The Interpretation of Realities*, London and New York: Routledge.

Hauke, C. and Alister, I. (2001) *Jung and Film: Post-Jungian Takes on the Moving Image*, London and New York: Routledge.

Herman, J. L. and Hirschman, L. (1981) *Father-Daughter Incest*, Cambridge, MA: Harvard University Press.

Hillman, J. (1976) *Revisioning Psychology*, New York: Harper Perennial.

Hillman, J. (1983) *Archetypal Psychology: A Brief Account*, Dallas, TX: Spring.

Hillman, J. (1985) *Anima: Anatomy of a Personified Notion*, Dallas, TX: Spring.

Hoberman, J. (2003) 'Along Came a Spider', *The Village Voice*, February 26 – March 4: 50–52.

Holden, K. J. and French, C. C. (2002) 'Alien Abduction Experiences: Some Clues from Neuropsychology and Neuropsychiatry', *Cognitive Neuropsychiatry*, 7(3): 163–178.

Homer (1976) *The Homeric Hymns*, trans A. N. Athanassakis, Baltimore, MD: Johns Hopkins University Press.

Hughes, D. (2001) *The Complete Lynch*, London: Virgin.

Hyde, L. (1998) *Trickster Makes This World: Mischief, Myth and Art*, New York: Farrar, Straus and Giroux.

Izod, J. (2001) *Myth, Mind and the Screen: Understand Heroes of our Time*, Cambridge: Cambridge University Press.

Jaffé, A. (1978) *Apparitions: An Archetypal Approach to Death, Dreams and Ghosts*, Dallas, TX: Spring.

James, H. (1898/1991) *The Turn of the Screw*, New York: Dover.

Jameson, F. (1985) 'Postmodern in Consumer Society', in H. Foster (ed.) *Postmodern Culture*, London: Pluto Press.

Jung, C. G.: Except where a different publication is noted below, all references are, by volume and paragraph number, to the *Collected Works of C. G. Jung (1953–91) (CW)*, H. Read, M. Fordham and G. Adler (eds), trans. R. F. C. Hull, London: Routledge and Princeton, NJ: Princeton University Press.

Jung, C. G. (1963/1983) *Memories, Dreams, Reflections*, London: Fontana.

Jung, C. G. (1964/1978) *Man and his Symbols*, London: Picador.

Jung, C. G. (1969) *On the Nature of the Psyche*, London: Ark Paperbacks.

Jung, C. G. (1973) *Letters 1: 1906–1950*, selected and ed. G. Adler and A. Jaffe, trans. R. F. C. Hull, London and New York: Routledge.

Jung, C. G. (1976) *Letters 2: 1951–1961*, G. Adler and A. Jaffe (eds), trans. R. F. C. Hull, London and New York: Routledge.

Jung, C. G. (1984) *Dream Analysis: Notes of the Seminar Given in 1928–1930*, W. McGuire (ed.), Princeton, NJ: Princeton University Press.

Jung, E. (1957/1985) *Animus and Anima*, Dallas, TX: Spring.

Kaplan, L. J. (1991) *Female Perversions: The Temptations of Emma Bovary*, New York: Doubleday.

Kayser, W. (1957/1981) *The Grotesque in Art and Literature*, trans. U. Weisstein, New York: Columbia University Press.

Keeley, B. (1999) 'Of Conspiracy Theories', *Journal of Philosophy*, 96: 109–126.

Kellner, D. (2002) *Media Spectacle*, London and New York: Routledge.

Kennedy, G. C. (1994) *Ancient Ireland*, Killala, Co. Mayo: Morrigan.

Kerenyi, C. (1949/1985) 'The Primordial Child in Primordial Times', in C. G. Jung and C. Kerenyi, *The Science of Mythology: Essays on the Myth of the Divine Child and the Mysteries of Eleusis*, London: Ark Paperbacks.

Kerényi, K. (1956/1972) 'The Trickster in Relation to Greek Mythology', in P. Radin, *The Trickster: A Study in American Indian Mythology*, New York: Schocken.

Kremer, J. W. (2000) 'The Maya Sape of Time', *ReVision*, 23(2): 24.

Kristeva, J. (1982) *The Powers of Horror*, trans. L. S. Roudiez, New York: Columbia University Press.

Kristeva, J. (1987) *Tales of Love*, trans. L. S. Roudiez, New York: Columbia University Press.

Kureishi, H. (1997) 'Nightlight', in *Love in a Blue Time*, London: Faber and Faber.

Lavery, D., Hague, A. and Cartwright, M. (eds) (1996) *'Deny All Knowledge': Reading the X-Files*, London: Faber and Faber.

Lechte, J. (1990) *Julia Kristeva*, London and New York: Routledge.

Lévi-Strauss, C. (1963) *Structural Anthropology*, trans. C. Jacobson and B. G. Schoef, London: Basic Books.

Lévi-Strauss, C. (1970) *The Raw and the Cooked: Introduction to a Science of Mythology: 1*, trans. J. Weightman and D. Weightman, London: Jonathan Cape.

Lightfoot, J. B., James, M. R. and Swete, H. B. (trans.) (1927) *Excluded Books of the New Testament*, London: E. Nash & Grayson.

Lucas, M. and Williams, D. (2004) *Little Britain: The Complete Scripts and Stuff: Series One*, London: HarperCollins.

Luckhurst, R. (1999) ' "Something Tremendous, Something Elemental": On the Ghostly Origins of Psychoanalysis', in P. Buse and A. Scott (eds) *Ghosts: Deconstruction, Psychoanalysis, History*, London: Macmillan.

Lyotard, J.-F. (1979/1984) *The Postmodern Condition: A Report on Knowledge*, trans. G. Bennington and B. Massumi, Minneapolis, MN: University of Minnesota Press.

Mack, J. E. (1994) *Abduction: Encounters with Aliens*, London: Simon and Schuster.

McNally, R. J. (2003) *Remembering Trauma*, Cambridge, MA: Harvard University Press.

Main, R. (1997) *Jung on Synchronicity and the Paranormal: Key Readings Selected and Introduced*, London and New York: Routledge.

Masson, J. (1992) *The Assault on Truth: Freud and Child Sex Abuse*, London: Fontana.

Mellencamp, P. (1992) *High Anxiety: Catastrophe, Scandal, Age and Comedy*, Bloomington, IN: Indiana University Press.

Miles, M. (1991) *Carnal Knowing: Female Nakedness and Religious Meaning in the Christian West*, New York: Vintage.

Mitchell, J. (2000) *Mad Men and Medusas: Reclaiming Hysteria and the Effects of Sibling Relations on the Human Condition*, London: Penguin.

Modleski, T. (1982) *Loving with a Vengeance, Mass-produced Fantasies for Women*, Hamden, CT: Archon.

Neville, B. (1989) *Educating Psyche: Emotion, Imagination and the Unconscious in Learning*, Melbourne: Collins Dove.

Neville, B. (2003) 'Taking Care of Business in the Age of Hermes', *Trickster's Way*, 2:1, Available http://www.trinity.edu/org/tricksters/TrixWay (accessed 20 March 2003).

Neville, B. (2004) 'Celebrating the Solstice', public lecture for the Jung Society of Melbourne, 19 November.

Nietzsche, F. (1889/1974) *Beyond Good and Evil*, trans. R. J. Hollingdale, London: Penguin.

Noyes, R. (1999) 'The Other Side of Plato's Wall', in P. Buse and A. Scott (eds) *Ghosts: Deconstruction, Psychoanalysis, History*, London: Macmillan.

Paz, O. (1970) *Claude Lévi-Strauss, an Introduction*, New York: Cornell University Press.

Pedler, M. and Walton, S. (2004) 'Wrapped in Plastic: Surrealism, Soap Opera and Mystery in Twin Peaks', in A. Rattigan and T. Waddell (eds) *Lounge Critic: The Couch Theorist's Companion*, Melbourne: Australian Centre for the Moving Image in association with La Latrobe University.

Pelton, R. D. (1980) *The Trickster in West Africa: A Study of Mythic Irony and Sacred Delight*, Berkeley, CA: University of California Press.

Pintchman, T. (1994) *The Rise of the Goddess in the Hindu Tradition*, Albany, NY: State University of New York Press.

Plato (1992) *The Trail and Death of Socrates: Four Dialogues*, trans. B. Jowett, New York: Dover.

Porton, R. (2001) 'Elusive Intimacy: An Interview with Patrice Chéreau', *Cineaste*, 27(1): 16–19.

Rabelais, F. (1530–1534/1990) *Gargantua and Pantagruel*, trans. R. Burton, New York: W. W. Norton.

Radin, P. (1956/1972) *The Trickster: A Study in American Indian Mythology*, New York: Schocken.

Rich, A. (1979) *On Lies, Secrets, and Silence: Selected Prose, 1966–1978*, New York: Norton.

Rowe, K. (1995) *The Unruly Woman: Gender and the Genres of Laughter*, Austin, TX: University of Texas Press.

Rowland, S. (2002) *Jung: A Feminist Revision*, Cambridge: Polity Press.

Rowland, S. (2005) *Jung as a Writer*, London and New York: Routledge.

Rowland, S. (2006) 'Jung and Derrida: the Numinous, Deconstruction, and Myth', in D. Tacey and A. Casement (eds) *The Idea of the Numinous*, London and New York: Routledge.

Russell, J. (1972) *Witchcraft in the Middle Ages*, London: Cornell University Press.

Russo, M. (1994) *The Female Grotesque: Risk, Excess and Modernity*, London and New York: Routledge.

Rychner, J. (ed.) (1963) *Les Quinze Joies de Mariage*, Geneva: Droz.

Sallmann, J.-M. (1993) 'Witches', in N. Zemon Davis and A. Farge (eds) *A History of Women: Renaissance and Enlightenment Paradoxes*, Cambridge, MA: Harvard University Press.

Samuels, A. (1985) *Jung and the Post-Jungians*, London and New York: Routledge.

Samuels, A. (1989) *The Plural Psyche*, London and New York: Routledge.

Samuels, A. (1990) 'Beyond the Feminine Principle', in K. Barnaby and P. D'Acierno (eds) *C. G. Jung and the Humanities: Toward a Hermeneutics of Culture*, Princeton, NJ: Princeton University Press.

Samuels, A. (1993) *The Political Psyche*, London and New York: Routledge.

Samuels, A., Shorter, B. and Plaut, F. (1986) *A Critical Dictionary of Jungian Analysis*, London and New York: Routledge.

Sanford, J. (1987) *The Strange Trial of Mr Hyde*, San Francisco, CA: Harper and Row.

Saunders, J. (1994) *Absolutely Fabulous 2*, London: BBC Books.

Seger, L. (1987/1994) *Making a Good Script Great*, Hollywood, CA: Samuel French Trade.

Shakespeare, W. (1980) *The Complete Works of William Shakespeare*, London: Octopus.

Shelburne, W. A. (1988) *Mythos and Logos in the Thought of Carl Jung*, Albany, NY: State University of New York.

Showalter, E. (1997) *Hystories: Hysterical Epidemics and Modern Culture*, New York: Columbia University Press.

Speaight, G. (1970) *Punch and Judy*, Boston, MA: Plays Inc.

Spinks, C. W. (1991) *Semiosis, Marginal Signs and Trickster: A Dagger of the Mind*, London: Macmillan.

Stallybrass, P. and White, A. (1986) *The Politics and Poetics of Transgression*, London and New York: Methuen.

Stein, R. (1973/1984) *Incest and Human Love: The Betrayal of the Soul in Psychotherapy*, Dallas, TX: Spring.

Stevens, A. (1990) *On Jung*, London and New York: Routledge.

Tacey, D. (1990) 'Incest, Society and Transformation', *Psychological Perspectives*, 23: 16–31.

Tacey, D. (2001) *Jung and the New Age*, London and New York: Routledge.

Taylor, T. (trans.) (1824) *The Mystical Hymns of Orpheus*, London: Chiswick.

Thompson, J. (1982) *Monty Python: Complete and Utter Theory of the Grotesque*, London: British Film Institute.

Ulanov, A. and Ulanov, B. (1994) *Transforming Sexuality: The Archetypal World of Anima and Animus*, Boston, MA: Shambhala.

Van der Helder, E. (1988) *Pope Joan in Legend and Drama: A Case Study in German Medieval Drama*, Armidale, NSW: University of New England.

Vogler, C. (1992) *The Writer's Journey: Mythic Structure for Storytellers and Screenwriters*, Studio City, CA: Michael Wiese Productions.

Waddell, T. (1998) 'Dana Scully and Gillian Anderson: Unresolved Sexual Tension without Mulder', *Metro* 117: 34–39.

Waddell, T. (1999) 'Revelling in Dis-Play: The Grotesque in *Absolutely Fabulous*', in A. Mills (ed.) *Seriously Weird: Papers on the Grotesque*, New York: Peter Lang.

Wakefield, S. R. (2001) 'Your Sister in St. Scully: An Electronic Community of Female Fans of *The X-Files*', *Journal of Popular Film and Television*, 29(3): 131–137.

Walker, J. S. (2002) ' "Cunnilingus and Psychiatry Have Brought Us To This": Livia and the Logic of False Hoods in the First Season of *The Sopranos*', in D. Lavery (ed.) *This Thing of Ours: Investigating The Sopranos*, New York: Columbia University Press.

Webster, R. (1995) *Why Freud was Wrong: Sin, Science and Psychoanalysis*, London: HarperCollins.

Wehr, D. (1987) *Jung and Feminism: Liberating Archetypes*, Boston, MA: Beacon Press.

Williams, L. (2001) 'Cinema and the Sex Act', *Cineaste*, 27(1): 20–25.

Winterson, J. (1987) *The Passion*, London: Penguin.

Woodroffe, J. (1925/2000) 'Foreword', in W. Y. Evans-Wentz (trans.) *The Tibetan Book of the Dead*, London and New York: Oxford University Press.

Young-Eisendrath, P. (1997) 'Gender and Contrasexuality: Jung's Contribution and Beyond', in P. Young-Eisendrath and T. Dawson (eds) *The Cambridge Companion to Jung*, Cambridge and New York: Cambridge University Press.

Film references

About Schmidt (2002) Alexander Payne.
Along Came a Spider (2001) Lee Tamahori.
American Beauty (1999) Sam Mendes.
American Psycho (2000) Mary Harron.
Amityville Horror (1979) Stuart Rosenberg.
Baise-moi (2000) Virginie Despentes.
Batman Begins (2005) Christopher Nolan.
Black Widow (1987) Bob Rafelson.
Blade Runner (1982) Ridley Scott.
Blue Velvet (1986) David Lynch.
Braveheart (1995) Mel Gibson.
Changeling (The) (1980) Peter Medak.
Damage (1992) Louis Malle.
David Lynch Interview, Mulholland Drive DVD featurette (2001)
Don't Look Now (1973) Nicolas Roag.
Dracula (1992) Francis Ford Coppola.
Election (1999) Alexander Payne.
Eraserhead (1977) David Lynch.
Evil Angels (1988) Fred Schepisi.
Exorcist (The) (1973) William Friedkin.
Following (1998) Christopher Nolan.
Freud (1962) John Huston.
Gilda (1946) Charles Vidor.
Gladiator (2000) Ridley Scott.
Harry Potter and the Sorcerer's Stone (2001) Chris Columbus.
Harry Potter and the Chamber of Secrets (2002) Chris Columbus.
Harry Potter and the Prisoner of Azkaban (2004) Alfonso Cuarón.
Harry Potter and the Goblet of Fire (2005) Mike Newell.
Haunted (1995) Lewis Gilbert.
Haunting (The) (1963) Robert Wise.
Hills Have Eyes (The) (1977) Wes Craven.
House on Haunted Hill (The) (1959) William Castle.

I Married a Witch (1943) René Clair.
Intimacy (2001) Patrice Chéreau.
In my Father's Den (2004) Brad McGann.
Jacob's Ladder (1990) Adrian Lyne.
Ju-on (2000) Takashi Shimizu.
Kill Bill, Vol. 1. (2003) Quentin Tarantino.
Kill Bill, Vol. 2. (2004) Quentin Tarantino.
L'Age d'Or (1930) Luis Buñuel.
Last Tango in Paris (1972) Bernardo Bertolucci.
Little Buddha (1993) Bernardo Bertolucci.
Lord of the Rings: The Fellowship of the Rings (2001) Peter Jackson.
Lord of the Rings: The Two Towers (2002) Peter Jackson.
Lord of the Rings: The Return of the King (2003) Peter Jackson.
Lost Highway (1997) David Lynch.
Mad Max (1979) George Miller.
Mad Max 2 (1981) George Miller.
Mad Max Beyond Thunderdome (1985) George Miller and George Ogilvie.
Magnolia (1999) Paul Thomas Anderson.
Man Who Wasn't There (The) (2001) Joel Coen and Ethan Coen.
Mask (The) (1994) Chuck Russell.
Matrix (The) (1999) Andy Wachowski and Larry Wachowski.
Matrix Reloaded (The) (2003) Andy Wachowski and Larry Wachowski.
Matrix Revolutions (The) (2003) Andy Wachowski and Larry Wachowski.
Meaning of Life (The) (1983) Terry Gilliam and Terry Jones.
Memento (2000) Christopher Nolan.
Million Dollar Baby (2004) Clint Eastwood.
Mulholland Drive (2001) David Lynch.
9 Songs (2004) Michael Winterbottom.
Open your Eyes (1997) Alejandro Amenábar.
Others (The) (2001) Alejandro Amenábar.
Poltergeist (1982) Tobe Hooper.
Psycho (1960) Alfred Hitchcock.
Ringu (1998) Hideo Nakata.
Ringu 2 (1999) Hideo Nakata.
River's Edge (1986) Tim Hunter.
Romance (1999) Catherine Breillat.
Rosemary's Baby (1968) Roman Polanski.
Sea Inside (The) (2004) Alejandro Amenábar.
Sex and Zen (1992) Michael Mak.
Shining (The) (1980) Stanley Kubrick.
Silence of the Lambs (1991) Jonathan Demme.
Sin City (2005) Frank Miller and Robert Rodriguez.
Sixth Sense (The) (1999) M. Night Shyamalan.
Solaris (2002) Steven Soderbergh.

Species (1995) Roger Donaldson.
Species II (1998) Peter Medak.
Species III (2004) Brad Turner.
Spellbound (1945) Alfred Hitchcock.
Spider (2002) David Cronenberg.
Spider-Man (2002) Sam Raimi.
Spider-Man 2 (2004) Sam Raimi.
Spider-Man 3 (in preproduction for a 2007 release) Sam Raimi.
Star Wars (1977) George Lucas.
Star Wars: Episode V – The Empire Strikes Back (1980) Irvin Kershner.
Star Wars: Episode VI – Return of the Jedi (1983) Richard Marquand.
Star Wars: Episode I – The Phantom Menace (1999) George Lucas.
Star Wars: Episode II – Attack of the Clones (2002) George Lucas.
Star Wars: Episode III – Revenge of the Sith (2005) George Lucas.
Superman (1978) Richard Donner.
Tatie Danielle (1990) Etienne Chatiliez.
Terminator (The) (1984) James Cameron.
Terminator 2: Judgment Day (1991) James Cameron.
Terminator 3: Rise of the Machines (2003) Jonathan Mostow.
Texas Chain Saw Massacre (The) (1974) Tobe Hooper.
To Kill a Mockingbird (1962) Robert Mulligan.
Twin Peaks: Fire Walk with Me (1992) David Lynch.
Uninvited (The) (1944) Lewis Allen.
Vertigo (1958) Alfred Hitchcock.
Wayne's World (1992) Penelope Spheeris.
Weaving the Web, Spider (DVD featurettes) (2002)
Wild at Heart (1990) David Lynch.
Witches of Eastwick (The) (1987) George Miller.
Wizard of Oz (The) (1939) Victor Fleming.

Television references

When citing television episodes, the episode name is followed by numerals indicating the season and the relevant episode number (e.g. *The X-Files* 'Home' 4×3). *Twin Peaks* does not have episode names so only season/episode numerals are cited.

Absolutely Fabulous (1992–) Jennifer Saunders (creator).
Angel (1999–2004) Jos Whedon and David Greenwalt (creators).
Astroboy (1963) Tezuka Osamu (creator).
Bewitched (1964–1972) Sol Saks (creator).
Bold and the Beautiful (The) (1987–) Lee Phillip Bell and William J. Bell (creators).
Buffy the Vampire Slayer (1997–2003) Jos Whedon (creator).
Charmed (1998–) Constance M. Burge (creator).
CSI: Crime Scene Investigation (2000–) Anthony E. Zuiker (creator).
CSI: Miami (2002–) Anthony E. Zuiker, Ann Donahue and Carol Mendelsohn (creators).
CSI: NY (2004–) Anthony E. Zuiker, Ann Donahue and Carol Mendelsohn (creators).
Dallas (1978–1991) David Jacobs (creator).
Dynasty (1981–1989) Esther Shapiro and Richard Shapiro (creators).
Enough Rope with Andrew Denton (2003–) Andrew Denton (exec. prod.).
Feeding the Monster (1992) Charles Brand and Helen Fraser (exec. prod.).
For One Week Only: David Lynch (1990), Andy Harries (dir. and prod.).
Frozen (1998) Chris Cunningham (dir.).
Games (The) (1998–2000) John Clarke and Ross Stevenson (creators).
I Dream of Jeannie (1965–1970) Sidney Sheldon (creator).
Just Shoot Me (1997–2003) Steven Levitan (creator).
Kath and Kim (2002–) Gina Riley and Jane Turner (creators).
L.A. Law (1986–1994) Steven Bocho and Terry Louise Fisher (creators).
Law and Order (1990) Dick Wolf (creator).
Law and Order: Special Victims Unit (1999–) Dick Wolf (creator).
Law and Order: Criminal Intent (2001–) Dick Wolf (creator).

Law and Order: Trial by Jury (2005) Dick Wolf (creator).
League of Gentlemen (The) (1999–2002) Jon Plowman (exec. prod.).
Little Britain (2003–) Matt Lucas and David Williams (creators).
Living with Michael Jackson: A Tonight Special (2003) Julie Shaw (dir. and prod.).
Monty Python's Flying Circus (1969–1974) Graham Chapman, John Cleese, Terry Gilliam, Eric Idle, Terry Jones and Michael Palin (creators).
Northern Exposure (1990–1995) Joshua Brand and John Falsey (creator).
Office (The) (2001–2003) Ricky Gervais and Stephen Merchant (creators).
Roseanne (1988–1997) Matt Williams (creator).
Simpsons (The) (1989–) Matt Groening (creator).
Sopranos (The) (1999–) David Chase (creator).
Twin Peaks (1990–1991) David Lynch and Mark Frost (creators).
Young and the Restless (The) (1973–) Lee Phillip Bell and William J. Bell (creators).
Young Ones (The) (1982) Paul Jackson (dir. and prod.).
X-Files (The) (1993–2002) Chris Carter (creator).
Xena Warrior Princess (1995–2001) John Schulian and Robert G. Tapert (creators).

Index

Page numbers for main headings which are sub-divided refer only to introductory/general aspects of that topic.
Figures appear in **bold** type and can been found in the plate section.